INDIAN POLITICS
Protests and Movements

INDIAN POLITICS

Protests and Movements

By

Mohammad Yasin
Srinanda Dasgupta

ANMOL PUBLICATIONS PVT. LTD.
NEW DELHI - 110 002 (INDIA)

ANMOL PUBLICATIONS PVT. LTD.
4374/4B, Ansari Road, Daryaganj
New Delhi - 110 002
Ph.: 23261597, 23278000
Visit us: www.anmolpublications.com

Indian Politics: Protests and Movements

First Published, 2003

ISBN 81-261-1565-3

PRINTED IN INDIA

Published by J.L. Kumar for Anmol Publications Pvt. Ltd., New Delhi - 110 002 and Printed at Mehra Offset Press, Delhi.

To

Our Son

Neel

Source of all our Inspiration, Energy and Joy

Contents

Foreword

The present volume which is the outcome of a serious and penetrating research by Dr. M. Yasin, Reader in Political Science, University of North Bengal and Dr. (Mrs.) Srinanda Dasgupta, Reader in Political Science, K.G.T. Mahavidyalaya, Bagdogra, deals with a subject of great contemporary as well as future relevance. It is true that the state in India today is in the multiple-crises stage and no single method can provide solution to this problem. It may be noted that immediately after the attainment of independence, the State in India had to undertake the twin tasks of 'nation-building' and 'state-building'. This called for a concerted and integrated action taking into consideration different social, political, economic, psychological and other related issues. A vast country with so many diversities needed a political framework which could bring all these forces and factors under one common umbrella – the Indian State.

The twin process of state formation and nation-building demanded larger sphere for accommodating diverse and often conflicting interests together. The infant state with a very weak economic support from a shattered economy had to spend a large part of the formative period to bear the impact of stresses and strains arising out of sudden release of socio-economic and political forces which had remained dormant under the oppressive measures of the imperialist power.

The adoption of a democratic polity provided a larger and effective platform to bring within its fold the major demands coming from different sections of the society. But the polity at that initial stage could not accommodate all kinds of demands many of which were not even crystallized and properly channelized.

That was perhaps the reason why the so-called "paradoxes of accommodative politics" so forcefully brought out by Francis Frankel became visible within the very first phase of the formative period. India's path to development, very often described as the capitalist path, may be the logical outcome of this 'accommodative' nature of India politics. But the mechanism of accommodation has its own limitations as it depends, to a large extent, upon two factors: capability of the system to accommodate and the nature of accommodation to be effected. The Indian polity, right from the beginning, was confronted with this problem – the problem of bringing 'unity in diversity'.

Contemporary India is passing through a multiple of crises of unprecedented nature the roots of which can be traced in the interplay of many forces. One may raise a very pertinent question: are the protest movements that have been confronted by the political system systemic or issue-based which is better called non-systemic? The answer lies in the proper perception of the protest movements and the contextual frame in which these movements take place. One look at the historical background of the freedom struggle in India will establish the fact that there had been numerous manifestations of protests at social, political and spiritual levels. The establishment of the Brahmo Samaj, the Arya Samaj, the Theosophical Society sought to launch reformist movements on socio-religious levels. Besides, the Wahabi Movement or the Ahmadia Movement were launched against the acceptance of Christianity and through its westernization. Moreover, the history of freedom struggle in India gives a clear picture of protests and dissents by the Indian people against the British imperialism.

The attainment of Independence evoked much enthusiasm and aspirations among the people in general in India. But the subsequent developments have clearly shown that instead of having a strong and unified India, there appeared 'two Indias' – one comprising the ruling elite and the other the general mass of people struggling to liberate themselves from economic exploitation in a new form. This has been compounded by the process of development and modernization which has created vast regional imbalances.

The State in India has been the victim of these developments and instead of being a vehicle for bringing all round economic development, it became a tool in the hands of the ruling elite for maximizing their own economic interests. Sometime, the state has been used in such a way as to expand what is called "lawlessness".

The present volume by the authors has made an in-depth study of this phenomenon. Rightly, they have tried, in an elaborate way, to situate protest movements in the proper perspectives, identifying the forces which operate at the core of the issue.

The present volume is undoubtedly a significant contribution and those interested in the changing dimension of the political process in contemporary India will find immense materials from this work.

—Pradip Kumar Sengupta
Professor of Political Science
&
Dean, Faculty of Arts, Commerce and Law
University of North Bengal

Preface

Since independence, especially since the 1970s, Indian political system has been witnessing a number of agitations and protests expressing dissent from conditions of powerlessness, deprivation, injustice or loss of identity. In many cases, the causes of the protests are assumed to lie in economic deprivation and exploitation while in others, the desire to assert the ethnic identity of the minority groups and sometimes, the people desiring to preserve the distinctive socio-cultural and tribal heritage. It is also assumed that the roots of India's growing problems of governability due to, and resulting from, numerous protests and agitations are political than socio-economic. A highly interventionist state dealing with a poor economy became an object of intense political competition leading to frustration for some in the game of politics thus resulting in the mobilization of common masses for growing access to and control over the political competition.

As such, so long as the feeling of discrimination, deprivation, injustive and denial of fair treatment continue to exist, the phenomenon of protest in one form or other will continue to operate. The past experience shows that these protest movements have influenced and tend to influence the working of the Indian social, economic and political system in general and the federal governance in particular.

Any protest can never be a sudden outburst; the root is to be found in the dynamic interaction of the various parameters of the Indian socio-economic and political system. As such, the causes of protests in India are thought to be rooted in the major contradictions of India's social, economic, cultural, religious and political life. By the logic of a plural society, India exhibits the heterogeneous presence simultaneously of modernity with tradition, relatively developed urban centres with all the modern amenities with the backward rural peripheries; all pervasive presence and getting ascendency in recent years of caste as a social phenomenon having large scale political penetration with pronounced constitutional equality. Similarly, a major contradiction revolves around nationalism on the one hand and subnationalism on the other. Varieties of subnationalism and the resultant regionalization of politics thus extend the contradiction to regionalism and national integration. Again, one of the most ominous aspects of the political crisis in India today is the conflict between a professed secularism and communalism spreading hatred and inflaming passions in the name of religion. The economic contradiction in Indian politics emanates from the disparity between growth and justice. Finally, the political contradiction centres around the principle of democracy and freedom as reflected from the legal-constitutional framework on the one hand and authoritarianism, interventionism, repression and hegemony in practice on the other.

Given these contradictions that are thought to be the breeding grounds for protest movements in India, one observes a large number of protest movements in India with different orientations and dimensions. These protest movements of different types and nature sometimes recede within absorbable time and scale without much challenge to the unity, integrity and existence of the system. But some protests, in course of time assume much higher scale and operational area posing substantial threat to the existence and functioning of the political system.

Given the background, the present volume is a modest attempt to explore the various aspects and dimensions of protest movements in India along with finding out the impact of these protest movements on the society, economy and polity of India. The book is an attempt to evaluate the two broad perspectives on the perception of protest movements in India – as potential instruments for bringing about desired change in the society and as antithetical to the smooth governance of the polity.

In preparing this volume, we have benefited from a number of sources. We like to put on record our sincere thanks and gratefulness to Dr. Pradip Kumar Sengupta, Professor of Political Science and Dean, Faculty of Arts, Commerce and Law, University of North Bengal for his critical comments throughout the preparation of the volume. In fact, we feel privileged to acknowledge that this problem of Indian politics was introduced to us by him. Sincere thanks are also due to him for his taking the pain to write down the foreword of the book despite his busy academic and administrative schedule. We also acknowledge the inspiration and encouragement we received from Dr. Dhruba Jyoti Bhowmick, Professor of Political Science and Director, Centre for Women Studies, University of North Bengal. Besides, we have benefited from formal and informal discussion on many of the areas of book with a number of academicians and administrators and as such, we take the opportunity to extend our thanks to them. Thanks are also due to R.K. Cyber Zone, Shivmandir, for their promptness, efficiency and sincerity in getting the manuscript ready.

We would also like to thank Mr. Kripal D. Joshi of Anmol Publications Pvt. Ltd., New Delhi for his interest on the subject that made the publication of the book possible within a reasonably short period of time.

Finally, we would fail in our duty if we do not acknowledge the inspiration and cooperation that we received from our son, Neel, who did not mind he was not getting proper attention and care he deserved for. The book is thus much more his than ours.

Limitations if any, are obviously ours.

Mohammad Yasin
Srinanda Dasgupta

Abbreviations

AASU	:	*All Assam Students Union*
AAGSP	:	*All Assam Gana Sangram Parishad*
ABSU	:	*All Bodo Students Union*
ABVP	:	*Akhil Bharatiya Vidyarthi Parishad*
AGP	:	*Assam Gana Parishad*
AIGL	:	*All India Gorkha League*
AJSU	:	*All Jharkhand Students Union*
AKSU	:	*All Kamtapur Students Union*
ATPLO	:	*Army of Tripura Peoples Liberation Organization*
ATTF	:	*All Tripura Tribal Force*
BCNSM	:	*Bihar Chhatra Naujavan Sangharsh Morcha*
BCSS	:	*Bihar Chhatra Sangarsh Samity*
BDSF	:	*Bodo Security Force*
BPAC	:	*Bodo Peoples Action Committee*
BLT	:	*Bodoland Liberation Tigers*
CPI	:	*Communist Party of India*
CPI (M)	:	*Communist Party of India (Marxist)*
CPI (ML)	:	*Communist Party of India (Marxist-Leninist)*
CPRM	:	*Communist Party of Revolutionary Marxist*
DGHC	:	*Darjeeling Gorkha Hill Council*
GNLF	:	*Gorkha National Liberation Front*
JAAC	:	*Jharkhand Coordination Committee*
JKLF	:	*Jammu and Kashmir Liberation Front*

JMM	:	*Jharkhand Mukti Morcha*
JP	:	*Jharkhand Party*
JPP	:	*Jharkhand Peoples Party*
KCP	:	*Kangli-Pak Communist Party*
KLO	:	*Kamtapur Liberation Organization*
KPP	:	*Kamtapur Peoples Party*
LIC	:	*Life Insurance Corporation of India*
MCC	:	*Maoist Communist Centre*
MNTAC	:	*Manipur Nagaland Tripura Assam Coordination*
MNF	:	*Mizo National Front*
NDFB	:	*National Democratic Front of Bodoland*
NNC	:	*Nagaland National Council*
NYS	:	*Navnirman Yuvak Samity*
NSCN	:	*National Socialist Council of Nagaland*
PTCA	:	*Plain Tribal Council of Assam*
PREPAK	:	*Peoples Revolutionary Party of Kangli-Pak*
PLA	:	*Peoples Liberation Army*
POTA	:	*Prevention of Organised Terrorist Activities Act*
PWG	:	*Peoples War Group*
RPF	:	*Revolutionary Peoples Front*
RSS	:	*Rashtriya Swayamsevak Sangh*
SGPC	:	*Shiromani Gurudwara Prabandhak Committee*
TSS	:	*Tarun Shanti Sena*
TNV	:	*Tripura National Volunteers*
ULFA	:	*United Liberation Front of Assam*
YSS	:	*Yuvak Sangram Samity*

Chapter – 1

Introduction, Theoretical Framework—Review of Literature

Over the last four decades, especially since the seventies, there has been a visibly dismal trend of erosion in stability and authority of India as a state leading to a situation which Kohli designates as the "crisis of governability"[1] – a situation more or less common to all the developing countries. The social and psychological elements that are thought to be the ingredients of crisis exist in contemporary Indian society – perception of generalized social and cultural alienation; an acute sense of indifference among the intelligentsia and the public; structural and operational imbalances in the society rendering older paradigm of national development open to doubts or even total rejection by some; and the breakdown of the national consensus on the social and cultural design of the society.[2] Socio-political indecisiveness, lack of priorities, massive state interventionism and widespread corruption in politics and administration – all these virtually challenge the very legitimacy of the system of governance.

In the initial two decades after Independence, many observers on Indian politics were sceptic about Indian political viability.[3] Even though the nation did not disintegrate and democracy has still been surviving, the questions that the Indian political system has been confronted with since the 1970s have been whether India's democratic governance possesses the capability to accommodate conflicting interests and promote development with social justice; whether the basic framework of the Indian political system is able to remain intact with its basic characteristics; and whether the society can remain integrated within a smooth state-society relationship. These questions become all the more relevant when one finds that Indian successive governments that have been elected with large majorities have repeatedly failed to translate popular support into effective policies. This has resulted in an inevitable distance of the ruling elite from the common people. Under the circumstances, the country is confronted with a phenomenon of peasant revolts, ethnic outbursts, urban tensions, religious and fundamentalistic revivalism, insurrections and unabated orgy of violence and terrorism. Violence, crime and corruption have come to be associated with political life at all levels and people of India feel deceived and disenchanted with the performance of the system.[4]

As such, one witnesses the proliferation of protest movements with the pronounced aims of expressing dissent from conditions of powerlessness, deprivation, injustice or loss of identity and seeking various remedial empowerments and entitlements. A number of protest movements are going on in India causing concern for the viability of the Indian political system and no serious effort has yet been made to find solution to them.

There is lack of unanimity among the scholars on the causes of these protest movements. In many cases, the cause of these protests is assumed to lie in the economic exploitation while in others, the fear of loss of ethnic identity of the minorities or the desire of a section of people to preserve their distinctive cultural and tribal heritage are thought to be the sole source of tension, conflict and agitation. In addition, some scholars also view that the protest movements actually reflect the anguish and resentment of a section of the society for being ignored by the ruling elite. It is also assumed that the roots of India's growing problems of governability due to numerous protests and dissents are more political than socio-economic. A highly interventionist state dealing with a poor economy has become an object of intense political competition leading to frustration for some in the game of politics thus resulting in the mobilization of common people for gaining access to and control over the political competition.[5]

It, therefore, implies that as long as the feeling of discrimination, deprivation, injustice and denial of fair treatment continue to exist, the phenomenon of protest in one form or other will continue to operate.[6] As such, past experience shows that these protest movements have affected and are capable of affecting the entire process of nation-building, national integration and the process of socio-economic development in a multi-lingual, multi-regional, multi-religious and multi-ethnic society and polity of India. These protest movements, in ways as varied as the movements themselves, have influenced and tend to influence the working of the Indian social, economic and political system in general and the democratic and federal governance in particular.

However, as remedial measures to counter the negative impact of these protest movements, India has witnessed a number of political accords concluded with the aim of meeting the grievances of the agitating sections of the people in a region. The objective of these accords may also be to contain the intensity and expansion of these movements beyond the region so that they cannot assume the national dimension thus challenging the legitimacy of the regime in power. Observations also show that accords are signed for short term political mileage by the party or leadership in power. Whatever may be the motive force behind the accords signed, these could not provide respite to the ongoing resentments of the agitating people for various reasons.[7] Hence, protest movements, later turned to be broader ethnic secessionist movements in many cases, continue to operate with more vigour and intensity thus leaving profound impact on the Indian society, economy and polity as a whole.

Two broad perspectives may be identified on the perception of protest movements in India. At one end lies the view that these protest movements are to be viewed as potential instruments for bringing about desired change in the society. In these perspectives, the protests are viewed as the instruments or avenues reflecting the aspirations of the people thus preventing the system from deviation and helping the system in refixing, redesigning and reorienting priorities and policies. On the other hand, there is the perception that the protest movements are antithetical to the smooth governance of the polity and as such, halt economic growth and social change. Accordingly, protest movements seem to pose threat to the basic structure and characteristics of the socio-political system and its legitimacy in general.

Objective of the Study

Given this background, the present study seeks to explore the various causes of protest movements, their nature, leadership pattern, ideological orientation, and their overall impact on the political system and process in India. The study, by way of examining the various perspectives and theoretical frameworks about the protest movements, also seeks to evaluate whether protest movements in India have been the rational instruments for bringing about desired social change or are responsible for growing systemic crisis leading to the so-called crisis of governability. In fine, the study moderately attempts at explaining the relationship between the protest movements on the one hand and the state and society on the other.

Theoretical Framework

It has been a worldwide phenomenon that the unprivileged and underprivileged sections of the society – whether racial, linguistic, religious or ethnic minorities or low castes and classes – organize themselves to fight against inequalities, injustices, discriminations or deprivations perceived to be addressed to them. They often resort to violent agitation for their perceived legitimate share in social position, economic opportunities and political power. Thus, widespread collective mobilizations centering around such objectives have resulted in organized social movements with defined ideologies and leadership and in this way, have brought about significant structural and organizational changes in the societies wherefrom they originate.[8]

Thus viewed, "Social movements and protests, which is the manifestation of the former, is an effort to redefine or recapture the past to restructure the present and reorient the future".[9] The English word 'movement' derives from the old French verb, 'movoir', which means to move, or stir or impel, and the mediaeval Latin 'movimentum'. The word has different connotations. In the past, it was used to denote certain 'liberal', 'innovatory' or 'progressive parties or functions' as in 'movement party' in early nineteenth century Britain. The other usage of the term refers to 'historical tendency', 'trend', 'current', or 'drift'. As against these, the general English usage of 'movement' as found in *Oxford English Dictionary*, points to a "series of actions and endeavours of a body of persons for a special object".[10]

However, there is no accepted precise definition of the term 'movement'. It has become "all things to all men".[11] Writing from a political scientist's point of view, Mackenzie argues that although "political science cannot afford to neglect politicized movements, it is very difficult, in practice, to prevent such work from becoming all inclusive and therefore vacuous".[12] Many writers use the word almost interchangeably with such words as 'organization', 'association', 'group' and 'union'. Writers sometimes appear to have hit on the word quite arbitrarily or for purely stylistic reasons.[13] Like many other words such as 'people', 'popular', 'democracy', 'equality', 'liberty', the term 'movement' is still regarded as a "hurrah! word".[14]

The word 'movement' got popularized in European language in the early nineteenth century when social upheaval of the period attracted the political leaders and scholars alike to use the word for the emancipation of the exploited classes and the creation of a new society by changing property relationship. However, since the early fifties, scholars have attempted to provide a comprehensive definition of the concept of social movement. The works of Rudolf Heberle, Neil Smelser,

John Wilson and Paul Wilkinson are important in this regard. Rudolph Heberle defines a social movement as a collective effort to transform established relations within a particular society.[15] A social movement in Heberle's analysis requires a collectivity and the objective of bringing about change in the existing social relationships. Neil Smelser views social movements as directly oriented towards a change in social institutions and social norms.[16] Thus, in Smelser's definition the desire for change is the prime motive for a social movement. Wilson defines social movements as a conscious, collective and organized attempt to bring about or resist large-scale change in the social order by non-institutionalized means.[17] According to Tilly, this definition by Wilson belong to the Weberian tradition in Sociology which says that a group of people somehow orient themselves to the same belief system and act together to promote changes on the basis of a common orientation.[18] Most of the writers tend to agree with Paul Wilkinson's comprehensive view that two basic elements – a minimum degree of organization and a commitment to change – are necessary for the existence of a social movement.[19] Paul Wilkinson gives the following working definition of the concept of 'social movement':

1. "A social movement is a deliberate collective endeavour to promote change in any direction and by any means, not excluding violence, illegality, revolution or withdrawal into utopian community".
2. "A social movement must evince a minimal degree of organization, though this may range from a loose, informal or partial level of organization to the highly institutionalized and bureaucratized movement and the corporate group".
3. "A social movement's commitment to change and the raison-detre of its organization are founded upon the conscious volition, normative commitment to the movement's aims or beliefs, and active participation on the part of the followers or members".[20]

An analysis of the working definition of the concept of social movement shows that it does not claim to provide a precise definition. It is too broad and comprehensive, and encompasses both institutionalized collective action through legal means as well as violent extra-institutional collective action. The 'minimum degree of organization' is problematic because it is difficult to say precisely what this 'minimum degree' is. It is also not clear whether movement begins with a self-organization with committed members, or the organization evolves in the course of time as the movement develops. Also, such a definition may exclude protests and agitations which may not have an organization to begin with. However, despite these difficulties in Wilkinson's working definition, it has indeed the heuristic value.[21]

Broadly thus, social movements may be defined as a wide variety of collective attempts in which the participants organize themselves to bring about a change in certain social institutions or to create an entirely new order, or to resist a change.[22] It has certain specific objectives to be achieved through the movement, an organizational structure, and may also have an ideology oriented towards change.

It appears from all the definitions cited above that social movements encompass both institutionalized collective actions such as petitioning, fighting legal battles in courts of law as well as non-institutionalized collective actions such as protests, agitations, strikes, gheraos, riots, etc. Thus, protests may not strictly seem to be social movements. But more often than not a social movement develops in course of time, and it begins with protest which may not have the 'organization' or 'ideology' for change. Taking an example from Shah, when the students of the engineering college in Gujarat protested against the mess bill, it was a relatively spontaneous act devoid of organization or ideology the necessary preconditions for a social movement. But that protest led to the Nav Nirman Andolon of 1974 in Gujarat.[23]

Thus, it can be safely said that protest is a form of social movement. It is a non-institutionalized mode of bringing about the desired state of affairs – either change in the existing socio-economic and political order or resist that change. There may be a large number of techniques of protests. These include small public meetings, leaf letting, postering, submitting memorandum, press conference, press statements, mobile announcements, street corner meetings, long marches on foot, holding meeting at public places, mass rallies, processions, celebrating protest days, political drama, mass deputation, torch light procession, demonstrations, hartals, strikes, picketing, satyagraha, dharna, fasting including chain fast, fast unto death, sympathetic fast, self-immolation, destruction of public property, holding up of transport, uprooting of railway tracks, damaging of control boxes, dislocating telephone and telegraph wires, burning of police stations and other government buildings, disturbing the public meetings of the opponents, go slow, mass casual leave, sit in demonstrations, looting of public and private property, riot, localized attempts to throw off state authority and run parallel administration, declared or undeclared warfare in a region, etc.[24] David Bayley[25], writing in the Indian context, speaks of six primary forms of protests: 1) processions and public meetings; 2) hartals (work stoppage), boycotts and strikes; 3) fasts; 4) obstructions; 5) courting of arrest; and 6) riots. These general forms of protests can be divided into two main groups: legal and illegal. Again, the category of illegal protests can be subdivided into violent and non-violent. These different categories have been schematically organized by Bayley as:

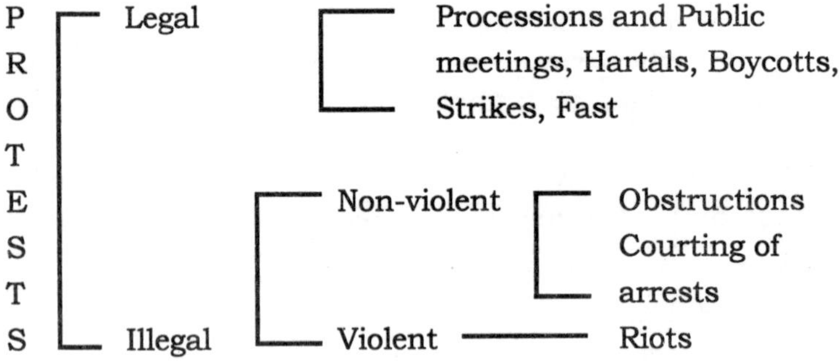

Though a distinction is sought to be made in terms of organization, ideology[26] and strength of participation, nature of the goal and coverage of area of operation between social movements and protest movements, these two virtually overlap. Sometimes social movements assume its form through protests while protests in any form happen to be precondition for social movement. For our purpose then, protests movements may be operationalized as those collective actions – legal and/or illegal, violent and/or non-violent – which seek to bring about a desired state of affairs either by bringing about change or resisting any change in the existing order. Since it is a collective endeavour, it needs to develop an organization and an amount of commitment to the goal and in turn, sharing to a set of ideas for legitimizing the goal and the means to reach the goal. The goal is, indeed, political though may appear to be social because, to differentiate between social power and political power in the contemporary world is to obscure the reality and ignore the complexities of political process.[27] Any collective endeavour to bring about social transformation inevitably involves capturing or influencing political authority even though it may not be on the immediate agenda.

This has been the general trend that analyses of protest movements follow either a Marxist or non-Marxist framework. Scholars following the Marxist framework locate the cases of protest movements in the economic structure and relations of the society. Conflicting interests between 'haves' and the 'have nots' are inherent in a class-divided society that generates contradictions. The 'have class' makes use of the coercive power of the state, as well as of other institutions, including religion, education, mass media to impose its ideology on the society and to control the exploited class. The 'have nots', on the other hand, resist and protest and occasionally revolt or launch organized and collective action against the dominance of the exploiting class. It is assumed that the members of the same class not only have common interest vis-à-vis other classes, but also share a common consciousness regarding their position in society and the common interest they share. This facilitates their collective action against the ruling class and the state.

However, the dominant Marxist approach has been subjected to criticism by a group of Marxist historians, the subaltern studies group. They advocate for studying history from below. They question the classical Marxists for ignoring the history of the masses and hold that 'subaltern' classes make history of their own and do not depend solely on the advanced classes or the elite for organization and guidance. It is argued by the subaltern historians that the classical Marxist scholars have undermined cultural factors and viewed a linear development of class consciousness.[28] On the contrary, the subaltern studies historians have been strongly criticized by other Marxist scholars for ignoring structural factors and viewing consciousness as independent of structural contradictions. They have been accused of being 'Hegelian idealists'.[29] Besides, the Marxist scholars, both the classical and the subaltern, find it difficult to analyze and accommodate the influences of race, ethnicity, caste, religion, community that transcend the class boundaries thus blurring the process of class formation on common class consciousness.

Non-Marxist scholars alike, while accusing the Marxist approach as being 'reductionist', 'mechanical, and of over-determining economic factors, also suffer from great deal of variations among themselves in their approach to the analysis of protest movements. It is argued that mass movements are the product of mass societies which are extremist and anti-democratic and hence, masses are to be excluded from the day-to-day participation in politics which hampers the efficient functioning of the government.[30] The scholars adhering to the theory of political development hold that the existing political institutions which are rigid and incompetent are not in a position to meet the rising aspirations of the people. As the gap between the two widens, political instability and disorder increases leading to protest in one form or the other.[31] Writing in the Indian context, some scholars view that the protest movements in post-independence India are the results of the conflict between tradition and modernity[32], while others blame the opposition leaders, parties and trade unions for instigating the masses to protest activities.[33] Rajni Kothari feels that protest movements 'are inevitable in the context of present day Indian parliamentary democracy because the general climate of frustration, the ineffectiveness of known channels of communication, the alienation and atomization of the individual, the tendency towards regimentation and the continuous state of conflict between the rulers and the ruled – all these make the ideal of self-government more and more remote and render parliamentary government an unstable form of political organization'.[34] Kothari goes on to argue that democracy in India has become a playground for growing corruption, criminalization, repression and intimidation of large masses of the people. The role of the state in social transformation has been undermined. Thus, people have started asserting their rights through various struggles.[35] Taking almost a similar stand, David Bayley observed that before and after independence, the institutional means of redress for grievances, frustrations and wrongs – actual or fancied were inadequate and hence, called for protest.[36]

However, the analyses of Kothari and Bayley are confined to the discussion of direct action that are against the government. But there may be issues and situations of equal concern for protests beyond the spheres of government. Actually, they do not consider the direct actions and protests against the socio-economic dominance and power structure in the society even though reference of social imbalances and injustices is found in Kothari's treatment. A.R. Desai joins issue with Kothari and Bayley and argues that protests of people will continue till adequate political institutional forms for the realization and exercise of concrete democratic rights are found.[37] He reiterates his position by saying that the civil and democratic rights of the people are not protected by the constitution and hence, the protests and movements for their protection have increased.[38]

Given the analyses of different dimensions of protest movements, theories which are generally accepted as explaining the structural conditions and motivational forces that give rise to a protest movement may be considered. There are three main theoretical frameworks that are relevant to the explanation of protest movements. These are: 1) Theory of Relative

Deprivation; 2) Theory of Strain; and 3) Theory of Revitalization. In addition, one more theoretical framework is sought to be suggested in this present study for explaining the causes of protest movements. This may be conceptualized as the Theory of Relative Deprivation of Elites of the Deprived.

The theory of Relative Deprivation centres around two different but important concepts – social mobility and social conflict. Although the authors of the 'American Soldier'[39] were the first to develop the notion of relative deprivation, it was Merton[40] who systematically developed the theory in relation to reference group theory and applied it to the analysis of social mobility. Later, following Merton, Runciman[41] developed the theory further in relation to reference group and problems of inequalities and social injustice. Marx and Engels[42] also recognized that dissatisfaction with the existing order was not determined by absolute condition but by relative expectations, thus leading to conflict situation. Aberle[43] defining relative deprivation as a negative discrepancy between legitimate expectations and actuality, considered it as the bed-rock for the study of social movements. Gurr[44] observed relative deprivation as a gap between expectations and perceived capabilities involving three general sets of values – economic conditions, political power and social status. This gap, according to Gurr, may originate when expectations remain stable but capabilities decline (detrimental deprivation); expectations rise but capabilities decline (progressive deprivation); and expectations rise but the capabilities remain stable (aspirational deprivation).

The theory of relative deprivation assumes that when a group of people in a society feels deprived of the social status or economic opportunities or political power or the combination of these in comparison to other group/groups, the group perceiving deprivation may resort to remedial measures including agitations and protests. Here, the deprivation is thus relative in nature as it may be real or fancied. Thus, the theory appears to be limited on the ground that the structural conditions of relative deprivation provide only the necessary conditions. Sufficient conditions that actually trigger the operational part are provided by the perceptions of a situation and by the estimate of capabilities by the leaders of the group that they can do something to remedy the situation.[45] The theory thus ignores the importance of consciousness and ideological aspects of the participants.[46] Similarly, the theory assumes movements as 'temporary aberration' rather than as 'ongoing process of change'.[47] Particularly for Gurr, deprivation is primarily psychological. Therefore, he does not deal with the socio-economic and political structure which is the source of deprivation.

The strain theory that was propounded by Neil Smelser[48] treats structural strain as the underlying factor that leads to collective mobilization and behaviour. Smelser considers from the structural functional framework, 'strain' as the impairment of relations among parts of a system leading to the malfunctioning of the system and causing deprivation under strain. This structural strain or impairment of smooth functioning of the system may occur at different levels of norms, values, mobilization and situation. Indeed, strain is assumed to provide the structural condition for protests but it is the generalized belief that marks the attempts of persons under strain to assess their situation, explain the situation and respond accordingly. Thus, both strain and generalized belief require participating factors to trigger off a movement.

The theory of revitalization was developed by Wallace.[49] According to the theory, when a group of people feels the urge for revitalizing the culture to which it belongs, it realizes the culture as a whole and for perceived fear of loss of cultural identity or cultural extinction moves towards a movement for cultural change. Thus, to Wallace, protest movements may develop out of a deliberate, organized and conscious effort on the part of members of a society to construct a more satisfying culture for themselves. He analyzed the dynamics of revitalization movements in four phases – period of cultural stability, period of increased individual stress, period of cultural disortion and consequent disillusionment, and period of revitalization.

In all these theories what is common is the prime emphasis on the participants of a movement. The assumption is that if the people feel deprived of, or are under strain due to malfunctioning of the system, or feel the necessity for cultural revitalization, the movement will emanate, as if other factors and conditions of the movement will automatically follow. To accept this basic analytical framework in its totality is to oversimplify the reality. May be that there exists the objective conditions for a movement, namely, deprivation, strain, and the urge for revitalization, but the mere presence of these necessary conditions will not lead to a protest or a movement unless driven by a driving force – leadership in the main followed by an ideology and organization. It is true that at the initial stage of a protest movement there may not be any well-defined organization and ideology and once the movement gets triggered off, organization and ideology will get articulated. But it cannot be denied that to trigger the protest movement off, leadership is a concomitant necessity with the prime necessary condition, that is, the people. Leadership actually provides the driving force for any protest movement. Under this framework of analysis, people's feeling and leadership to channelize the feeling need to be present simultaneously along with, of course, the necessary objective conditions for protests.

It is on this that the present study seeks to float an analytical framework that movements, and for that matter, protests do not originate; they are made to originate and are imposed on the passive, ignorant masses. Taking cues from Kedourie's 'Nationalism'[50] and 'Nationalism in Asia and Africa'[51] that nationalism is not a reaction against European political or economic exploitation (feeling of deprivation causing strain and/or, urge for revitalization) but essentially an emotional reaction by Asian and African intellectuals against their rejection by Europeans. Taking a similar stand, Banton observes, "National consciousness was not an inherent feeling, but something taught and cultivated to serve specific ends".[52] The roles of elites in the emergence of nationalist movements is critical in Smith's analysis also.[53] If we stretch the argument further it leads to the observation that consciousness is created, mobilized and imposed by the few for their own narrow interest but garbed as universal interest for legitimacy. Political elites exploit situation of regional deprivation and unrest and convert them into movements to forge and strengthen their individual and factional support bases.[54] In other words, political leaders excite regional or nativist sentiments for their political ends. The framework may be elaborated further as under.

As has already been stated, the poor economy and the limited economic resources on the one hand, and almost inevitably, the interventionist nature of the state in the developing countries basically safeguarding and promoting the interest of a particular class entails intense political competition. Remaining in and around the power centre only ensures access to and control over the poor but otherwise lucrative economy and thus begets social and political position. Hence, one witnesses intense political competition among the aspirants of power and the aspirants even go to the extent of adopting irrational means to be in and around the power centre. In view of the intense competition, some of the aspirant political leaders in the game of politics inevitably get frustrated when they are defeated in the game of power. This section of the frustrated leaders who are out of the helms of power centre (s) but want to be around mobilize the already deprived common people, mostly on primordial considerations, to protest against their injustice, discrimination and deprivation. In reality, however, this section of the leadership wants to serve its personal parochial interest of achieving or regaining social, economic and political position and that too, in the name of universal common interest. Thus, it implies that objective conditions of deprivation and discrimination alone may not necessarily lead to the protests and movements as is assumed by the relative deprivation theorists. Observations show that in most of the cases, it is the frustration of the section of political elites and its desire to be near the power centre that actually leads the actual or perceived deprivation to be channelized into protests and agitations. Hence, it is not the existence and content of deprivation but the politics of deprivation that originates protest movements.

Review of Literature

Over the years, sociologists and social anthropologists have been showing considerable interest in the study of protest movements – a field that has long been considered to be the field of the historians. Political scientists have, by and large, ignored this area.[55] Political scientists have been found paying little attention to the study of the politics of masses, their aspirations and demand, the articulation of their problems and their modus operandi in the assertion of their demands outside the formal institutional framework.[56] The reasons for this apathy on the part of the political scientists to ignore the socio-political dynamics may be attributed to the value-oriented and formal institution-oriented trend of traditional political science and excessive dominance of positivism under the influence of behaviouralism. Besides, due to the dominance of the post World War-II liberal political ideology and the structural functional approach, there has been greater emphasis in the social science literature on 'equilibrium and harmony' rather than on conflict and change. Political Science, though primarily concerned with power and conflict has mostly refrained, with, of course, the exception of the Marxist Scholars, from researching the issue of societal conflict for social change.[57] However, a small section of political scientists, both liberal and radical, have started exploring the area of protest movements for greater understanding and identifying their impact on the social, economic and political environment.

At the outset, mention must be made of Ghanashyam Shah's "Social Movements in India: A Review of Literature".[58] In this volume, Shah reviews the literature available on social movements in India in general in an exhaustive and intensive manner thus making the task of a researcher on social movements in India easier. His other two works, namely, "Protest Movements in Two Indian States"[59] and "Caste Association and Political Process in Gujarat: A Study of Kshatriya Sabha"[60] deal exclusively with protest movements, their origin, expansion, consolidation and impact in specific context.

David Bayley[61], writing in the early sixties, observed that parliamentary form of government in India could not redress the grievances of large number of people and hence, justified the functional utility of public protests. Rajni Kothari, taking a similar stand, argues that protests in the form of direct action are inevitable in India's present day parliamentary democracy[62] and feels that mass mobilization at the grassroots level is both necessary and desirable.[63] His other works – 'State Against Democracy'[64], 'Transformation and Survival'[65], 'Rethinking Democracy'[66], 'Politics and People'[67] also deserve mentioning as he, in all his studies, succinctly analyzes the internal dynamics of Indian politics.

Taking an opposite stand, scholars like Phadke[68], Aiyer[69] and Srinivasan[70] disapprove agitations and protests in India after independence because they feel that recognized formal and constitutional means are enough for redressing the grievances of the people. Similarly, some other scholars feel that protests are redundant in the Indian culture and civilization due to its 'multilinear character' and 'all pervasive hierarchy'. Moore[71], Chandra[72] and Badrinath[73] observe that because of the Brahminical ideology and hierarchical social structure the oppressed classes have become docile, obedient and fatalist. But Gough[74], Thapar[75], Damle[76] and Dhanagare[77] refute such assertions and point to a number of protests and struggles by the deprived and oppressed classes in the pre and post independence India.

A.R. Desai, a noted Sociologist, has made significant contribution to this field. As a sociologist and social activist, he has analyzed the problem mainly from human rights perspective. He feels that the parliamentary form of government, as a political-institutional device, has proved to be inadequate to sustain or expand democratic rights of the people. The protests by people will thus continue till adequate political-institutional forms for the realization and exercise of concrete democratic rights are found.[78] Desai reiterates his position that civil and democratic rights of the people are not protected by the constitution. Consequently, protests for their protection have increased.[79, 80]

T.K. Oommen[81] analyzes the potentiality of protest as a source of change. He argues that the basic sources of change have been taken to be the economy or the agrarian, industrial or information revolution. In contrast, political revolutions, by definition, imply the transfer of power from one group to another. Those likely to be deprived of it, as also those sections of the population who support the ruling elite, disapprove protest. This 'displacement syndrome', Oommen says, reduces the potential of protest as an instrument of change. In another book[82], Oommen explores and analyzes the problematiqe of nation-building in India. Some of these problems, the author argues, are the result of erroneous conceptions arising out of misplaced polarities juxtaposing nation vs. state, political nationalism vs. cultural nationalism, Indianism vs. localism. These dimensions coexist and are mutually reinforcing and enriching. The Indian genius is one of gradual transformation, piecemeal accretion and cautious reconciliation. Therefore, the real task of nation building entails nurturing pluralism in all contexts – values, technology and culture.

Atul Kohli[83], in his penetrating and insightful study on Indian politics, describes how and explains why India has become difficult to govern. Kohli observes that the roots of India's growing problems of governability are more political than socio-economic. A highly interventionist state dealing with a poor economy has become a subject of intense political competition. The spread of egalitarian political values and the opportunities provided by democracy have, in turn, helped to transform what was once a heterogeneous social structure into many groups of mobilized activists. Failure of leaders to make timely concessions has only intensified political demands and activity.

Paul R. Brass[84], in his stimulating analyses of 'Indian Politics since Independence', has argued that the Indian state, society and economy are in the midst of a systematic crisis which has intensified, revealing itself in secessionist movements and in increased inter-caste and inter-religious conflicts. The issue before the country, Brass feels, is whether or not it can find within its own traditions the moral and material resources and the leadership to restore a political and communal balance in state and society. In another work[85], Brass looks at elite competition as the basic dynamics which precipitates ethnic conflict under specific conditions. These conditions arise from the broader economic and political environment. He feels that the political economy of India induces strong conflicting drives towards centralization and decentralization in the Indian polity and this in turn, manifests itself in various forms of ethnic upsurges.

Zoya Hasan *et al.*[86], in an edited volume, discuss and explore the potentially dangerous challenges posed to Indian polity. The essays in the volume examine in particular the unprecedented upsurge in communal, sectarian and regional tensions in the recent past and simultaneous emergence of religious, class, and caste groups as powerful expression of political consciousness. Taken together, these developments have had the effect of bringing the very nature of the Indian state into question.

Another edited volume by Upendra Baxi and Bhiku Parekh[87] addresses *inter alia* on the problematique of tradition and modernity shaping religious and secular identities. Again, it focuses on the issues of civil loyalty and primordial politics emerging as a part of a dialectic shaping of modern India, the crisis of governability and the nature of Indian politics.

Rudolph and Rudolph[88], accepting the modernization paradigm, seek to explain how the state in India came to play a dominant role in the economy and how the interplay between the state as an interest group and other interest groups in the society brought about a centrist thrust to economic policies. The book's basic thesis appears to be that the formulation and the implementation of economic policies in India have been influenced by the "overload" on the state which has changed its character from "being autonomous" to "being constrained". In a similar way, Bardhan[89], Frankel[90] and Bhambri[91] deal with the economic dimensions of various problems confronting the Indian polity and the resulting dissentions.

David Taylor and Malcolm Yapp's[92] edited volume deals with the relationship between language, religion and political identity in South Asian perspective. Primary attention in the volume has been paid to linguistic and religious factors in the making of political identities and the formation of new political demands, but the operation of these factors is seen as being conditioned and in some cases determined by grander political and economic forces.

M.S.A. Rao's edited volumes[93] are the attempts to bring together twelve studies of diverse social movements in different parts of India. The papers included in the volumes provide valuable insights into the genesis of the concerned movements, their ideological foundations, organization and leadership, event structure, integral dynamics and social and cultural consequences.

Besides these general studies, there are some important contributions on specific studies of protest movements in India. On peasant protests studies by Mishra[94], Kling[95], Mitter[96], and Natarajan[97], deal with indigo movement in Bengal and Bihar; studies by Gopalan[98], Dale[99], Hardgrave[100], Choudhury[101], Hitchock[102], deal with the Moplah rebellion in Malabar region, Kerala; studies by Dhanagare[103], Sarkar[104], Custers[105] examine the Tebhaga movement in Bengal; studies by Rao[106], Dhanagare[107], Elliott[108], Pavier[109], deal with the Telengana movement in Andhra Pradesh; and the Naxalite movement in West Bengal, Bihar and Andhra Pradesh has been studied by Dasgupta[110], Ghose[111], Banerjee[112], Sengupta[113]. Historical analysis of peasant movements have been offered from different perspectives by Chaudhury[114], Kaviraj[115] and Sen[116] on Bengal; Das[117] and Henningham[118] on Bihar; Ranga[119] on Andhra Pradesh; and by Namboodiripad[120], Oommen[121], and Kannan[122] on Kerala. However, a comparative approach to regional struggle is missing in these studies though the studies by Dhanagare[123] and Custers[123] are the exceptions to that directions.

Various studies on tribal and ethnic movements highlight militancy of tribals in various struggles during pre and post independence period. These studies point out the line between the changing nature of issues that the tribals raised in the past and the peasant movement is getting blurred as tribals become peasants. Though the number of studies on tribal movements is large, only a few are intensive and well documented. Mention may be made of the studies by Singh[125], Anand[126], Augustine[127], Sareen[128], Weiner[129], Bhattacharjee[130], Chattopadhyay[131], Das[132], Dutta[133], Hall[134], Hussain[135], Goswami[136], Mathur[137], Nibedan[138], Phukan[139], Bhattacharjee[140], Lama[141], Subba[142], Syangden and Moktan[143] and Mukherjee[144].

The studies on the Dalit protests in pre and post independence period are not many. Most of the studies available so far are confined to Maharastra. These studies include those by Pimpley and Sharma[145], Kamble[146], Lynch[147], Rajendran[148], Rao[149], Shah[150], Shyamlal[151], Verba, Ahmed and Bhatt[152], and Kothari[153].

The theme of protest movements has also attracted, though marginally, the scholars dealing with state politics in a general way. The studies conducted so far from different perspectives of states politics either as a specific case study or in a general comparative way have touched upon this vital aspect affecting the governing process of India. In this connection, mention may be made of Innaih[154], Irani[155], Kapoor[156], Katzenstein[157], Narang[158], Nayar[159] and the like.

On the government response to various protest movements by way by signing accords the study by Dutta[160] deserves special mention. In this volume, the author brings together the full text of all the peace accords since 1947 signed between various protesting groups and the government.

Besides, there are innumerable research articles published in periodicals on various aspects and dimensions of protest movements. These too provide sufficient insight into the different contours of protest movements and their impact on the socio-political and economic environment in India.

Significance of the Study

It is evident from the literature reviewed above that in most of the cases, the studies are unidimensional in character. Hardly, in any work, specific, in-depth analyses of the political implications of protest movements in India has been made. The present study, in this sense, seeks to bridge the existing research gap and thus opens the possibility of formulating a broad theoretical framework to understand the political process of the developing countries in general and India in particular. The study seems to be relevant in the context of the theoretical framework that has been suggested in the section of the theoretical framework for further test and applications.

Methodology

The method for collecting information for the present study was essentially historical-analytical and as such, exploratory in nature. As such, the information were collected from the documents and/or reports by the Governments and movements as also from published books and articles on protest movements. As the purpose of the study was to explore, reliance was on review of literature available on the subject. By its own logic, the study is thus limited on the ground that it could not undertake any fieldwork for collecting primary data. But it is also obvious that the objective of the study was too broad to permit fieldwork and the nature of the study was so that there was, in fact, little scope for field study. Besides, one of the important techniques to understand properly any movement is to resort to participatory action research, that is, study of ongoing movements. The present study could not go for participatory action research too because the objective was a holistic one to cover a large number of protest movements to arrive at generalized formulation of the impact of the movements on the political system and processes in India. In fact, impact study can be made only after some amount of progress has been there in a movement.

NOTES & REFERENCES

1. Kohli, Atul: *Democracy and Discontent: India's Growing Crisis of Governability*, New Delhi: Cambridge University Press, 1991, p. IX.

2. Singh, Yogendra: "Contemporary Social 'Crisis' in India and its Dimensions" in *Man and Development*, Vol. XIV, No. 4, December, 1992.
3. *Ibid.*, p. IX.
4. Singh, Dalip: "Protest Movements in India", *Indian Journal of Political Science*, Vol. 52, No. 4, 1991, p. 448.
5. Kohli, Atul: *op. cit.*, p. 3.
6. Singh, Dalip: *op. cit.*, pp. 456-457.
7. *Ibid.*, pp. 454-455.
8. Rao, M.S.A.: *Social Movements and Social Transformation: A Study of Two Backward Classes Movements in India*, Delhi: Macmillan, 1979, p. 1.
9. Oommen, T.K.: *Protest and Change: Studies in Social Movements*, New Delhi: Sage, 1990, p. 13.
10. Cited in Wilkinson, Paul: *Social Movement*, London: Macmillan, 1971, p. 11.
11. *Ibid.*, p. 14.
12. Mackenzie, W.J.M.: *Politics and Social Science*, Harmondsworth, Middlesex, 1967.
13. Wilkinson, Paul: *op. cit.*, p. 15.
14. Weldon, T.D.: *The Vocabulary of Politics*, Harmondsworth, 1955.
15. Heberle, Rudolph: *Social Movements: An Introduction to Political Sociology*, New York: Appleton-century-crofts Inc., 1951, p. 2. Also Herbert Blummer: "Collective Behaviour" in Gittler (ed.): *Review of Sociology: Analysis of a Decade*, New York: Wiley, 1957, p. 145.
16. Smelser, Neil J.: *Theory of Collective Behaviour*, London: Routledge and Kegan Paul, 1962, p. 14.
17. Wilson, T.H.: *Introduction to Social Movements*, New York: Basic Books, p. 8.
18. Tilly, Charles: *From Mobilization to Revolution*, Mass: Addison-Weskly, 1965.
19. Wilkinson, Paul: *op. cit.* p., 26.
20. *Ibid.*, p. 27.
21. Shah, Ghanshyam: *Social Movements in India: A Review of Literature*, New Delhi: Sage, 1990, p. 17.

22. Heberle, Rudolf: "Types and Functions of Social Movements" in *International Encyclopaedia of the Social Sciences*, New York: Colliev Macmillan, 1968, pp. 438-439. Also Bhattacharjee, Chandana: *Ethnicity and Antonomy Movement: Case of Bodo-Kacharis of Assam*, New Delhi: Vikas, 1996, p. 2.

23. Shah, Ghanshyam: *Protest Movements in Two Indian States*, Delhi: Ajanta Publishers, 1977, p. 19.

24. Mahendru, K.C.: "Public Protests and Civil Liberties in India" in *Political Science Review*, Vol. XIII, No. 1-4, 1974, p. 197.

25. Bayley, David H.: "The Pedagogy of Democracy: Public Protest in India" in *American Political Science Review*, Vol. 56, No. 3, September, 1962, pp. 663-664.

26. Wilkinson, Paul: *op. cit.*, pp. 26-28. Also Rudolph Heberle: *op. cit.*

27. Frank, Andre Gunder and Marta Fuentes make a distinction between social and political movements. According to them, social movements do not strive for state power. Frank, Andre Gunder and Marta Fuentes: "Nine Theses on Social Movements" in *Economic and Political Weekly*, Vol. 32, No. 35, August 29, 1987. Dhanagare and John feel that Frank and Fuentes are committed to process of 'depoliticization of social realism and believe that the difference between social and political movement is merely semantic. Dhanagare, D. and John, J.: "Cyclical Movement towards the "Eternal" – "Nine Theses on Social Movements: A Critique" in *Economic and Political Weekly*, Vol. 33, No. 21, May 21, 1988.

28. Guha, R.: *Elementary Aspects of Peasant Insurgency in Colonial India*, Delhi: Oxford University Press, 1983.

    Guha, R.: "The Process of Counter-Insurgency" in Guha, Ranjit (ed.): *Subaltern Studies*, Vol. II, Delhi: Oxford University Press, 1983.

    Chatterjee, P.: "Peasants, Politics and Historiography: A Response" in *Social Scientist*, Vol. II, No. 5, May 1983.

    Chatterjee, P.: "Models of Power: Some Classifications" in *Social Scientist*, Vol. 13, No. 2, February 1985.

    Hardiman, David: *The Coming of the Devi: Adivasi Assertion in Western India*, Delhi: Oxford University Press, 1987.

29. Chopra, Suneet: "Missing Correct Perspective" in *Social Scientist*, Vol. 10, No. 8, August 1982.

Alam, Zaveed: "Peasantry, Politics and Historiography: Critique of New Trend in Relation to Marxism" in *Social Scientist*, Vol. II, No. 2, February 1983.

Singh, Sangeeta; Menon, Minakshi *et al.*: Subaltern Studies 11: A Review Article in *Social Scientist*, Vol. 12, No. 10, October 1984.

Gupta, Dipankar: "On Altering the Ego in History: Paradoxes of the Ethnic Option" in *Peasant Studies*, Vol. 13, No. 2, Fall, 1985.

30. Kornhouser, W.: "Mass Society" in Shills, David (ed.): *International Encyclopaedia of Social Sciences*, Vol. 9, New York: Macmillan, 1968.

Kornhouser, W.: *The Politics of Mass Society*, Glenco: Free Press, 1959.

Nisbet, R.: *The Quest for Community*, New York: Oxford University Press, 1953.

Shills, Edward: "The Political Class in the Age of Mass Society: Collectivistic Liberalism and Social Democracy" in Czudnowski, M. (ed.): *Does who Govern Matter? Elite Circulation of Contemporary Societies*, De Kalib: Northern Illinois: University Press, 1982.

31. Huntington, S.: *Political Order in Changing Societies*, New Haven: Yale University Press, 1968.

Johnson, Chalmers: *Revolutionary Change*, Boston: Litter Brown, 1966.

32. Moris-Jones, W.H.: *The Government and Politics of India*, Bombay: Manaktalas, 1966.

33. Aiyar, S.P. (ed.): *The Politics of Mass Violence in India*, Bombay, Manaktalas, 1966.

Srinivasan, R.: "Democracy and the Revolt of the Masses" in Aiyar, S.P. (ed.): *The Politics of Mass Violence in India*, Bombay, Manaktalas, 1966.

34. Kothari, R.: "Direct Action: A Pattern of Political Behaviour" in *Quest*, 24, January March, 1960, pp. 26-27.

35. Kothari, R.: "The Non-Party Political Process" in *Economic and Political Weekly*, Vol. 19, No. 5, February 4, 1984, p. 218.

36. Bayley, David H.: *op. cit.*

37. Desai, A.R.: "Public Protest and Parliamentary Democracy" in Aiyar, S.P. and R. Srinivasan (eds.): *Studies in Indian Democracy*,

Bombay: Allied Publishers, 1965, p. 323.

38. Desai, A.R. (ed.): *Violation of Democratic Rights in India*, Bombay: Popular Prakashan, 1986.

39. Stouffer, Samuel A. *et al.* (eds.): *The American Soldier: Adjustment During Army Life*, Vol. 1, Princeton: Princeton University Press, 1949.

40. Merton, R.K. and Rosset, Alice Kitt: "Contribution to the Theory of Reference Group Behaviour" in Merton, R.K. and Lazarsfeld, P.F. (eds.): *Continuities in Social Research*, New York: The Free Press, pp. 40-106.

41. Runciman, W.C.: *Relative Deprivation and Social Justice*, London: Routledge and Kegan Paul, 1966.

42. Marx, Karl and Engels, Frederick: *Selected Works* (Three Volumes), Moscow: Progress Publishers, 1973.

43. Aberle, D.F.: *The Peyote Religion Among the Navaho*, Viking Fund Publications in Anthropology, No. 42, New York: Wenner-Gren Foundation, 1966.

44. Gurr, T.R.: *Why Men Rebel*, Princeton N.J.: Princeton University Press, 1970.

45. Rao, M.S.A. (ed.): *Social Movements in India*, Vol. 1, New Delhi: Manohar, 1979, p. 5. Also Rao, M.S.A.: *Social Movements and Social Transformation: A Study of Two Backward Class Movements in India*, Delhi: Macmillan, 1979, p. 207.

46. Shah, Ghanshyam: "Direct Action in India: A Study of Gujarat and Bihar Agitation" in *Contribution to Asian Studies*, 14, 1979, p. 207. Also Shah, Ghanshaym: *Social Movements in India*, *op. cit.*, p. 26.

47. Oommen, T.K.: "Sociological Issues in the Analysis of Social Movements in Independent India" in *Sociological Bulletin*, Vol. 26, No. 1, 1977.

48. Smelser, Neil: *The Theory of Collective Behaviour*, New York: Free Press, 1963.

49. Wallace, A.F.C.: "Revitalization Movements" in *American Anthropologist*, 58, April, pp. 264-81.

50. Kedourie, Elic: *Nationalism*, London: 1960 cited in Taylor, David and Yapp, Malcolm (eds.): *Political Identity in South Asia*, London: Curzon Press, 1979, pp. 5-6.

51. Kedourie, Elic: *Nationalism in Asia and Africa*, London: 1971 cited

in Taylor and Yapp, *op. cit.*, p. 6.

52. Banton, M.: "Ethnic Groups and The Theory of Rational Choice" in *Sociological Theories: Race and Colonialism*, Paris: UNESCO, 1980 cited in Richmond, Anthony H.: "Ethnic Nationalism: Social Science Paradigms" in *International Social Science Journal*, III, February 1987, p. 11.
53. Smith, A.D.: *Theories of Nationalism*, London: Duckworth, 1971, p. 256.
54. Narain, Iqbal: "A Conceptual Analysis in Indian Context" in Akhtar, Majeed (ed.): *Regionalism: Developmental Tensions in India*, Delhi: Cosmo Publication, 1984.
55. Shah, Ghanshyam: *Social Movements in India, op. cit.*, p. 13.
56. *Ibid.* p. 14.
57. Sathyamurthy, T.V.: "Contemporary European Scholarship on Political and Social Change in South Asia: An Essay in the Sociology of Knowledge" in *Economic and Political Weekly*, Vol. 22, No. 11, March 14, 1987.
58. Shah, Ghanshyam: *Social Movements in India: A Review of Literature, op. cit.*
59. Shah, Ghanshyam: *Protest Movements in Two Indian States, op. cit.*
60. Shah, Ghanshyam: *Caste Association and Political Process in Gujarat: A Study of Kshatriya Sabha*, Bombay: Popular Prakashan, 1975.
61. Bayley, David H.: *op. cit.*
62. Kothari, Rajni: "Direct Action: A Pattern of Political Behaviour", *op. cit.*
63. Kothari, Rajni: "Masses, Classes and the State" in *Economic and Political Weekly*, Vol. 21, No. 5, February 1, 1986.
64. Kothari, Rajni: *State Against Democracy: In Search of Humane Governance*, Delhi: Ajanta, 1988.
65. Kothari, Rajni: *Transformation and Survival: In Search of a Humane World Order*, Delhi: Ajanta, 1988.
66. Kothari, Rajni: *Rethinking Development: In Search of a Humane Alternatives*, Delhi: Ajanta, 1989.
67. Kothari, Rajni: *Politics and the People: In Search of a Humane India*, Delhi: Ajanta, 1989.

68. Phadke, U.D.: "The Historical Background of Mass Violence in India" in Aiyar, S.P. (ed.): *op. cit.*

69. Aiyar, S.P. (ed.): *op. cit.*

70. Srinivasan, R.: *op. cit.*

71. Moore, Barringter Jr: *Social Origins of Dictatorship and Democracy*, London: Allen Lane, 1967.

72. Chandra, Pratap: "Study of Ideological Discord in Ancient India: Search for a Suitable Model" in Malik, S.C. (ed.): *Dissent, Protest and Reform in Indian Civilization*, Simla: Indian Institute of Advanced Study, 1977.

73. Badrinath, C.: "Dissent, Protest and Social Reform: The Historical Context" in Malik, S.P. (ed.): *op. cit.*

74. Gough, Kathleen: "Indian Peasant Uprising" in *Economic and Political Weekly*, Vol. 9, No. 32-34, special number, August 1974.

75. Thapar, Romila: "Ethics, Religion and Social Protest in the First Millennium B.C. in Northern India" in Malik S.C. (ed.): *op. cit.*

76. Damle, Y.B.: "Protest, Dissent and Social Reform: A Conceptual Note" in Malik, S.P. (ed.): *op. cit.*

77. Dhanagare, D.: *Peasant Movements in India 1920-50*, Delhi: Oxford University Press, 1983.

78. Desai, A.R.: "Public Protest and Parliamentary Democracy" in Aiyar, S.P. and Srinivasan, R. (eds.): *op. cit.*

79. Desai, A.R. (ed.): *Violation of Democratic Rights in India*, Bombay: Popular Prakashan, 1986.

80. Desai, A.R.: *Repression and Resistance in India*, Bombay: Popular, 1990.

81. Oommen, T.K.: *Protest and Change: Studies in Social Movements*, New Delhi: Sage, 1990.

82. Oommen, T.K.: *State and Society in India: Studies in Nation-Building*, New Delhi: Sage, 1990.

83. Kohli, Atul: *Democracy and Discontent: India's Growing Crisis of Governability*, *op. cit.* Also (ed.): *India's Democracy: An Analysis of Changing State-Society Relation*, Princeton N.J.: Princeton University Press, 1988.

84. Brass, Paul R.: *The Politics of India Since Independence*, New Delhi: Foundation Books, 1994.

85. Brass, Paul R.: *Ethnicity and Nationalism: Theory and Comparison*, New Delhi: Sage, 1991.
86. Hasan, Zoya, Jha, S.N. and Khan Rasheeduddin (eds.): *The State, Political Process and Identity: Reflections on Modern India*, New Delhi: Sage, 1989.
87. Baxi, Upendra and Parekh, Bhikhu (ed.): *Crisis and Change in Contemporary India*, New Delhi: Sage, 1995.
88. Rudolph, Lloyd I. and Rudolph, Susanne H.: *In Pursuit of Lakshmi: The Political Economy of the Indian State*, New Delhi: Orient Longman, 1987.
89. Bardhan, Pranab: *The Political Economy of Development in India*, Oxford: Basil Blackwell, 1984.
90. Frankel, Frencise: *India's Political Economy, 1947-1977: The Gradual Revolution*, Princeton N.J.: Princeton University Press, 1978.
91. Bhambri, C.P.: *Politics in India, 1947-87*, New Delhi: Vikas Publishing House, 1988.
92. Taylor, David and Yapp, Malcolm (eds.): *Political Identity in South Asia, op. cit.*
93. Rao, M.S.A.: *Social Movements in India*, Vols. 1&2, *op. cit.*
94. Mishra, Girish: "Socio-Economic Background of Gandhi's Champaran Movement", in *The Indian Economic and Social History Review*, Vol. 5, No. 3, September, 1968.
95. Kling, B.B.: *The Blue Mutiny: The Indigo Disturbances in Bengal, 1859-1862*, Calcutta: Firma K.L.M., 1977.
96. Mitter, S.K.: *Peasant Uprising and Mahatma Gandhi in North Bihar*, Meerut: ANU Prakashan, 1978.
97. Natarajan, L.: "Indigo Cultivator's Strike, 1860", in Desai, A.R. (ed.): *Peasant Struggle in India*, Delhi: Oxford University Press, 1979.
98. Gopalan, N.C.: *The Moplah Rebellion*, Calcutta: The Author, 1921.
99. Dale, Stephen: "The Mappila Outbreak: Ideology and Social Conflict in 19th Century Kerala", in *Journal of Asian Studies*, Vol. 33, No. 1, 1975.
100. Hardgrave, Robert Jr.: "The Mopilla Rebellion 1921: Peasant Revolt in Malabar", in *Modern Asian Studies*, Vol. 2, No. 1, 1977.
101. Choudhury, Sukhbir: *Moplah Uprising (1921-23)*, Delhi: Agan

Prakashan, 1979.

102. Hitchock, R.H.: *Peasant Revolt in Malabar: A History of Malabar Rebellion, 1921*, Delhi: Usha Publication, 1983.

103. Dhanagare, D.: "Peasant Protest and Politics – The Tebhaga Movement in Bengal (India), 1946-47", in *The Journal of Peasant Studies*, Vol. 8, No. 3, April, 1976.

104. Sarkar, K.K.: "Kakdwip Tebhaga Movement" in Desai, A.R. (ed.): *Peasant Struggle in India, op. cit.*

105. Custers, Peter: *Women in the Tebhaga Uprising*, Calcutta: Naya Prakash, 1987.

106. Rao, R.: *The Historical Telengana Struggle*, New Delhi: Communist Party of India, 1972.

107. Dhanagare, D.: "Social Origins of the Peasant Insurrection in Telengana" 1946-51", in *Contributions to Indian Sociology* (New Series) 8, 1974.

108. Elliot, C.M.: "Decline of a Patrimonial Regime: The Telengana Rebellion in India 1946-51", in *The Journal of Asian Studies*, Vol. 32, No. 1, 1974.

109. Pavier, B.: *The Telengana Movement, 1944-51*, Delhi: Vikas Publishing House, 1981.

110. Dasgupta, Biplab: *The Naxalite Movement*, Bombay: Allied Publishers, 1974.

111. Ghose, Sankar: *The Naxalite Movement: A Maoist Experiment*, Calcutta: Firma K.L.M., 1974.

112. Banerjee, Sumanta: *In the Wake of Naxalbari*, Calcutta: Subarnarekha, 1980.

113. Sengupta, Pramod: *Naxalbari and Indian Revolution*, Calcutta: Research India Publications, 1983.

114. Chaudhury, B.B.: "Peasant Movements in Bengal 1850-1900", in *19th Century Studies*, 3, July 1973.

115. Kaviraj, Narahari: *A Peasant Uprising in Bengal*, New Delhi: Peoples' Publishing House, 1972.

116. Sen, Sunil: *Agrarian Struggles in Bengal 1946-47*, New Delhi: Peoples' Publishing House, 1972.

117. Das, Arvind N.: *Agrarian Unrest and Socio-Economic Change in Bihar 1900-1980*, New Delhi: Manohar, 1983.

118. Hennigham, Stephen: *Peasants Movements in Colonial India, North Bihar 1917-1942*, Canberra: Australian National University, 1982.

119. Ranga, N.G.: *Revolutionary Peasants*, New Delhi: Amrit Book Company, 1949.

120. Namboodripad, E.M.S.: *A Short History of the Peasant Movement in Kerala*, Bombay: Peoples' Publishing House, 1943.

121. Oommen, T.K.: *From Mobilization to Institutionalization: The Dynamics of Agrarian Movement in 20th Century Kerala*, Bombay: Popular Prakashan, 1985.

122. Kannan, K.P.: *Of Rural Proletarian Struggles, Mobilization and Organization of Rural Workers in South West India*, Delhi: Oxford University Press, 1988.

123. Dhanagare, D.: *Peasant Movements in India 1920-50*, Delhi: Oxford University Press, 1983.

124. Custers, Peter: *op. cit.*

125. Singh, K.S. (ed.): *Tribal Movements in India*, Vols. 1&2, Delhi: Manohar, 1982 and 1983.

126. Anand, V.K.: *Conflict in Nagaland*, Delhi: Chanakya Publications, 1980.

127. Augastine, P.A.: *Suppression of Valia Tribals: A Case of Human Rights Violation*, Delhi: Indian Social Institute, 1984.

128. Sareen, H.K.: *Insurgency in North East India: A Study of Sino-American Role*, New Delhi: Sterling Publishers, 1980.

129. Weiner, M.: *Sons of the Soil*, Delhi: Oxford University Press, 1978.

130. Bhattacharjee, S.: *Genesis of Tribal Extremism in Tripura*, New Delhi: Gyan Publishing House, 1991.

131. Chattopadhyay, D.K.: *History of the Assam Movement since 1947*, Calcutta: Minerva Associates, 1990.

132. Das, Victor: *Jharkhand: Castle Over the Graves*, New Delhi: Inter-India, 1978.

133. Dutta, P.S.: *Autonomy Movements in Assam: Documents*, New Delhi: Omsons, 1993.

134. Hall, R.L.: *Ethnic Autonomy – Comparative Analysis: The Americans, Europe and the Developing World*, Vol. II, New York: Macmillan, 1933.

135. Hussain, M.: *The Assam Movement: Class, Ideology, Identity*, Delhi: Har Anand, 1983.

136. Goswami, B.B.: *The Mizo Unrest*, Jaipur: Alekh, 1979.

137. Mathur, L.P.: *Resistance Movement of Tribals of India*, Udaipur: Himansu Publications, 1988.

138. Nibidan, N.: *North-East India: The Ethnic Explosion*, New Delhi: Lancers, 1981.

139. Phukan, Girin: *Assam's Attitude to Federalism*, New Delhi: Sterling Publishers, 1984.

140. Bhattacharjee, Chandana: *Ethnicity and Autonomy Movement: Case of Bodo-Kacharis of Assam*, New Delhi: Vikas, 1996.

141. Lama, M.P.: "Unquiet Hills" in *The Statesman*, April 19, 20 and 21, 1988.

142. Subba, T.B.: *Ethnicity, State and Development: A Case Study of the Gorkhaland in Darjeeling*, New Delhi: Har-Anand Publications, 1992.

143. Syangden, Bipin and Moktan, Ashok: *Gorkhas Speak*, Darjeeling: B.B. Tamang Publishers, 1986.

144. Mukherjee, Partha: "The Gorkhaland Movement: Some Theoretical Formulations and Propositions", in *Social Action*, Vol. 46, April-June 1996.

145. Pimpley, Prakash and Sharma, Satish (eds.): *Struggles for Status*, Delhi: B.R. Publishing Corporation, 1985.

146. Kamble, J.R.: *Rise and Awakening of Depressed Classes in India*, Delhi: National, 1979.

147. Lynch, Owen: *The Politics of Untouchability*, New York: Columbia University Press, 1969.

148. Rajendran, G.: *The Izhava Community and Kerala Politics*, Trivandrum: The Kerala Academy of Political Science, 1974.

149. Rao, M.S.A.: *Social Movements and Social Transformation*, *op. cit.*

150. Shah, Ghanshyam: *Politics of Scheduled Castes and Scheduled Tribes*, Bombay: Vohra Publishers, 1975.

151. Shyamlal: *Caste and Political Mobilization*, Jaipur: Panchsheela Prakashan, 1981.

152. Verba, S.; Anand, B. and Bhatt, A.: *Race, Caste and Politics*, New York: Sage Publishers, 1972.

153. Kothari, Rajni: *Caste in Indian Politics*, Delhi: Orient Longman, 1971.

154. Innaih, N.: *Saffron Star Over Andhra Pradesh*, Hyderabad: Book Links Corporation, 1984.

155. Irani, C.R.: *Bengal: The Communist Challenge*, Bombay: Lalvani Publishing House, 1968.

156. Kapoor, Rajiv: *Sikh Separatism: The Politics of Faith*, London: Allen and Unwin, 1986.

157. Katzenstein, Mary F.: *Ethnicity and Equality: The Shiv Sena Party and the Preferential Policies in Bombay*, Ithaca, New York: Cornell University Press, 1979.

158. Narang, A.S.: *Storm Over the Sutlej: Akali Politics*, New Delhi: Geetanjali Publishing House, 1983.

159. Nayar, Baldev Raj: *Minority Politics in Punjab*, Princeton N.J.: Princeton University Press, 1966.

160. Dutta, P.S.: *Ethnic Peace Accords in India*, New Delhi: Vikas Publishing House, 1995.

Chapter – 2
Indian Political System: Major Contradictions and Paradoxes

India stands for an ideal example of a plural society – a society that is divided by what Eckstein calls, "Segmental Cleavages". These segmental cleavages, he writes, may be of racial or ethnic in nature.[1] Another characteristic that is implied in Eckstrin's definition is that political parties, interest groups, media of communication and other voluntary associations tend to be organized along the lines of segmental cleaveages.[2] This tendency has been more manifest in India from the early eighties with the consolidation of the Bharatiya Janata Party and the 'Sangh' family on the one hand, and the Muslim counter groups and the dalits on the other. It has been a well-established proposition that in a plural society, it is difficult to achieve and maintain stable democratic government.[3] The root of this proposition may be traced to Aristotle's observation that "a state aims at being, as far as it can be, a society composed of equals and peers".[4] Social homogeneity and political consensus are thus treated as necessary conditions for, or factors strongly conducive to, stable democracy while deep social divisions and political differences within plural societies are regarded as responsible for instability and breakdown in democracies.[5]

As such, India, like other plural societies, has been witnessing a spurt of protest movements and these protests emanate mostly from the plural character of Indian society leading to, and resulting from, the crisis of governability. The hopes and aspirations that were aroused during the freedom struggle and as a result, incorporated in the Constitution are found to have turned bitter leading to a sense of despair thus strengthening the already existing segmental cleavages and finding avenues of expression through different forms of protests. Under the circumstances, India had moved from stability to instability and has even acquired the reputation of a "functioning anarchy".[6]

Under the circumstances, an understanding of the genesis, nature, content, direction and impact of protest movements in India would inevitably require an analysis and understanding of the social, economic and political dynamics of the system involving major contradictions operating at different levels. The root of dissent, agitation and protest can never be a sudden outburst. It is to be found in the dynamic interaction of various parameters of the system covering the social, cultural, ethnic, religious, economic and political dimensions. The plural society of India exhibits the blatant operation of all these parameters in view of the fact that during the colonial rule these were systematically encouraged and patronized for sustaining colonial interest.

Social Contradictions

By the logic of a plural society, India provides an ideal example of formalism – the discrepancy between what is apparent and what is real – exhibiting the heterogeneous presence simultaneously of modernity with tradition, relatively developed urban areas with all the modern facilities and amenities with the backward rural peripheries struggling for minimum subsistence; on the one hand, while the upper class and the upper middle class urban people commanding all the avenues of a lavish life with the slum-dwellers counting their days and the rural landed class benefited heavily from the politics of Panchayati Raj with the landless marginalized labourers looking for their emancipation in the old traditions on the other; all pervasive pressure and getting ascendancy in recent years, of caste as a social phenomenon having large scale political penetration and leading to a situation characterized by caste hierarchy with pronounced equality; constitutional guarantee for non-discrimination on sex with the politics of gender disparity; and rampant corruption at all spheres of the society. Undoubtedly, all these distinct poles exhibit social systemic contradictions that tend to impair the legitimacy of the political system.

In terms of population, India is the second most populous polity in the world. The beliefs and behaviour of the vast mass of India's population are characterized by great antiquity, continuity and diversities and that also on a scale unmatched by any other political system.[7] The Indian actually live in one country but in many centuries. The scientists working in the most sophisticated laboratories with rational beliefs and outlook spatially coexist with millions of people plying bullock-carts and depending on the 'ojhas' in the villages. These two represent two extreme cultural polarities in their outlook and lifestyle but yet also be congruent in some respects.[8] There have been great techno-economic achievements in the fields of science, technology and engineering but most Indians still continue to subscribe to beliefs whose philosophical foundations were moulded several centuries ago and whose ideational core has remained intact, despite momentous changes in the political realm and regular contacts with different and/or divergent cultural traditions.[9] This marginalized sector of Indian population is thus bound to be vulnerable to the influences of the influentials of this section for agitation and protest to bring about change in their lives and social relations.

Observers like Morris-Jones[10] and Weiner[11] have attempted to encapsulate the process of contradiction and adjustment that is going on in India by arguing that there are several "idioms" or "cultures" that are in fundamental conflict with each other. A "modern" idiom, according to Morris-Jones, centres in the ideas of the nationalist elite and in the institutions in the capital while a "traditional" idiom is rooted in the caste, kin and communal relations of villages, localities and provinces. It has a complete social ethos and comes into politics not with a list of demands but with a way of life. A "Saintly" idiom is characteristically Indian and is associated with Gandhi and his disciples involving selfless devotion to constructive work for the good of the society and immune from the mimicking of foreign models or from being contaminated by the archaic superstitions and feudal practices of the Indian society.[12]

According to Weiner, two political cultures emerged at different levels of Indian society after independence. One is rooted in the districts permeating local politics, local party organizations and administration. The second predominates in the national capital and is found among planners, many national political leaders, and in the administrative cadre. The first may be called an emerging mass political culture and the second, an elite political culture. While the mass political culture is an expanding political culture, the elite political culture is a defensive one and very critical of the emerging more popular mass political culture, its own creation.[13]

If one compares the characteristics of the two main political idioms of Morris-Jones with those of the two political cultures of Weiner, it becomes clear that the "traditional idiom" is the idiom of "mass political culture" and the "modern idiom", the idiom of "elite political culture". The first idiom and culture are found in the cities. In fine, two basic and general pattern of political culture are found in India from the village to the national level denoting a distinct manner of political thinking and behaviour.[14]

The analyses of Indian scenario made by Morris-Jones and Weiner make an obvious reference to the distinct contradiction between modernity and traditions – a situation more or less common in the developing societies. Even though there has been attempts to rationalize and legitimize the contradiction in the name of a unique feature of the Indian system – "unity in diversity" – the tradition-bound mass political culture cannot be expected to be dominated and colonized for long by the modern elite political culture. Thus, quicker the divide is minimized, the less possibility and potentiality would be for a collision resulting in a fatal outburst and thus threatening the very foundation of the society.

Closely related to the modernity-tradition dichotomy, there exists the rural-urban divide and the intra-rural and intra-urban divide. The urban areas actually monopolize most of the modern and basic amenities of life. The rural areas are left to the basic minimum, even less of the basic needs. In terms of education, health, marketing the products and purchasing for sustained livelihood the rural areas have virtually no option but to look to the urban areas. The consequences become deplorable when the people of the rural areas cannot afford to go to the urban areas for education or for medical purposes. Under the circumstances, they are left with the predestined option of remaining uneducated or half-educated, unemployed or underemployed, traditional in outlook, and victims of traditional ways of medical treatment by the 'ojhas' or the local quacks. Even now, when the human civilization has entered in the twenty first century, human beings are brutally killed after being branded as witches, perceived to cause damage to other fellows in rural India.

However, during the last few years, the picture has started changing. With the revitalization of Panchayati Raj, the horizontal and vertical penetration of political parties in the rural areas, particularly in West Bengal, and the policy of the central government to allocate more funds for agriculture and rural development, the level of the consciousness of the rural people is expected to have become high and the rural people are supposed to feel integrated with the mainstream of the socio-political system. But it cannot be denied that much still remains to be achieved. If the rural people are left to feel alienated and if the rural-urban divide is allowed to continue it will not be a healthy sign for the development, integrity and cohesion of the system.

Besides, the intra-urban divide that manifests the conditions of the slum-dwellers lacking the minimum basic needs on the one hand and the rest of the people living in the urban areas with access to all modern amenities of life. Lack of proper planning and implementation, lack of popular initiative, insecured rural life and above all, politics of support make the problems in the urban areas worse confounded. Similarly, the conditions of the marginal farmers and particularly the landless labourers in the rural areas are bound to create an atmosphere of distrust between this class of the rural society and the landed class. By virtue of their class position, the upper class in the rural areas controls the political process to its advantage and thus the intra-rural divide gets widened.

Another social contradiction that affects the social, economic and political system in a big way is the organization and persistence of the society on caste hierarchy and the legal-constitutional declaration for equality. It is not surprising to note that – "a homogeneous, endogamous social organization with distinctive rituals, especially those pertaining to religious purity" [15] – has not disappeared from the society in independent India. Rather, the new constitutional arrangements and the politics of mustering support base have given a fresh lease of life to caste politicization. A close examination of the social and political process in India reveals that, in a wider sense, caste ties have grown significant and every political party, including the Communists have taken due note of it though overtly caste factor has been denounced by most[16] of the parties and their leaders. In this connection, Kothari observes that relative decline in the importance of pollution as a factor in determining caste hierarchy and the diminishing emphasis on the summation of roles as involved in the 'Jajmani' system do not by themselves involve any basic destruction of the caste system but only a shift in the critical criteria of social awareness and the structural differentiations through which such an awareness is mobilized and organized.[17] Thus, the process of transformation revealing certain notable changes in the Indian social system does not at all mean end of caste framework.[18]

There was a common belief before independence, particularly subscribed by the British rulers of India, that parliamentary democracy was not suited to a society like India which was intensely divided into religious and communal groupings and whose social structure was basically characterized by an ideology of hierarchy rather than equality. It was also argued that caste Hindus and the untouchables and other low castes could hardly be in a position to work together as equals in a democratic political order. The former would continue to maintain, even under constitutional guarantee for equality, the rigidity of traditional hierarchies and cause discriminations which would prevent the poor and disadvantaged low castes from participating effectively in the political process and social interaction.

Indian nationalists, however, argued strongly against such ideas. Thus, at independence, though they resisted any efforts to create separate electorates for the low castes, the Constitution and the government policies instituted mechanisms and procedures to ensure their full participation as equal citizens in the new order. These mechanisms and proceedings included reservations of seats in the legislatures and other bodies, the maintenance of a list of low caste groups on a schedule entitling them to special privileges and preferential policies of all sorts, the abolition of untouchability, and the like. But these mechanisms and procedures have further aggravated the caste relationship in India and thus have provided fresh impetus to caste induced social tensions.

True it is that the role of caste in Indian society has been decried as a fissiparous threat to national unity.[19] But it has also been appreciated as a channel of communication thus being conducive to societal integration. Rudolph and Rudolph observe, "by mobilizing...jatis of village and locality in horizontal organizations with common identities, caste associations have contributed significantly to the success of political democracy by providing bases for communication, representation and leadership. They have taught illiterate peasants how to participate meaningfully and effectively in politics. Lower castes, whose large members give them an advantage in competitive democratic politics, have in many areas gained influence, access and power in state and society. With these at their command, they can change in their favour the allocation of resources, privileges and honours. Rather than providing the basis for a reaction, caste has absorbed and synthesised some of the new democratic values".[20] This view of caste and caste associations has been shared by a number of social scientists.[21]

But, however, strengthening of the democratic values has seldom been the aim of the caste associations.[22] In practice, the leaders of the caste associations project their interests as those of their castes and their interests are generally directed towards gaining or retaining or promoting their own political and economic dominance. Caste conflicts are thus more an extension of the conflict of interests of caste leaders. Such conflicts promote what Rajni Kothari calls "negative communalism".[23] As such, violence in the name of caste is growing both in number and severity.

The division between the caste Hindus and the lower castes is not the only kind of problems posed by the caste hierarchy. In most villages, one or two large elite castes control most of the land and other resources constituting, what anthropologists call "dominant castes". After independence, these dominant castes have often been able to control and mobilize the role of their clients among the low castes who are considered to constitute the "vote banks". Since independence, the spread of conflict between these "forward" or elite castes and the backward castes has become a major source of social tension.[24] Leaders are found to utilize reservations – the Indian version of affirmative actions – as the means to gain the electoral support of numerically significant backward castes. Higher castes, feeling that their interests are threatened have resisted their moves. The acceptance of the recommendations of the Mandal Commission extending the coverage of reservations for the backward castes and the subsequent anti-reservation movement throughout the country is a case in point. In fact, once set in motion, those who have been mobilized have been difficult to be satisfied or controlled. Conflict has often been the result.[25] The issue of the integration of the low castes as effective participants in a democratic political order and of caste conflict between the elite castes and backward castes have persisted throughout the post-independence period upto the present and have posed recurring challenge to the maintenance of an integrated society, an egalitarian polity and non-violent mechanisms of conflict resolution.[26]

Even though gender disparity has been a worldwide phenomenon, Indian society exhibits an organized, institutionalized and legitimized character of gender disparity. The contradiction relating to gender relations lies in women-in-theory – adorned and worshipped as Goddess and projected as mother – and women-in-action – the marginalized lots. When women constitute 50 per cent of world's population and account for 66 per cent of the work done, they have a share of 10 per cent in the world's income and they own only one per cent of the world property. Thus, woman is an epitome of global gender injustice and inequality. All this is due to the anti-female psyche of the male chauvinists.[27] The Human Development Report, 1993 states: "Women, a majority of the world's population, receive only a small share of the developmental opportunities. They are often excluded from education or from better jobs, from political system or from adequate healthcare".[28]

In India, gender inequality and injustice is found in an institutionalized and legitimized form – institutionalized and legitimized by religious norms, social traditions, belief system and practices. Thus, the constitutional guarantee against discrimination on sex has remained merely as a rhetoric far outweighed by the reality of subjugation, domination and exploitation of women by men. This phenomenon explains the emergence of a number of women's groups and association for the cause of women's rights and interests. The recent trend of globalization of national economy has tended to further widen the gap between men and women and has intensified the feminization of poverty. Under the circumstances, women's movements are found to be rational and justified for resolving the contradiction between the rhetoric of gender equality and the practice of gender disparity.

Finally, of late, the society is experiencing unprecedented amount of corruption, moral degradation, and erosion in the integrity in the component parts of the system, thus questioning the very legitimacy of the system itself. Previously, petty corruption at the bottom level of administration was within the limits of tolerance of the society. But the extensive level of corruption at the top level politics and administration like the Bofors pay off scam, Security scam, Tahelka scam, Hawala scam, Fodder scam, Urea scam and the like has virtually shattered the foundation of the trust of the society over politics. Excepting the left political parties, all the national political parties and their leaders have been indicted on charge of corruption. This has led to the distrust of the people to the politicians and the political parties. This also signifies the institutionalization of corruption and the elasticity of the social system to absorb the vice without much resistance. This itself signifies a contradiction in the social system of India – the contradiction between the rhetoric of the claims of moral considerations and the reality of moral degradation.

Ethno-Cultural Contradictions

In the Indian political system, a major contradiction revolves around the ethnic and cultural domain – the contradiction between 'nationalism' – an attachment to the broad identity of being Indian – and a variety of what is called 'subnationalisms' – cultural, linguistic, and ethnic – denoting narrow loyalty or attachment to a particular culture or language or group as constituting primary identity. All these varieties of subnationalism actually lead to the regionalization of politics thus extending the contradiction to national integration and regionalism.

There are two broad schools of thought on the role and impact of these micro nationalistic variations. One school believes that the activities of the groups at micro level certainly hamper the nation-building process and consequently destabilize the balance of the state system.[29] The other school does not find any reason to believe that micro loyalties are disastrous moves of the human collectivities to thwart the very basis of the corrupt 'nation-state'.[30] Rather, these may contribute to the strengthening of the nation-state.[31] Thus it is argued that no contradiction need to be perceived in describing India as 'multinational nation state' based on the principles of democracy, federalism, and secularism.[32]

Viewed thus, a distinction between 'state formation' and 'nation-building' is considered to be necessary. Most of the developing countries in general and Indian in particular emerged as 'states' but they have yet to mature as 'nations'. Maturity to a nation implies an emotional-affective attachment of an average citizen to one's own country transcending those based on his primordial attachments of religion, race, caste, language, etc.[33] This passage from a 'nation-in-the becoming' to a 'nation-in-the being' is the period of 'nation-building'. The coming into being of a 'nation-state' implies a national consensus on the institutions and mechanisms of the state through which social conflicts get articulated and resolved. But before such a consensus is reached, more often than not, this period is likely to witness strifes and conflicts overclashing values and interests, over issues of discrimination, domination, exploitation and oppression. Hence, conflicts taking place within the state need not be interpreted necessarily as destabilizing, anti-national forces bent upon destroying the country. On the contrary, these should be considered as constituting the very stuff out of which a nation-state will get galvanized.[34]

Indeed, the explanation of the second school of thought points to an optimism worthnoting. But the period of 'nation-building' in which the internal strifes and conflicts over clashing values and interests are considered to be the 'stuff' of the nation-state need not and should not be an unlimited period widening the gap in the society. Thus, there must be a border line beyond which the conflicts in the society should be considered as destabilizing and anti-national and as such, appropriate measures should be taken to thwart those anti-national forces from destroying the society into pieces.

The Indian situation in the recent past shows that the optimism of the second school of thought stands on weak foundation. The reorganization of the states on linguistic consideration has not contained the proliferation of regional movements. Rather, regional movements on ethnic grounds having secessionist as well as autonomy orientations have been going on with considerable intensity and as such, pose challenge to the very foundation of national integration and the state itself. All these movements vindicate the divide between secular-national identity and primordial regional identity. The institutional and procedural incapacity of the political system to tackle and resolve these conflicts further aggravate the perceived feeling of deprivation, discrimination and oppression of one group by the other. Logically, concomitant option to this feeling further widens the gap between nationalism and regionalism and the alienation of the deprived section from the mainstream of the Indian political system. Thus, whatever may be the cause of their origin, these regional movements pose threat to the national identity of India. The intensity of these movements is such that questions like "Is the Republic breaking up?", are raised.[35]

The foremost threat to national integration comes from the movements in the North-Eastern States, Punjab, Jammu and Kashmir, and to a limited extent, from the Gorkhaland movement and Kamtapuri movement in West Bengal and the Jharkhand movement in Bihar and West Bengal. From the North-East, the threat is apparent from Naga National Council (NNC), National Social Council of Nagaland (NSCN), Mizo National Front (MNF), Peoples Liberation Army (PLA), Peoples Revolutionary Party of Kangli-Pak (PREPAK), All Tripuras Tribal Force (ATTF), Tripura National Volunteers (TNV), United Liberation Front of Assam (ULFA), Bodo Security Force (BDSF), All Bodo Students Union (ABSU), National Democratic Front of Bodoland (NDFB), Bodoland Liberation Tigers (BLT) and the like. Armed rebellion has been organized by these organizations and thus insurgency has been the most popular method for the realization of the goal. It started with Nagaland as late as in 1956 and inspired the other disgruntled underground tribal leaders to demand sovereignty from the Indian State. It is argued that their ethno-cultural background is derived from the Astro-Mongoloid origins and their territory has been subjugated by India. They claim that neither the Hindu norms nor any Indian traditional pattern match with the conglomeration of the myriad ethnic tribes in the region.

In Nagaland, NSCN came into being in 1979 as a reaction to the NNC's (pro-Phizo) acceptance of the Constitution of Indian in 1975 as per the Shillong Accord. Since then, the NSCN has been carrying out an armed struggle to bring an end to Indian rule over the Naga people. Only recently, the NSCN has agreed to a moratorium to its armed struggle for the sake of negotiation with the Government of India. The secessionist movement in Mizoram is led by the MNF which has been campaigning for a sovereign Mizoram since 1968. It has created tension between Mizos and non-Mizos and has gone to the extent of identifying the Mizo as non-Indians. In Manipur, separatist movement is spearheaded by the Revolutionary Peoples' Front (RPF) and its army wing PLA and PREPAK and its offshoots like the armed wing of PREPAK called the Red Army and the Kangli Pak Communist Party (KCP) and KCP's Red Army. The declared objectives of these organizations are the formation of an independent Manipur. The RPF, which appeared in May, 1989, is running a sort of government in exile in Bangladesh. In Tripura, it is the TNV, which is organizing and leading the secessionist movement. The tribal extremists have also organized an armed wing called the Army of Tripura Peoples' Liberation Organization (ATPLO). In Assam, the fear of the Assamese of becoming a minority in their own state led to the rise of the separatist organization like the Lachit Sena in 1960s. Then, the ULFA came into being in 1979 – a direct descendent of the AASU, which spearheaded the anti-foreigner agitation in Assam between 1979 and 1985. The ULFA is the proponent of sovereign Assam. 'It has vowed to liberate Assam from the exploitation of the Centre which is treating the State as its colony'.[36] Within the State of Assam, there has emerged the demand for separate State of Bodoland spearheaded by All Bodo Students Union (ABSU) against Assamese chauvinism. The phases of Bodo movement ascertain the inability of the caste Hindu Assamese governing elite whether belonging to national or regional political parties to appreciate the aspirations of the tribals thereby pushing the leadership from softer options to violent methods from Plain Tribal Council of Assam (PTCA) via All Bodo Students Union, Bodo Peoples Action Committee to Bodo Security Force (BDSF) and again pushing the leadership from matured politicians to the young and militant blood. The whole situation has been emotionalized, bloodshed continues and ethnic divide continues to expand in a land known for its capacity to absorb people from various parts of the country belonging to various ethnic groups.[37] Another development in this connection to be noted in relation to the identity formation in this region is that recently the rebel groups have formed a sort of a pan-Mongoloid federal set-up called Manipur-Nagaland-Tripura-Assam Consolidation (MNTAC) for tactical coordination.

In Punjab, Sikhs constituted the minority before 1947. To safeguard the Sikh position, the Akalis submitted a memorandum to the minorities sub-committee of the Constituent Assembly demanding some statutory rights. As the demands were rejected, the Akalis formulated their demands as a cry for 'Punjabi Suba'. Later, the efforts of the orthodox Akalis to mobilize the Sikh population under the slogan of a Shikh Theocratic State – 'Raj Karega Khalsa' – gradually made an impact on the growing vested interests, and on the unemployed, little educated, rural youth.[38] As the Jan Sangh became a potential contender of Congress Hindu vote bank, the Congress started, as a reciprocal move, playing the communal card. This was the background of the emergence of Sant Jarnail Singh Bhindranwala and the demand of Khalistan – an independent sovereign state. The widespread terrorism and the resultant state repression are the factors that come in the way of the bridge between Punjabi identity and India's national identity.

In Kashmir, the fear of the Kashmiri Muslims, who constitute about 95 per cent of the population of the valley, of cultural marginalization due to a process of state-sponsored imposition of sanskritized pan-Indianness along with manipulative politics of the ruling elites, impoverishment, unemployment, corruption and adhocism of the Government, acted in favour of exclusivist interest and ideology.[39] The Jammu and Kashmir Liberation Front (JKLF) leads the agitation in Kashmir valley and demands a totally independent state of Kashmir although a number of Pakistan-based and sponsored terrorist groups like Harkat-ul-Mujahadin, Harkat-ul-Ansar, Jaish-E-Mohammad, Hijbul Mujahidin also operate in the valley leaving a profound impact on the society, economy and politics of the state as well as on the state and society of India.

As against these anti-Indian movements, the movements for Gorkhaland, Jharkhand and Kamtapur do not pose serious threat to the unity of the country though they impair substantially the integrity of the society. Though ethnic movements in Darjeeling of West Bengal have a history of over eighty years, the threat to the Indian political system actually came with the demand by the Communist Party of India (CPI) in April, 1947 for 'Gorkhasthan', an independent nation comprising Nepal, Darjeeling district and parts of Sikkim. However, this demand was in line with Soviet concept of right to self-determination and the CPI being ideologically close to the Soviet Union supported Gorkhasthan till 1951 after which they started propagating for 'regional autonomy'. Systematic demand for separate statehood for the district of Darjeeling and its adjoining areas surfaced via the Nepali Bhasa Movement with the establishment of Pranta Parishad in 1980 (April) and the Gorkha National Liberation Front (GNLF) in July 1980. The basic thrust of the GNLF movement was for a separate state of Gorkhaland so that Bengali hegemony over the hill people could no longer be there. However, the GNLF movement was not basically a secessionist movement. It was the movement of the hill people with distinctive identity against the 'Bengali hegemony'. And the gap between these two identities has not yet been bridged even though partially, the demand of the GNLF has been fulfilled with the formation of the Darjeeling Gorkha Hill Council.

The Jharkhand demands should be viewed in the context

of identity formation. Inconsiderate industrialization and deforestation of the area has severely affected the life style of the indigenous tribal population. Tribal movements in this area for pursuing the distinctive tribal identity have also a long history. However, after the formation of the All Jharkhand Students Union in 1986, the movement acquired a new dimension. The charter of demands published by the activists of the movement contained among others – demand for a separate state within the Indian Union, stoppage of anti-people industrialization and urbanization policies and uprooting the tribal population from their traditional homeland; inclusion of all tribal languages into the Eighth Schedule of the Indian Constitution; acceptance of the old Panchayati System and the System of 'para-pathi-majhi-pargana' in all social, religious and land questions related to the tribal population. An analysis of these demands indicates that these were related more to the intricate process of nationality formation – an identity which is to be different from the mainstream national identity. Thus, the Jharkhand movement that came to an end with the formation of the separate Jharkhand State actually reflected the divide or the contradiction between broad Indian national identity and the narrow regional tribal identity – a divide between nationalism and regionalism.

Similarly, in the northern part of West Bengal, particularly in the districts of Cooch Behar, Jalpaiguri and the plains of Darjeeling, a movement based on regional cultural identity has been in vogue, spearheaded by the Rajbangshis of the region leading to a divide between the Bengali identity and the local Rajbangshi identity – the cultural expression of which being the Kamtapuri identity. Though initially the movement was for cultural homogenization and identity it has assumed militancy for a separate state of Kamtapur within Indian Union since 1980s under the influence and leadership of the Kamtapur Liberation Organization, the militant outfit of the Kamtapur Peoples Party and the All Kamtapur Students Union. Though the movement is not that organized and mobilized, it poses threat to the age-old harmony and integration in West Bengal.

Contradiction Relating to Communalism and Secularism

One of the most ominous aspect of the political crisis in India today has been the conflict between professed secularism on the one hand and widespread communalism on the other spreading hatred and inflaming passions in the name of religion. In recent years, these two ideals have reached to such a pass that the century old Indian traditions of communal assimilation and harmony have been subjected to major challenge acquiring truly explosive dimensions.[40]

In common parlance, the idea of secularism is identified with three western connotations: (a) separating man and society from the transcendental and divine; (b) institutionalizing rationality through a process of displacing religiosity; and (c) relegating religion to the private realm of human activity. However, all these connotations are found to be conceptually untenable and empirically impossible.[41] As a way out of this impasse and empirical deadlock, secularism may be conceptualized as religious pluralism – a societal situation in which different religious collectivities would not only respect one another in terms of their beliefs and worship patterns, but would be eager to enter into creative and critical dialogue so that they could empathetically understand one another and collectively shape a humane and just society.[42]

In defining secularism in the Indian context, Donald Smith refers to three provisions that have been incorporated in the Constitution of India: (i) freedom of religion, both individual and corporate; (ii) citizenship based on equality of all individuals regardless of religious persuasion; and (iii) separation of state and religion.[43] Thus, a secular state is a state that guarantees individual and corporate freedom of religion; deals with the individual as a citizen irrespective of his religion; is not constitutionally connected with a particular religion; does not seek either to promote or interfere with religion.[44] Secularism actually reflects something rational based on reason.

Communalism, on the other hand, is generally viewed as the degenerated manifestation of religion. It is believed to be a negative social force. Smith views communalism as the functioning of religious communities and organizations, which claim to represent them in a way which is considered detrimental to the interests of other groups or of the nation as a whole.[45] Communalism thus includes an appeal to a common religious heritage – an appeal for politicized goal. It involves the politicization of religious rituals and symbols and religion becomes transformed into a political instrument. Communalism goes further and attempts to eliminate the natural heterogeneity which exists within the Hindu as well as the Muslim communities in India and transform the community into a unified political corporate group.[46] It not only stresses unity in the community but also the antagonism between communities, that is, between Hindus and Muslims. In socio-economic terms, W.C. Smith defines communalism as the ideology which emphasizes, as the social, political and economic unit, the group of adherence of each religion and emphasizes the distinction, even the antagonism between such groups.[47]

Communalism in India has been viewed from three perspectives by different scholars. First, despite considerable variation in their treatment of the subject, the works of Bipan Chandra, P.C. Joshi and Asghar Ali Engineer may be clustered as the left-oriented perspective. Bipan Chandra[48] traces the growth of communal ideology and politics to the social framework provided by the colonial economy and polity. Colonial underdevelopment and the crisis of the colonial economy resulted in widespread unemployment which led to widespread scramble for jobs among the middle class. This helped communalism acquire its real mass base. To him, the Hindu-Muslim contradiction had no basis in reality; it was not an efficient or real causation of communalism. The basic contradiction during the colonial period was between the Indian people and colonialism. P.C. Joshi[49], while discussing the causes that led to the Muslim separation, utilizes the model of 'cumulative causation'. For the Indian Muslims, the British colonial policy led to a setback in the economic and political sphere vis-à-vis the majority community. And this engendered in them the feeling of deprivation, which ultimately prepared the ground for secessionist demands. Asghar Ali Engineer[50], viewing the subject from the Marxist perspective and also recognizing the great mobilizational potential of religion, observes that communalism emerged during the struggle for independence and kept on going into higher and higher gear as the day of independence drew nearer and nearer. The explanation has to be sought, apart from other factors, in the socio-economic situation and socio-political climate in the country.

The second perspective is associated with the works of prominent Indian and Western sociologists and some historians who have tried to explain communalism through their insight into the social structure, cultural heritage and social change in India. Under the perspective come the studies of Louis Dumont, Satis Saberwal and Ratna Naidu. Louis Dumont's[51] cultural historical perspective shows that the more or less peaceful coexistence of the two communities after the Muslim conquest did not produce any "general ideological synthesis" and lack of this ideological synthesis created "lasting social heterogeneity of the two communities". Satis Saberwal[52] emphasizes the role of ideas and traditions, religious beliefs and institutions for understanding communalism. He establishes the linkage of religious ideas and symbols to the social structure. Naidu's[53] work is more definitive and she explains communalism in terms of politico-economic and cultural factors.

Finally, studies of Paul R. Brass[54], Joseph Rothschild[55] and Francis Robinson[56] treat the phenomenon of ethnic identities and ethnic conflict from political perspective assigning primacy to political determinants that is, to political elites, party organizations in mobilizing communal and/or ethnic consciousness among the competing groups.

The history of communalism in India dates back to the later half of the 19th century although a few communal riots had taken place as early as 1781.[57] It was mainly because of the growth of consciousness that one community is being subjugated by the other and also because of the competition between these two people in economic field that their relations got strained in the later centuries. The British became cautious from the lesson they derived from the 1857 Mutiny and hence, adopted the policy of balancing one community against another for weakening the nationalist movement and perpetuating their rule in India. Besides, the English education not only gave tremendous opportunities of employment to the Hindus, but it also broadened their mind to accept the challenges of new industrial age. A number of endeavours by intellectuals came forth to reform the Hindu society on modern and rational lines. As for the Muslims, the introduction of English education by the British for administrative and other purposes belittled the importance of Arabic and Persian and adversely affected the position of the Muslim intelligentsia. As such, the advancement of the Hindus in all walks of life and their rapid march towards monopolizing the administrative, industrial and commercial fields raised a fear among the intellectual elite of the Muslims that their own existence as a major group and hitherto enjoying an elite position was in jeopardy and, instead of blaming themselves for their lagging behind in the race, the Muslim leaders started expressing the fear that the Muslims would be dominated by the Hindus in future India. Moreover, some of the revivalist movements among the Hindus like the Arya Samaj, had a narrow Hindu basis, a negative attitude towards Islam that led the Muslims to mobilize themselves on a corresponding communal basis.[58]

In such an environment of mutual distrust coupled with irrational perceptions, no social movement of secular character came on the scene to bring these two communities together. Even the political movement of national independence could not unite them. Besides, a number of organizations on communal lines gradually sprang up among both the communities, like the Muslim League, Jamat-Ul-Ulema, Hindu Mahasabha and Rashtriya Swayamsevak Sangh and alienated both the communities from one another. The establishment of two separate states, namely, India and Pakistan in 1947, after partition on communal lines, could not solve the problem as, by that time, the cancer of communalism had spread its virus too wide and deep in the body politic of India.[59] The partition, as it was expected, did not put an end to communalism but instead it proved to be the beginning of a series of new conflicts and problems on the basis of communalism.[60]

The violent partition of the country and the Hindu-Muslim killings which preceded and accompanied it discredited for several decades the ideologies of both Hindu-nationalism and Muslim separatism and made secularism appear the only possible basis of the modern Indian State. But during the last five decades after the partition, Hindu-Muslim communal division has been a central feature of Indian politics and brutal communal killings have been increasing in numbers and frequency in recent years. The root of this phenomenon may be found in the divergent perception that exists in both the communities. The Congress Party that was the ruling party for a number of decades, has been viewed by the conservative or extremist Hindus as pro-Muslim and this made the Hindu communalism more aggressive in the post-independence period. The Congress Party's approval to the scheme of partition, Nehru's opposition to the revivalist tendencies among the Hindus, prominent positions assigned to Muslims in political and administrative fields, reluctance shown by the Congress to initiate reforms in Muslim Personal Law and instead, defending the latter in the event of the Shahbano Case, and above all, its alliance with the Muslim League in Kerala are the reasons that contributed to develop a pro-Muslim and communal image of the Congress among the Hindus. The frustration of the Hindus in prevailing upon the ruling party to follow the harsh policy towards the Indian Muslims made them adopt aggressive attitudes towards the Muslims.[61] As a result, Hindu nationalism represented in the RSS and its "family" of organizations[62] – the Bharatiya Jana Sangha and now the Bharatiya Janata Party, Vishwa Hindu Parishad and the Bajrang Dal – has reached a new peak of popular support and political alliance. Besides, the cross-border terrorism sponsored by Pakistan and the subversive activities by Pakistan-sponsored different Islamic Jehad groups inside the territory of India, like ones in the Jammu and Kashmir Assembly House and the Indian Parliament House have contributed to strengthen the RSS-brand of Hindu nationalism and harsh attitudes towards the Muslim community.

Muslim solidarity as a counterforce has increased in recent years as well, as a consequence of the perception that the constitutional protection and the secular overtone of the Congress Party have proved to be too inadequate to wipe out the Muslim fears about the growing and militant Hindu communalism. Legislations passed by the states like Uttar Pradesh, Madhya Pradesh, Bihar and Rajasthan banning cow slaughter, government's lukewarm attitude towards Urdu, less opportunities given to them or received by them in the key fields of social life, deliberate ineffectiveness shown by the law and order machinery at the time of communal riots[63], shifting alliance and endeavours of the Congress Party during Indira Gandhi, Rajiv Gandhi and Narasimha Rao by way of allowing the opening of the gate of the Ramjanam Bhumi-Babri Masjid structure, 'Sheela Puja' (worshipping of the stone) and ineffective handling of the situation causing the demolition of the Babri Masjid, to play the Hindu card for neutralizing the growing popularity of the Bharatiya Janata Party and rewinning the majority Hindu votes, the demolition of Babri Masjid itself and the worst-ever communal riot in Gujarat – all these make the Muslims think that the constitution is not an adequate safeguard for them. Thus, the Muslims in India perceive that "the state has remained committed to secularism but the widely diffused communalism and the highly strung atmosphere of the country has made it impossible for the secular values and ideals to be realized".[64]

Under the circumstances, in view of this phenomenon of intensified Hindu nationalism and Muslim consciousness, the secular ideology has been subjected to challenge from several quarters. Hindu nationalists consider it false, a 'pseudo-secularism' which actually favors the Muslims and other minorities. Similarly, the Muslims find that the 'so-called' secular state has not been able to protect their lives, property, and even their places of worship against Hindu attacks. Even some intellectuals who are neither Hindu nationalists nor Muslim separatists, also now argue that India needs a new state ideology that recognizes religious pluralism and the importance of faith in peoples' lives, and stresses the message of tolerance said to be present in all the Indian faiths rather than secular neutrality.[65]

Economic Contradictions

The economic contradictions in India emanate from the disparity or contradiction between growth and equity, that is, economic growth on the one hand and the pattern of distribution of the growth on the other. This has been the inevitable result of the contradiction between the rhetoric of welfarism and populism and the reality of feudalism and capitalism.

India, besides being plural, is a multi-structural society where the archaic feudal and semi-feudal relationships coexist with pre-capitalist and highly developed capitalist formations. One of the most important characteristics of the Indian society has been the absolute unequal distribution of social, political and economic powers in the various segments of the society. In the rural areas, the largest cultivable land area is owned by a small minority of the society and with it, all the amenities of modern means of life leaving the majority in poverty and destitution. In the urban sectors are found slum-dwellers with all miseries, petty-shopkeepers and small entrepreneurs in thousands overshadowed by the economic empires of the big industrial and business houses. In this social milieu of absolute unequal distribution of resources and power, the state in India operates.

After independence, the public policy makers opted for rapid industrialization of the country in the overall framework of centralized economic planning and mixed economy. The pronounced objective of the policy was to raise the standard of living of the masses and to eradicate poverty and gross inequalities. The draft of the First Fiver-Year Plan stated that

"It is essential that private enterprise should function in conformity with the social and economic policy of the State, recognize its full responsibilities and cooperate in the implementation of such measures of control and regulation as are considered necessary...."[66] Similarly, the Second Five-Year Plan defined the appropriate role of the private and public sectors in the economic and social development of the country. The Plan document stated: "For creating the appropriate conditions, the State has to take on heavy responsibilities as the principal agency speaking for and acting on behalf of the community as a whole. The public sector has to expand rapidly.... The private sector has to play its part within the framework of the comprehensive plan accepted by the community".[67]

The Constitution of India also lays down the objective of harmony between economic development and social justice. The Directive Principles of State policy under Article 39 (B) and (C) of the Constitution, stipulates:

> " The State shall in particular divert its policy towards securing (i) that the ownership and control of the national resources of the community are so distributed as best to subserve the common good, and (ii) that the operation of the economic system does not result in the concentration of wealth and means of production to the common detriment."

However, the framework for economic development that was provided by the Five-Year Plans and the Directive Principles of State Policy got distorted in actual operation. Despite over four decades of Planning under the mixed economy which was meant to reconcile growth with justice, the scenario of the national economy remains dismal.[68] Soaring prices, increasing unemployment and the decreasing purchasing power of the rupee are the visible and alarming symbols of the malady. Hence, India has witnessed growth and poverty, not growth eliminating poverty.[69] The root of this phenomenon may be found in the evolution of capitalism in India.

Capitalism in India did not emerge as a natural

transformation from one stage to other, but it was the product of colonial development. The modern Indian State, like capitalism in the country, was established by the British to safeguard the class interests of the metropolitan capitalism. Thus, the indigenous capital found a powerful colonial State as an objective obstruction to its development. As a result, the Indian bourgeoisie involved itself in the struggle for transfer of state power from the capitalist class of the metropolis to the bourgeoisie of the exploited society.[70] The bourgeois-led Indian nationalism thus fought against imperialism, mobilized the Indian masses for struggle but did not allow radicalization of the mass struggle against internal and external oppressors and exploiters.[71]

Under the circumstances, when power was transferred, it was handed over to the bourgeoisie and their political representatives and hence, the state became the instrument in the hands of the bourgeoisie for their development. Thus, the post-colonial state in India was actually the instrument to achieve the development of capitalism and to subserve the interests of exploiting class over the exploited.

The consequences of capitalist path of development in India have been lopsided and hence, contradictory. On the one hand, the social base of Indian capitalism has expanded by bringing numerous social groups into the capitalist process. Similarly, despite the Monopoly and Restrictive trade Practices Act, indigenous monopoly capitalism has grown to a leading group of the capitalist classes. Under the circumstances, politics in India has become an instrument to exercise power and use public resources for sectional and personal political advancement.[72] The political legitimacy for the system has been sought to be accorded through electoral alliances based on caste, communal, religious, linguistic and regional loyalties and identities and the overall deceptive framework of universal adult franchise. There have also been some rhetorical forms like 'Socialist pattern of Society', 'Socialism', 'Garibi Hatao', 'Development', 'Development with social justice', 'empowerment' of political legitimation. This distorted path of capitalist development has thus been under severe strains impinging, in the process, on the vulnerable and deprived sections of the population and thereby leading to social tensions and conflicts of various sorts.[73] As such, the state has increasingly to be a coercive apparatus to be used to manage and sustain the system.

Since the early 1990s, there has been a formal shift of policies from mixed economy with centralized planning to liberalization of the economy and its concomitant outcome, privatization and globalization. The combined policies of liberalization of import-export regime, dismantling of state-detailed planning, and export-led growth have been adopted with the pronounced expectation that such policies would lead to expansion and diversification of manufacturing capacities, increased employment and stimulation of agricultural production. These policies, like the capital intensive heavy industrialization policies that preceded them, only expect that the conditions of the poor would improve through the general 'trickle down' affects of an expanded economy. But in reality, these policies offer no direct benefits to the poor. In fact, the New Economic Policy of India has been the reflection of the interests of the India's capitalist class that grew under state protection as well as the interests of the international capitalism. Indian capitalism that developrd under State protection during the last four decades has reached to such a stage that the domestic market is not adequate enough for its operation and as such, needs foreign markets. Similarly, under state protection, Indian capitalism has developed to the extent of competing with the foreign and transnational capital either individually or in collaboration. The interests of international capitalism lie in bringing the Indian economy with a huge potentiality of market into the fold of globalization for its unified and effective operation.

Under the circumstances, one can safely say that the pronounced rhetoric of peoples' welfare as found in the

Constitution of India and other policy documents have little relevance for the reality. Rather, the reality is that the assets of the big business and industrial houses are ever increasing while poverty in India is not eradicated. So comes the contradiction leading to social tension and conflict.

Political Contradictions

Closely linked with the economic contradiction of growth and justice, emanating from the inevitable outcomes of capitalism is the political contradiction centering around the principles of democracy and freedom on the one hand, and authoritarianism, interventionism, repression and hegemony on the other. An analysis of the composition of the personnel of the state system, its ideology, policies pursued by the government, the relationship between the ruling class and the state, and the relationship between the rulers and the ruled clearly manifests the character of the Indian State. It is intolerant of all dissent, hostile to the demands of the toiling masses. It claims to be wedded to democracy but that democracy with elite foundation. If this foundation is threatened then curbing freedom, enactment of anti-people legislation, suppressing the opposition leaders, brutally murdering the dissenters or rebels, promoting extra-constitutional centres of authority, personalizing power and imposing emergency – official or otherwise – is permitted under the cover of "national interest".[74] Given this, one would agree with the assessment of E.M.S. Namboodiripad that the state in India has run from 'crisis to chaos'.[75]

An analysis of over five decades of the functioning of the democratic, secular, federal and activist political system in India reveals its achievements and failures – failures far out-weighting the achievement. However, the more important achievement of the Indian political system is the holding of periodical elections on the basis of universal adult franchise and at regular intervals. The impact of elections on Indian society is claimed to have been qualitative, the percentage of voters' turnout has been extremely satisfactory, competition in politics has been legitimized. Participatory policies, particularly through local self-governments at the rural and urban areas, has raised the level of political awareness of the masses and the government has become a critical factor in voters' life. Politicization of an indifferent and apathetic community is the first step towards advancement of a society and elections at various levels have achieved this in India.[76]

But there are negative forces which tend to blur the achievement of the democratic process in India. The appearance of democracy is different from the reality of democracy in India. Elections actually legitimize the weilders of political power and thus this does not determine the totality of politics.[77] In practice, the power coalition which wields power in India consists of the exploiting classes, that is, the capitalist classes, landlords, rich peasants and petti bourgeoisie and their power goals are different from what they appear to be. Thus, the division of the society into classes makes the constitutional guarantees for freedom, equality, justice – all the foundations of democracy – unattainable for the bulk of the population in India.

Since independence, India has been involved in building a capitalist society and in this basic task the political system is actively involved. The industrial policy of the Government of India recognizes the supportive role of public policy for the development of the private corporate sector. All important infrastructural industries are owned and managed by the government and through infrastructural support the government has facilitated the growth of private corporate sector during the last decades. Similarly, the government is found to mobilize national resources for industrial development and these resources are shared by the state capitalist sector and the private corporate sector. The nationalized banks, the LICI, the IDBI, the ICICI and other financial institutions owned by the government provide financial resources for private capitalist enterprises. Moreover, the government controls the setting up of industries and thus has facilitated the development of private capitalism by regulatory, supportive and subsidiary mechanisms. Besides, the existence of a separate ministry for disinvestment under the present BJP government and the concerted bids to divest and sale of public enterprises one after another to private hands manifest the trend of favouring the private capitalist sector. Thus, the expansion and diversification of private capitalism has taken place under the protective umbrella provided by the Indian government during last few years. The government legislation to check monopolies under MRTP Act is merely a formal cover-up devoid of any real implications. Under the circumstances, one can easily smack of the real and operational motive of the private capitalism and the Indian State vis-à-vis the needs and aspirations of the common people. The logic of capitalism and capitalist development constraints the State to look for and serve the interests of the common people.

Even since the days of the freedom movement, people were given hopes and promises of plenty and prosperity, even the rudiments of which remain like something fashionable in a dream out of reach of the bulk of the population.[78] The very development programmes initiated by the government have thus contributed at least two kinds of imbalances in the society – the regional imbalance and the class imbalance. Thus, the post-Nehru era has witnessed a remarkably rapid escalation in confrontations between the government and the people all over the country. Wherever these confrontations tend to challenge the foundation of the existing order, the state – the instrument in the hands of the ruling capitalist class favouring the maintenance of the existing order – intervenes with all its resources and becomes more and more repressive and authoritarian. Given this background, democracy in India remains a rhetoric; the reality is the repression and hegemony of the state acting on the behest of the ruling class. And hence, this contradiction of democracy and authoritarianism provides ground for social tension and social conflict thus paving the way for more organized protest movements.

NOTES & REFERENCES

1. Eckstein, Harry: *Division and Cohesion in Democracy: A Study of Norway*, Princeton: Princeton University Press, 1966, p. 34. Also,

   Zuckerman, Alan: "Political Cleavages: A Conceptual and Theoretical Analysis", *British Journal of Political Science*, Vol. 5, No. 2, April, 1975, pp. 231-248. And

   Schermerhorn, R.A.: *Comparative Ethnic Relations: A Framework for Theory and Research*, New York: Random House, 1970, pp. 123-127.

2. Lijphart, Arendt: *Democracy in Plural Societies: A Comparative Exploration*, Bombay: Popular Prakashan, 1989, p. 4.

3. *Ibid.*, p. 1.

4. Aristotle: *Politics*, translation by Ernest Barker, New York, Oxford University Press, 1958, p. 181.

5. Lijphart, Arendt: *op. cit.*, p. 1.

6. Reddy, K. Madhusudhan: "Indian Polity: From Consensus to Fragmentation" *Indian Journal of Political Science*, Vol. 54, Nos. 3-4, July-December, 1993, pp. 313-324.

7. Basham, A.L.: *A Cultural History of India*, London: 1975 cited in Narayan, Iqbal and P.C. Mathur, : *Politics in Changing India*, Jaipur: Rawat Publications, 1994, p. 34.

8. Singh, Yogendra: *Modernization of Indian Tradition*, Delhi: Thomson Press (India) Ltd., 1973. Also

   Srinivas, M.N.: *Social Change in Modern India*, Los Angels: California University Press, 1966.

9. Narain, Iqbal and Mathur, P.C.: *op. cit.*, pp. 34-35.

10. Morris-Jones, W.H.: *The Government and Politics of India*, London: Haertchinesm University Library, 1964, ch. 2.

11. Weiner, Myron: "India'a Two Political Cultures" in Weiner, Myron (ed.): *Political Change in South Asia*, Calcutta: Firma KLM, 1963.

12. Morris-Jones, W.H.: *op. cit.*

13. Weiner, Myron: *op. cit.*

14. Rao, C.R.M.: "The Levels of Indian Politics: A Problem of Authoritarian Tradition and Democratic Modernity", in Aiyer, S.P. and Srinivasan, R. (eds.): *Studies in Indian Democracy*, New Delhi: Allied Publishers, 1965, pp. 133-50.

15. Fairchild, H.P. (ed.): *Dictionary of Sociology*, New York: Philosophical Library, No year, p. 33.

16. Exception to this general pattern is Kansiram and his political party – Bahujan Samaj Party – which is organized exclusively on caste line.

17. Kothari, Rajni: *Politics in India*, New Delhi: Orient Longman Limited, 1995, p. 227.

18. Srinivas, M.N.: "The Indian Road of Equality", *Economic and Political Weekly*, Vol. 12, June (Special Number), 1960, pp. 867-872.

19. Harrison, Sleig: *India: The Most Dangerous Decades*, Princeton: Princeton University Press, 1960.

20. Rudolph, L.I. and Rudolph, S.H.: *In Pursuit of Laxmi: The Political Economy of the Indian State*, New Delhi: Orient Longman, 1987, pp. 63-64.

21. Blair, Marry W.: *Voting, Caste, Community, Society*, New Delhi: Young Asia Publications, 1979, p. 7.

Singh, Yogendra: *Modernization of Indian Tradition*, Delhi: Thomson Press, 1986, p. 58.

22. Jha, Hetukar: "Tradition, Violence and Modernization: Understanding the Legitimation Crisis of Indian Political Order", in *The Eastern Anthropologist*, Vol. 47, No. 4, 1994, pp. 327-340.

23. Kothari, Rajni: *Rethinking Development: In Search of Human Alternatives*, Delhi: Ajanta Publications, 1988, p. 197.

24. Brass, Paul R.: *The Politics in India since Independence*, New Delhi: Foundation Books, 1995, p. 6.

25. Kohli, Atul: *Democracy and Discontent: India's Growing Crisis of Governability*, New Delhi: Foundation Books, 1995, p. 8.

26. Brass, Paul R.: *op. cit.*, p. 6.

27. Dandavate, Madhu: "Social Roots of Gender Injustice", *Mainstream*, December 23, 2000, pp. 23-27.

28. Quoted in Mohan, Purnima: *Encyclopaedia of Women*, Delhi: Indian Publishers Distributors, 2000, p. 92.

29. Kedourie, E.: *Nationalism*, London: Hurchinsen, 1960.

Kedourie, E. (ed.): *Nationalism in Asia and Africa*, London: Weidenfeld and Nicolson, 1971;

Minogue, K.: *Nationalism*, London: Batsford, 1967;

Smith, A.D.: *Theories of Nationalism*, London: Duck-Worth, 1971.

30. Enloe, C.H.: *Ethnic Conflict and Political Development*, Boston: Little Brown and Company, 1973.

    Thompson, D.L. and Roness, D. (eds.): *Ethnicity Politics and Development*, Colorado: Lynne Reisner Publishers, 1986;

    Palanithurai, G.: "Ethnic Identity and National Loyalty of An Ethnic Group in India", *Indian Journal of Political Science*, Vol. 51, No. 1, 1990, pp. 84-97.

31. Gupta, Dipankar: "The State and Ethnicity in India", in *Asian Studies*, No. 10, 1992, pp. 62-71.

32. Banerjee, Ashis: "The Ideology and Politics of India's National Identity" in Hasan, Zoya; Jha, S.N. and Khan, Rasheeduddin (eds.): *The State, Political Process and Identity*, New Delhi: Sage Publications, 1989, pp. 289-96.

33. Mukherjee, Partha N.: "Social Conflicts in India: Nation-Building or Nation-Destroying? An Agenda for Urgent Research", *Man and Development*, Vol. 14, No. 4, 1992, pp. 21-32.

34. *Ibid.*

35. *Sunday*, Calcutta: February 20, 1986.

36. Kakati, S.C.: "From Fizo to ULFA in North East: in *The Statesman*, Calcutta: February 14, 1991.

37. Bhattacharjee, Chandana: *Ethnicity and Autonomy Movement: Case of Bodo-Kacharis of Assam*, New Delhi: Vikas, 1996, p. 134.

38. Sarkar, Ajeya: "Regionalism, State and Emerging Political Pattern in India", *Indian Journal of Political Science*, Vol. 51, No. 4, 1990, pp. 477-90.

39. *Ibid.*

40. Chandra, Bipan: *Communalism in Modern India*, New Delhi: Vikas Publishing House, 1993, p. IX. To him, until 1937-38, both Hindu and Muslim Communalists stood for Hindu-Muslim unity and a United Indian Nation.

41. Oommen, T.K.: *State and Society in India*, New Delhi: Sage Publications, 1990, pp. 116-118.

42. *Ibid.*, p. 120.

43. Smith, Donald E.: *India as a Secular State*, Princeton: Princeton University Press, 1963, p. 4.

44. *Ibid.*, p. 4.

45. *Ibid.*, p. 454.

46. Brass, Paul R.: "Language, Religion and Politics", in Roy, Subroto and James, William J. (eds.): *Foundations of India's Political Economy: Towards an Agenda for the 1990s*, New Delhi: Sage Publications, 1992, p. 88. Also

    Ahmed, I.: "Secularism and Communalism", in *Economic and Political Weekly*, Vo. 4, Nos. 28, 29 and 30 (Special number), 1969.

47. Smith, W.C.: *Modern Islam in India*, quoted in Engineer, Asghar Ali: "Socio-economic Basis of Communalism", in Grover, Verinder (ed.): *Sociological Aspects of Indian Political System*, New Delhi: Deep and Deep Publications, 1990, pp. 335-346.

48. Chandra, Bipan: *Communalism in Modern India*, New Delhi: Vikas Publishing House, 1993, pp. 4-5.

49. Joshi, P.C.: "Economic Background of Communalism in India: A Model of Analysis", in Nanda, B.R. (ed.): *Essays in Modern Indian History*, Delhi: Oxford University Press, 1980, pp. 167-80.

50. Engineer, Asghar Ali: "A Theory of Communal Riots", *Seminar*, 291 (November), 1983. Also "Socio-economic Basis of Communalism", in Grover, Verinder: *op. cit.*

51. Dumont, Louis: "Nationalism and Communalism" in *Religion, Politics and History in India: Collected Papers in Indian Sociology*, Paris: Mouton Publishers, 1970, pp. 89-110.

52. Saberwal, Satish: "Elements of Communalism, I and II", in *Mainstream*, Nos. 29 and 30, 21-28 March, 1981.

53. Naidu, Ratna: *Communal Edge to Plural Societies: India and Malayasia*, Delhi: Vikas Publishing House, 1980.

54. Brass, Paul R.: *Language, Religion and Politics in North India*, Cambridge: Cambridge University Press, 1974.

55. Rothschild, Joseph: *Ethno Politics: A Conceptual Framework*, New York: Columbia University Press, 1981.

56. Robinson, Francis: "Nation Formation: The Brass Thesis and Muslim Separatism", in *Journal of Commonwealth and Comparative Politics*, Vol. 15, No. 3, 1977, pp. 215-230.

57. Zakaria, R.: *Rise of Muslims in Indian Politics*, Bombay: Somaiya Publications, 1970, p. 279.

58. Desai, A.R.: *Social Background of Indian Nationalism*, Bombay:

Popular Book Depot, 1954, p. 257.

59. Rai, S.M.: "Gandhi and the Communal Politics in India", in *Indian Political Science Review*, Vol. 4, No. 1, 1969-70, p. 156.

60. Murti, V.V. Ramana: "Nationalism and Sub-Nationalism in Contemporary India", in *Quest* (Bombay) No. 56, 1968, p. 35.

61. Puranik, S.N.: "The Problem of Communal Harmony in India", in Grover, Verinder (ed.): *op. cit.*, p. 200.

62. For a detailed discussion on the RSS "family" of interrelated organizations, see Anderson, Walter K. and Damle, Shridhar D.: *The Brotherhood in Saffron: The Rashtriya Swayamsevak Sangh and Hindu Revivalism*, New Delhi: Vistaar Publications, 1987.

63. Mohammad Aslam shows that the Moradabad riots of 1980 was a riot between Provincial Armed Constabulary (PAC) of Uttar Pradesh and Muslims. He observes: "The trend in Uttar Pradesh now is that whenever there is communal tension leading to minor altercations (almost ever present in the prevailing environment) the PAC is moved in to disperse the more volatile elements of the two communities, curfew is imposed and the PAC is let loose on the Muslims like a pack of hounds hunting hares.... Allahabad riot of June 1986 is classic example of one such communal riot". Aslam, Mohammad: "State Communalism and the Reassertion of Muslim Identity", in Hasan Zoya; Jha, S.N. and Khan, Rasheeduddin (eds.): *The State, Political Processes and Identity: Reflection of Modern India*, New Delhi: Sage Publications, 1989, pp. 270-81. Also the reported involvement of the State machinery in the recent Post-Godhra Communal riot in Ahmedabad, and other parts of the State of Gujarat and the statements of the Sangh Parivar that the riots in Ahmedabad was the reaction against Muslim fundamentalism manifest how organized communal riots may be.

64. Ahmad, I.: "Secularism and Communalism", *Economics and Political Weekly*, Vol. 4, Nos. 28, 29 and 30 (special number), 1969, p. 1156.

65. Nandy, Ashis: "The Politics of Secularism and the Recovery of Religious Tolerance", in *Alternatives*, No. 13, 1988, pp. 177-194. Also,

    Madan, T.N.: "Secularism in Its Place", *Journal of Asian Studies*, Vol. XLVI, No. 4, 1987, pp. 747-760.

66. Government of India, *The First Five Year Plan* (A Draft Outline), Delhi: Planning Commission, 1951, p. 155.

67. Government of India: *The Second Five Year Plan*, Delhi: Planning Commission, 1956, pp. 22-23.

68. Mukherjee, I.N.: "Economic Growth and Social Justice in South Asia: Growing Potential for Domestic Conflict", in Phadnis, Urmila; Muni, S.D. and Bahadur, Kalim (eds.): *Domestic Conflict in South Asia*, New Delhi: South Asian Publishers, pp. 1-15.

69. Khan, Rasheeduddin: "The Total State and the Indian Political System", in Hasan, Zoya; Jha, S.N. and Khan, Rasheeduddin (eds.): *op. cit.*, p. 54.

70. Bhambri, C.P.: *Politics in India: 1947-1987*, New Delhi: Vikas Publishing House, 1988, p. 3.

71. *Ibid.*, pp. 3-4.

72. Quoted in Phadnis, Urmila; Muni, S.D. and Bahadur, Kalim (eds.): *Domestic Conflicts in South Asia*, New Delhi: South Asian Publishers, 1986, p. XVI.

73. Bhambri, C.P.: "Indian Political System: Nature of Contradictions", in Phadnis, Urmila; Muni, S.D. and Bahadur, Kalim (eds.): *op. cit.*, pp. 84-104.

74. Shakir, Moin: "Class Character of the Indian State", in Grover, Verinder (ed.): *op. cit.*, p. 28.

75. Namboodiripad, E.M.S.: *Crisis into Chaos*, New Delhi: Sangam Books, 1981.

76. Bhambri, C.P.: *Indian Political System, op. cit.*, p. 88.

77. *Ibid.* pp. 89-90.

78. Maheshwari, S.R.: "Anomic Situations and Political Legitimacy in India", in *Political Science Review*, Vol. 13, Nos. 1-4, 1974, p. 190.

Chapter – 3

Protests and Movements in India: Historical Setting, Economic Imperatives and Social Dynamics

The preceding chapter has shown the contradictions obtaining in the Indian society, economy, and polity that suggest the objective conditions for dissent and protest. However, it should be noted that the historical experiences of the protests of the Indian people against the repressive and discriminatory policies of earlier rulers give us meaningful clue to the understanding of the protest movements in India. The mode, mechanism, organizational structure, ideology, leadership – all these of protests in India have been partly influenced by historical legacies and partly on account of the prevailing conditions in contemporary society.

Protests of different forms and dimensions have been witnessed throughout the history of India. But the protests assumed a new significance during the British rule that provided a new source of legitimacy to the protest movement.[1] With the colonial rules and its effects being felt, a number of new avenues for claiming higher status in social, economic, political and cultural fields opened up and there was greater scope for the channelling of new aspirations. Thus, the socio-religious revivalist movements of the nineteenth century and the early twentieth century and the launching of the liberation movement against the colonial rule of the British not only influenced the social and political outlook of the people but significantly added new dimensions to the form, content and pattern of protests and dissent. The Brahmo Samaj, founded in 1825, the Prarthana Samaj, in 1867, the Arya Samaj in 1875 and the Theosophical Society in 1875 were all reformist protest movements that influenced the Hindu society to a considerable extent as well as contributed significantly to the growth of Indian nationalism by raising the sense of pride about India's past traditions. Being influenced by European enlightenment, the Brahmo Samaj organized welfare works for the depressed classes under the leadership of Raja Rammohun Roy and Keshab Chandra Sen. The influence of the Brahmo Samaj spread from Bengal to Madras where a theistic society was started in 1864 under the name of Veda Samaj which was later changed to Brahmo Samaj of South India.[2] In Bombay, the Prarthana Samaj worked actively for the depressed section of the society under the leadership of M.G. Ranade, R. Bhandarkar and N.G. Chandravarkar. The Arya Samaj started working with the downtrodden sections mainly with a view to preventing conversion to Christianity and regain converts to Hinduism. It launched the 'Suddhi' movement in 1891 under the leadership of Lala Munshi Ram aiming at reconverting to the Arya Samaj the Christian and Muslim converts who were mostly from the lower caste Hindus.[3] It also extended to the new recruits from the lower castes and the oppressed classes the right to wear the sacred thread – the symbol of high caste status. Gradually, the movement of the Arya Samaj gathered momentum and spread to Punjab, Kashmir, parts of UP and Bihar. The Theosophical Society, established in Madras under the leadership of Ms. Annie Besant and the Ramkrishna Mission under the leadership of Swami Vivekananda worked hard for the weaker sections especially in the field of education.

All these early protest movements were basically reformist in character aiming at bringing about certain changes in the Hindu socio-religious life. These movements were in the main, reactions in organized form against the conservative and irrational aspects of contemporary version and practice of Hindu religion and society. In fine, these reform movements were basically inward looking and sought to abolish customs and mores that seemed contrary to the liberal ideas of the French Revolution.[4]

Among the Indian Muslims, there arose similar but less organized movements. The Wahabi movement laid emphasis on the virtues of Islam and the oneness of God. Sir Syed Ahmed and Syed Amir Ali through their Aligarh movement wanted the Indian Muslims to accept the western culture and education and reconstruct the Indian society in accordance with it. The Ahmadia movement founded by Ghulam Ahmed was a protest movement against Christianity and westernization.

These reformist protests among the Muslims, except that of Sir Syed Ahmed, were basically conservative in character and aimed at purifying the so-called distorted Islamic customs and practices. But it was the Aligarh movement that wanted to adopt the modern values of rationalism and accommodate those into the mainstream Islamic culture and way of life.

However, all these movements among the Hindus and Muslims reflected religious and sectarian basis and as such, had some unfortunate repercussions arising from the fact that while the Hindus went back to their religious and historical past to assert their self-confidence, the Muslims went back to early Islam and the past history of Arabia. Among many other factors, this also contributed to the widening of the gap between the Hindus and the Muslims because the Hindu religious reform movements and the Muslim reform movements tried to rely on the two separate sources of spiritual and intellectual sustenance.[5]

The liberation movement in India reflects three phases of political protests. The first phase (1885-1905) was led by the moderates who are often referred to as the liberals and owed their allegiance to western political ideas. Consequently, they were not in favour of adopting the methods of violence, force, agitation and bloodshed for the redressal of grievances of the people of India. These moderate leaders believed in the peaceful presentation of their grievances to the government and in requesting the latter to redress them, "Petition and prayers" were the usual tools that they employed for attaining their goals.[6]

The second phase of the liberation movement (1905-1919) saw the emergence of the extremists who challenged the leadership and political ideas of the moderates. This political radicalism was the outcome of the activities of the earlier phase of the nationalist movement that were viewed to be of little impact as far as the goal of independence of India was concerned. This negative assessment of the moderate phase of the nationalist movement caused frustration among a section concerned for India's independence and hence, paved the way for political radicalism. Besides, the increasing authoritarianism and repression by the British colonial government in India aroused significant political awakening among the people. Under the circumstances, the political agitation of the extremists, unlike the moderates, brought larger number of people to the political field and in this way, inculcated among the people the spirit of sacrifice for the cause of the nation.

Among the extremists, however, there arose three distinct groups – the terrorists, the revolutionaries and the militant nationalists. The terrorist group believed in the philosophy of organized conspiracies and planned murder of Britishers and their agents as the method of attaining independence. The revolutionaries, on the other hand, disapproved the mode of activities of the terrorists and instead believed that only a mass uprising would drive the British out of India. As such, they advocated for the use of strikes, 'hartals', guerrilla warfare to be carried on with arms from foreign countries for the purpose. Finally, the militant nationalists, unlike the terrorists and revolutionaries, devised a three-fold programme for effective political action that comprised boycott, 'Swadeshi', and national education. This group also believed in "passive resistance", that is, non-violent civil disobedience and non-cooperation with the government to achieve the goal of independence.[7]

The third phase of the nationalist movement (1919-1947) was guided and directed according to the philosophy of

Gandhian protest. Under the mass appealing leadership of Gandhi, several movements were launched to assert the urgency for granting independence to India. The Non-cooperation Movement of 1920-21 was one of the important phases of India's liberation movement during the Gandhian era that exhibited the force of the use of peaceful protest on the part of the Indian people on a massive scale. The Civil Disobedience Movement of 1930-31 and the Quit India Movement of 1942-43 showed the different variety of protests against the British colonial government.[8]

All these protest movements of pre-independent India left a deep imprint on the minds of Indian people. Obviously, therefore, those modes of protest that the Indian nationalist leaders used for raising their grievances against the British began to be used by the Indian masses in the post-independence India. However, an understanding of the historical analytical aspect of protest movements in India needs to be viewed from the survey of the different types of protest movements that took place in the post-independent India. Broadly, these different variants may be peasant protests, working class protests, students' protests, women protests, ethnic protests, secular political protests and the like. Though all the types of protests are invariably bound to be politically-oriented, the secular political protests are those which aim exclusively to affect the political process and the political system in an organized and sustained manner.

Peasant Protests

India has predominantly been an agricultural country. About seventy per cent of its population still depends on agriculture for their livelihood. They are differentiated in terms of their relationship with the ownership of land, such as supervisory agriculturists, owner-cultivators, share-croppers, tenants, and landless agricultural laborers. In common parlance, they are known as 'Kisans' and 'Kisan' is often translated as 'peasant' in English. However, the term peasant is ambiguous and used differently by different authors or variously by the same author in different studies. Eric Wolf emphasized in 1955 that ownership of land should be the critical criteria for defining 'peasants'[9] but in 1966, he defined peasants as those who were 'rural cultivators' whose surpluses were transferred to a dominant group rulers.[10] Again, in 1970, his emphasis was neither on ownership nor exploited surpluses but peasants were defined as "populations that are existentially involved in cultivation and make autonomous decisions regarding the process of cultivation".[11] The category is thus made to cover tenants and sharecroppers as well as owner-operators as long as they are in a position to make the relevant decisions on the process of cultivation. Besides this different use of the concept of peasant by Wolf, it is, on the one hand, used for those agriculturists who are homogeneous with small holdings operated mainly by family labor and on the other hand, it includes all those who depend on land, including landless laborers as well as supervisory agriculturists.[12] Andre Beteille feels that the term 'peasantry' is misleading in the Indian context.[13] In the conventional meaning of peasant, the agricultural laborers, small and marginal farmers were not properly taken into consideration. Irfan Habib argues that the history of agricultural laborers remains part of peasant history.[14] Similarly, the problem becomes worse confounded with the coinage of the typology of 'bullock capitalism' by Rudolph and Rudolph. The bullock capitalism "operate family farms that rely on household labor (and) are 'non-capitalist' in the sense that, because they are self-employed, their relations of production remain relatively undifferentialed and non-antagonistic.... If there is exploitation involved in their relations of production, it is self-exploitation; they benefit from the 'surplus value' of their own labour".[15] Under the circumstances, the term 'peasantry' is preferred to be used for the analysis of agrarian relationship in the subcontinent.[16]

Regarding peasant protests in India, Barrington Moore Jr. questions the revolutionary potential of the Indian peasantry.[17] To him, peasant rebellions in pre-modern India were relatively rare and completely ineffective and it is modernization that impoverished the peasant over a long period of time. In his own words, the Indian peasant is traditionally docile and passive.[18] In the similar vein, Eric Stokes also finds that peasant protests look strangely absent in Indian history and he attributed this situation to the peculiar Indian social structure, that is, the caste system and the village structure.[19]

Moore's contention regarding the 'passive' and 'docile' character of Indian peasants and Stokes obstructive nature of the Indian social structure have been challenged by Kathleen Gough, A.R. Desai, D.N. Dhanagare, Ranjit Guha and others. Gough argues that peasant revolts have been common during the last two centuries in every state of present day India. She disagrees with Stokes regarding the obstructive role of caste in peasant protest movements and observes that a number of movements were led by lower caste Hindus. Therefore, it is an over-simplification to say that caste system has seriously impeded peasant rebellion in times of trouble.[20] Desai observes that "the Indian rural scene during the entire British period and thereafter has been bristling with protests, revolts and even large-scale militant struggle involving hundreds of villages and lasting for years".[21] Guha is of the opinion that agrarian protests of different forms and scale were endemic throughout the first three quarters of the British rule and during this period, there were no fewer than 110 known instances of revolts during the 117 years though forms of resistance varied.[22] Dhanagare also argues that Moore's conclusion is not deduced from any systematic theory and as such, needs reexamination in the light of a more extensive survey of various peasant resistance movements and revolts in India.[23]

Available literature suggests that peasant protests have been widespread in both the pre and post independence periods. Indeed, the intensity and nature of the protests vary and certain geographical areas appear to have a strong tradition of peasant movements. Kathleen Gough observed that Bengal has been a hotbed of revolt, both rural and urban, from the earliest days of the British rule. Some districts in particular, such as Mymensingh, Dinjapur, Rangpur and Pabna in Bangladesh and the Santhal regions of Bihar and West Bengal figured repeatedly in peasant struggle and continue to do so. The tribal areas of Andhra Pradesh and the state of Kerala also have long traditions of peasant protests. Hill regions where tribal or other minorities retain a certain amount of independent ethnic identity and tactical maneuverability and where the terrain is suited for guerrilla warfare, are especially favourable for peasant struggles but these have also occurred in densely populated plain regions such as Tanjavur where rock-renting, land hunger, landless labour and unemployment cause great suffering.[24] According to Andre Betteille, the areas with a larger number of agrarian revolts are predominantly rice-producing regions. These regions not only have a large proportion of agricultural labourers but land is also unequally divided among those who cultivate either as tenants or owners.[25]

An analysis of the peasant protest movements in India shows that the organizational development of the peasant protests was slow and as such, the landlord groups were able to influence the state legislation on agrarian reforms. Thus, Weiner has rightly observed that "the success with which the landlord groups have influenced state legislation calls attention to the weakness of peasant movements in India".[26]

There were many peasant agitations in the nineteenth century – the famous Santhal and Indigo revolts in Bengal, and others in Punjab and Maharastra. But these movements could not survive in the form of organized groups. In the early twentieth century, Gandhi and his supporters organized the peasants of Champaran, Bihar against the exploitation of the indigo planters in 1917; and in Gujarat, Gandhi led the famous Kaira Satyagraha against the realization of land revenue in 1918. In 1928, Sardar Patel organized the Bardoloi Satyagraha against the enactment of land revenue. Throughout the 1920s, the Congress penetrated into the countryside and mobilized the peasants for 'Swaraj' – the Gandhian vision of freedom – freedom from deprivation as well as freedom from the British Raj. At the Lucknow session of the Congress, an agrarian programme was adopted demanding the removal of British imperialist exploitation, a thorough change of the land systems and a recognition by the state of its duty to provide work for the unemployed rural masses.

In the same year, a group of Congressmen, some members of the Communist section, some from the newly formed Congress Socialist Party, and some of the Gandhian persuasion, formed the All India Kishan Congress to articulate the problems of the peasants and work for their remedies. But, however, many sections of the Congress Party itself criticized this attempt to form a peasant movement distinct from the Congress organization. Their uneasiness grew into antagonism in some states when the Kishan Congress became critical of the agrarian policies of the new Congress-controlled state governments. In 1937, the Kishan Congress dropped the suffix 'Congress', renamed itself the All India Kishan Sabha, and adopted the Red Flag, the symbol of leftist groups.

In his presidential address before the All India Kishan Sabha national convention in 1939, Acharya Narendra Dey explained why a separate kishan group was necessary even though the Congress membership was predominantly peasant and many of peasant demands had been incorporated into the Congress agrarian programmes of Faizpur and the Economic Rights Resolution of Karachi. Narendra Dev argued that the Congress was a multiclass organization within which the peasants were not fully able to exert their influence and many Congress resolutions could not be implemented because of the control of the parts of the Congress organization by the landlords and other rich peasants. Thus, a separate kishan organization was needed for exerting greater pressure on the Congress to adopt and carry out the demands of the peasants.[77]

The new organization of the Kishan Sabha was a federation of state peasant organizations and movements the largest of which were in Bihar, Andhra, Punjab and the United Provinces. In both Punjab and Bihar, the Kishan Sabha launched mass movements against the government; in Punjab, it opposed the new system of tax assessment; in Bihar, it pressed the government to abolish the Zamindari system, reduce rents, pass new survey legislation, place a moratorium on debts, and guarantee higher price for crops.[28] During the Second World War, the Kishan Sabha virtually became the frontal organization of the Communist Party of India. With the attainment of independence, the Communist Party along with its frontal organizations launched an insurrectionary movement to overthrow the newly independent government. As such, the Communist Party of India was banned in several states; so also the Kishan Sabha. The ban continued upto 1950-51.

However, in the post-independence India, the Kishan Sabha proceeded along the belief that the interests of the agricultural laborers and the Kishans were the same. This belief was reflected in the Telangana and Tebhaga movements launched by the Communist Party of India. In both these movements rich as well as poor peasants were mobilized to capture state power though in the process one class of peasants was more active than the other.[29] In the Naxalite movement in West Bengal in the late sixties, the participants ran from rich peasants to agricultural labourers.[30] Besides, the agrarian mobilization and protests organized by Charan Singh, Mahendra Singh Tikait and Ajit Singh in northern India, Sharad Joshi in western India and left parties in eastern India are worth mentioning. It should be noted in this connection that there has been a debate over the ideological issues regarding the nature of mobilization and leadership pattern of the agrarian peasants. Hamaza Alavi argues that the middle peasants who were economically somewhat more independent have grater potential than other peasant classes to play a revolutionary role and the poor peasants are initially the least militant class because of their dependence on landlords or rich peasants.[31] But scholars like Sarkar[32], Parier[33] and Dhanagare[34] do not accept Alavi's thesis. However, the agrarian protests organized and launched by the left political parties had been influential in the past, even to the extent of challenging the base of socio-economic and political system as in the Naxalbari movement and that protests are influential in contemporary India too though there operation are limited to some pockets of the country. The peasant organizations of the left political parties, particularly those of the Communist Party of India (Marxist) and the Communist Party of India (Marxist-Leninist) are successfully operating in West Bengal, Kerala, Tripura, Andhra Pradesh and Bihar. It is mostly due to the sustained movements of the peasants under the leadership of the left political parties, Communist Party of India (Marxist) in particular that the successful registration of the sharecroppers (Operation Barga) took place in West Bengal that led to substantial changes in the agrarian relations in West Bengal. In Bihar, the lower caste and class peasants have been mobilized under the umbrella of Maoist Communist Centre (MCC), a radical outfit of the Communist Party of India (Marxist-Leninist) and have been fighting for their cause against the age-old oppression by the upper caste landed class and their private army. This suggests that a unique form of class war based on caste is going on in some areas of Bihar. In some areas of Andhra Pradesh too the Peoples' War Group (PWG) has been waging an undeclared war against the upper landed class and its alleged sponsor, the state machinery.

All these suggest that there have been peasant mobilization and protests throughout India but these mobilizations and protests could not and do not assume a universalized phenomenon. One of the important impediments of the universality of peasant mobilization and protest in India has been the non-emergence of the peasants as a class with the perception of common sufferings and hence, common cause in view of the overlapping of caste in class apart from the subversive role of the state in subserving the interests of the upper castes and class.

Ethnic Protests

India is a plural society with a large number of ethno-cultural categories. This plural character of Indian society is also characterized by socio-economic inequality. Given this, it is obvious that Indian society will confront various types of protests on ethnic lines and identities. The socio-economic inequality of the sections of the society led them, and often are made, to search for separate identity and assert on these perceived separate identities. And this assertion on ethnic identities has culminated in the regional secessionist movements threatening the country's unity and integrity. Movements in the North-East, the Jharkhand movement, the Gorkhaland movement, the Kamatapuri movement, the Kashmir movement and the Khalistan movement are the important cases of protests on ethnic considerations.

North-East

North-East India, as we find it today, is essentially the creation of the British for their colonial and imperialist interests. Assam was known as Praghayotishpur in ancient times. The Ahoms who came from Burma around the year 1226 established themselves firmly in upper Assam. By 1750 AD, they conquered the whole of the Brahmaputra valley. However, the decline of the Ahom rule began with the Maomari rising in 1769. Later on, Burmese invaded Assam. Then, the British drove out the Burmese and concluded the Treaty of Yandavoo in February 24, 1826 by which the whole of Assam came under the British rule.

Similarly, Cachar, presently a part of Assam, was an independent state. After the expulsion of the Burmese, the British annexed it to Assam, and in 1853, the whole of Cachar was transferred to the Dacca division and retransferred to Assam in 1874. The British gradually annexed the Khasi, Garo, Jaintia and Naga hills and on capturing the hitherto isolated tribal land of Arunachal Pradesh, constituted the North-Eastern Frontier Agency (NEFA). Only Manipur and Tripura were left to remain as the princely states during the British rule.

The British, with the colonial interests in mind, experimented with different administrative arrangements in North-Eastern region. Indeed, the basic objective was to create a permanent rift between the different ethnic groups so that they could not offer organized resistance against the colonial rules. In the process, the British also divided most of the tribes into splinters. Thus, the Nagas were divided and dispersed into Assam, Manipur, and Burma; Mizos into Manipur, Burma. The

Khasis, the Garos and the tribes of Arunachal Pradesh also met the same fate. In fine, the political objective of the British was regime-maintenance and regime-sustenance while the economic objective was to extract surpluses in the interests of the colonial subservience. And needless to say, they were successful in their primary mission.

After independence, the Constituent Assembly constituted a sub-committee under the chairmanship of G.N. Bardoloi to report on the organization and administration of the North Eastern Frontier Area of Assam and the tribal and excluded areas. As such, the Bardoloi Committee recommended for the setting up of the administration of the hill areas based on the concept of regional autonomy in all matters affecting their customs, laws of inheritance etc. The pattern of administration took shape in the form of the Sixth Schedule. Under this Schedule, six autonomous districts were created in Assam – United Khasi and Jaintia Hills, Garo Hills, Lushai Hills, Naga Hills, North Cachar Hills and Mikir Hills. There was provision for a District Council for each autonomous district.

The district councils that were set up with a view to democratizing the administration of the hill people were found to have failed to fulfill the aroused expectations. The bureaucracy of the State looked at the district councils as subordinate organs of the state while the tribals viewed them as symbols of supra-administrative authority not subservient to the interests and identity of the tribal. Given the varied and often conflicting perceptions, the district councils became the source of growing distrust among the tribal people against the Assam administration. Under the circumstance, there arose the demand for the creation of a hill state comprising the autonomous districts of Assam. In 1955, the Aizal Conference of the Khasi and Jaintia Hills, Garo Hills, Mikir Hills and the Mizo Hills resolved to demand for a separate state. The matter was examined by the State Reorganization Commission in 1955 but the demand was rejected. Then came the Pataskar Commission in 1965 that recommended the appointment of a minister for the hill areas and the Ashok Mehta Committee felt that the federal structure should not be the basis of reorganization of Assam. But the tribal leaders of the hills were not willing to accept anything short of autonomous state. However, the Government of India had to accept the demand of an autonomous state within the state of Assam comprising the autonomous Khasi Hills, Garo Hills and Jaintia Hills. The relevant legislation also provided for an advisory council to be called the North Eastern Council. The autonomous state of Meghalaya thus came into being in 1970. The Mizo Hills and NEFA were made the union territories and Manipur and Tripura became full-fledged states in 1972. The Naga problem, however, could not be sorted out so easily as it had many dimensions and ramifications.

An assessment of the evolution of the administrative arrangements of the North East shows that the colonial administrative system was retained after independence with certain minor modifications. But it was not taken into consideration that the colonial administrative system was designed to create a rift between the peoples of the plains and those of the hills with a view to carrying on uninterrupted colonial rule and exploitation. Thus, the administration that was inherited and maintained was mostly suited to colonial interests and as such, not adaptable to the new situation obtaining after independence. As a result of growing pressures and movements, therefore, autonomous states were created but no attempt was made to address to the concrete problems of the states. The creation of new states, by its very logic, aroused enormous hopes and expectations of the different nationalities. But a highly centralized political and bureaucratic system with a very powerful center stood in the way of the fulfillment of their aspirations. Added to the problem was the capitalist path of development that generated unevenness in the development process.[35] This model of development, instead of providing sense of fulfillment and thereby emotional attachment to Indian nation-state, strengthened the sense of deprivation. And as a result, insurgency became the mode of protest that engulfed the entire North East thus making the entire region volatile and leaving a direct threat to the unity and integrity of the country and in the main, posing a question mark to the very notion of Indian nationhood.

Thus, in the case of the North East movement, though it is believed in some quarters that the movement was basically for maintaining the basic ethnic character of the people of the region either by dispersal, or disenfranchisement or by another boundary reorganization, an in-depth analysis of the movement shows that in the context of a stagnated economy, incessant flow of immigrants was viewed as a threat by the people of the region, squeezed as they were between the extra-regional bourgeoisie and the immigrants.[36] Again, regional protest movements in the North East was essentially a middle class phenomenon. These were led by the middle class people who were perceived to be deprived of the benefits of the system and thus suffered because they found their middle class position already occupied by migrants or their descendents in a highly competitive labor market. It made them resentful against the migrant population. Thus, protest movements in the region were primarily protectionist movements. The middle class people in general and the leadership of the class in particular wanted protective privileges by imposing restrictions on the migrant population. In line with these preferred policy options, they also demanded for the reorganization of the distribution of state resources. Thus, by the inherent logic of the movements in the region, no substantial and lasting breakthrough could be found even though geographic reorganization on demographic considerations was tried, special provisions for constitutional autonomy were undertaken and special legislations were passed imposing restrictions on immigrants with a fixed cut of date in the event of the movement by Assam Gana Parishad and the All Assam Students Union in the 1980s. The recurrence and sustenance of movements in the region as they are found in the entire region spearheaded by various militant groups till now suggest that the root of these movements lie not in the so-called deprivation of the common masses but of the elites of the so-called deprived lots.

Jharkhand

In India, there has been a large number of tribal movements launched to protest against the oppression and exploitation of their distinct culture, value and way of life. Among these, the movement of the tribals for a separate Jharkhand state acquired the dubious distinction of being one of the oldest movements in the country. The movement of the tribals of the South-central part of the country for a separate state of Jharkhand was in very many ways the continuation and extension of their heroic tradition of struggle against the British imperialism and local feudalism. A series of tribal protests and revolts marked the Jharkhand history in the eighteenth and nineteenth centuries – the revolt of Tilka Majhi (1780), the Kol revolt (1834), the Santhal Hul (1855) and the Birsa revolt (1900), to mention only the very well known and important ones. Even prior to the advent of British rule, the zamindars and petty 'rajas' of the area tried hard but failed to subdue the tribals.[37] In fine, Jharkhand had remained a battlefield of protests, uprisings, revolts and rebellions for more than three hundred years against zamindars, moneylenders, 'dikus' (outsiders), exploiters and the British.[38] Thus, prior to independence, the tribal movements had two distinct features: (1) mobilization of masses against appropriation of native resources such as forests and minerals by the outsiders, and (2) social and cultural upliftment of the adivasis through various organizations such as Unnati Samaj (1912), Adivasi Mahasabha (1938) with the basic motive to retain the distinct 'adivashi' identity.[39] Thus, the process continued in a more organized and mobilized way with the formation of the Chhotonagpur Unnati Samaj in 1912 to the emergence of the so-called United Jharkhand Party in the early 1990s and during this period, the tribals of Chhotonagpur and Santhal Parganas began to struggle for separate statehood within the Indian Union. Subsequently, however, the Jharkhand movement became divided between several groups and parties and had to struggle hard to maintain its distinct ideology and organizational identity in the face of the national political parties' bid to hijack their agenda for narrow political mileage.

Such a state of affairs within the movement had often been blamed for the character of the tribal leadership and its narrow personal political outlook, the divide and rule policy of the government and the weak pan tribal consciousness that eased the process of the penetration of the dominant political parties among the tribals.

The progressive erosion of the tribal ways, values of communal and cooperative systems, the breakup of the land systems and land alienation on the one hand and the imposition of the values and dominance of the non-tribals in collaboration with the British power provoked the tribals in general and their leaders in particular for a distinct culture, life style and socio-economic system and accordingly, administrative arrangements were made granting the tribals a large measure of internal autonomy and protection through a series of legal measures such as Regulation XIII of 1833 applicable to Santhal Parganas. But after independence, the substance of the tribal autonomy was more or less eroded keeping only its apparent form through the Schedules V and VI of the Constitution.[40]

The two main objectives that the Adivasi Mahasabha rolled for were: (i) the protection of the Adivasis from the 'dikus' or aliens and (ii) the granting of statehood for the Jharkhand region. These two objectives were thought to be realized by mobilizing and vocalizing the tribals politically as envisaged by the leader of the Mahasabha, Jaipal Singh. These objectives clearly reflected the Jharkhandi sub-nationality. Thus, Jaipal Singh decided to form the Jharkhand Party in 1950 replacing the parent organization, the Adivasi Mahasabha. This Jharkhandi tribal identity got concretized with the upstaging of the Jharkhand Mukti Morcha (JMM), Jharkhand Coordination Committee (JCC) and the All India Jharkhand Students Union (AJSU). Thus, in the later years before the formation of the separate Jharkhand State, it was not merely a geographic region inhabited by the tribals but it was viewed and made to view as a land of oppressed people adjectively characterized by a mass of destitute. Thus, Nirmal Sengupta has tried to capture the dimensions of the socio-political and economic situation of the Jharkhand region and observed that "Jharkhand is developing; but not the Jharkhandis. Thus the identity is not to be seen in terms of its conventional meaning, namely homogeneity of ethnicity, language, caste, religion etc. In the Jharkhand region, now the language spoken by the oppressed and the exploited is the basis of their identity formation".[41]

Similarly, the question of tribal identity got further setback leading to further frustration, alienation and ultimately resistance on the 'Sons of the Soil' thesis that was being applied in Jharkhand. In fact, the 'Sons of the Soil' thesis is replete with enormous contradictions. Technically, those who received education for one or two years or whose parents served in the state could be considered as the 'Sons of the Soil'. But those who were born and lived for generations did not become 'Sons of the Soil' in the technical sense as they neither had the privilege of going to school or college nor their parents had been in the employment of the government. Hence, they remained deprived of the privileged jobs and positions which in fact went to 40 per cent of those people who settled in the Jharkhand region – the fortunate north Biharis. Precisely due to this reason, bifurcation of the Santhal Parganas district into three districts was opposed by the Adivasis as it would have benefited only the non-adivasis. Similarly, opening of new developmental programmes and projects was resisted fearing that its dividends would be harvested by the outsiders.[42]

Thus, the tribal movement in Jharkhand, until the attainment of statehood, was, like all other tribal movements, a holistic movement in protest against the totality of non-tribals' intrusion and dominance at all levels of life. The movement specifically was against non-tribal dominance which was becoming more and more articulate and aggressive. The great revolts of the past highlighted this protest in the areas of autonomy, protection of land, and of honour of their women; but submerged within these was the persistent cry against the exploitative system into which they were increasingly being drawn. It was precisely this all embracing quality of tribal protest as well as non-tribal intrusion and exploitation that kept the movement alive and evoked sympathetic chords in the hearts of the tribal masses even when the movement often fell into the hands of the degenerate leadership.[43] In other words, it implies that the objective situation of the deprivation and exploitation of the tribals in their own land by the outsiders was ripe enough for exploitation by the elites of the tribals for their own social, economic and political interests but in the name of the general interests of the innocent and passive tribals. Thus, the Jharkhand movement may be viewed as a struggle to resist the imposition of ideology and dominance of the non-tribal communities and the ruling structure created by them that did not suit the tribal elites.

Punjab

The protests in different forms organized by the Sikhs in Punjab over the decades reflect the potential of ethnic and religious considerations for widespread mobilization. Paul Brass has rightly observed that the Sikh protest movements demonstrate that when an ethnic group turns to politics to achieve group demands, the political movement takes a life of its own to such an extent that political organizations may shape communal identities as well as be shaped by them.[44] The doctrine of Sikh nationhood, which figures so prominently in the Sikh agitational protests, implies a repudiation of Punjabi nationality based on territory, language and culture.

The assertion of the Shiromani Gurudwara Prabandhak Committee (SGPC) and the Akali leaders that Sikhs constitute a nation and the consequent demand for a state for the Sikhs may generate apprehensions and confusions but it is worthwhile to take note of the political aspirations of the Sikh community that spring from a widespread sense of collective group identity. During the last one century the subjective ethno-religious consciousness of identity supplemented by objective marks of differentiation has been vigorously articulated and developed giving to the community a sense of distinctive heritage and destiny. Until 1880s, "the Sikhs regarded themselves and were regarded by everybody else as an integral part of the Hindus".[45] The Sikh Sabha movement that was initiated during that decade by a small section of Sikh landed gentry, theologicians and the emerging urban middle class aimed at producing the Sikhs from their absorption in Hinduism. This process initially got encouragement from the British historians of the Sikhs, Cunningham and Macaulitte, as also from the British military authorities for their colonial interests indeed.[46] Subsequently, this communal identity found its formal form and content in the form of chief Khalsa Dewan and the Akali Dal. The initiation in the 1920s of the Guruduwara Reform movement further contributed to the sharpening of this separate identity. In this connection, Paul Brass observes that the Sikh historians and politicians got engaged in symbol selection from the past, adopting those which would best support contemporary self-consciousness and rejecting those which would not.[47]

But a close look at the evolution of the separate Sikh identity reveals that the religious cleavages in Punjab were only the apparently visible part of the iceberg, a mere façade for social and economic cleavages under which the economic disparity found its channel in the religious mobilization. Thus, the basic cleavages were between the agriculturalists and non-agriculturists, which further coincided with rural vs. urban, urban caste Hindus vs. rural dominant castes, and finally weak class conflict between the landlords and the tenants but a stronger conflict between the peasants and finance capitalists.[48] Under the circumstances, party alignments among the Sikhs proceeded along the economic interests. But in spite of this basic root of conflict, communal identity retained a very powerful mobilizatory potential for all the classes.

Before 1947, Sikhs were a minority in Punjab. In order to safeguard Sikh interests in general, the Akalis thus submitted a memorandum to the Minorities Sub-Committee of the Constituent Assembly demanding some statutory rights. These included: (i) 50 per cent seats in the Punjab Assembly for the Sikhs; (ii) 5 per cent seats in the central legislature; and

(iii) communal representation of the Sikhs. But the demands were rejected. Under the circumstances, the Akalis refashioned their demands as a cry for a 'Punjabi Suba' which was made a part of agitational protests and politics in the subsequent years.

After the death of Chief Minister Pratap Singh Kairon in a terrorist attack, class alignments within Punjab politics began to change. This process of change was aggregated for two reasons: First, the Green revolution changed the agricultural scenario of rural Punjab, as a result of which a new class of rich peasants emerged with a more articulate political aims and a more aggressive class attitude. They had marketable agricultural surplus in their hands. But in spite of this economic development, unemployment among the youths of the comparatively low income peasant family grew mainly because of the fall of military recruitment. Secondly, religion continued to constitute an integral part of the psyche. 'Raj Karega Khalsa' was a politico-religious chant, which Sikhs dutifully recite in their religious congregations. Thus, the efforts of the Akalis to mobilize the Sikh population under the slogan of a theocratic state made an impact on the growing vested interests, and on unemployed little educated rural youth.[49] On the other hand, during this period, Jan Sangh and later the Bharatiya Janata Party became a political contender of Congress Hindu votebank. Under the circumstances, Congress started playing the communal card. This precisely was the background of the emergence of Sant Jarnail Singh Bhindranwala as the leader of the most orthodox, backward looking, reactionary but economically prosperous section of the Sikh peasantry, who played with both the Congress and the Akalis with equal command the result of whose growing influence was the development of the demand of Khalistan.[50] This demand for Khalistan continued to be exploited by the sections of the community disillusioned from the existing socio-political equations and this disillusionment resulted in the mobilization of the hardcore militant organizations based on communal identity like Khalistan Liberation Organization for an independent sovereign state of Khalistan. As a result, widespread terrorist techniques were adopted for the perceived and propagated goal that resulted in the massive state repression and thus widened the gap between Sikh ethno-communal identity and the Indian national identity.

Kashmir

The history of protest movement in and on Kashmir dates back to the days of Hindu-Muslim divide created and sustained by the British for ensuring their rule over the subcontinent particularly after the threat that came in the event of the revolt of 1857. Since a sizeable section of the Muslims were actively involved in the revolt because of their disadvantaged position with the fall of the Muslim rule over India and the British taking over the throne and since a sizeable section of the Hindus adapted themselves to the British culture and education and in return, occupied privileged positions in the British courts that were hitherto monopolized by the Muslims, the British perceived threat to their colonial rule from the Muslims. This led them to pursue the policy of divide and rule. When the subcontinent was divided on Zinnah's Two-Nation Theory that Hindus and Muslims of undivided India had already constituted two distinct nations by virtue of their perceived separate identity mainly on religion They should also have separate state of their own on religion. But the fate of Kashmir, which was inhabited by 95 per cent of the Muslims was not resolved along the principle of the Two Nation Theory. The then ruler of Kashmir, Maharaja Hari Singh declared to remain as an independent sovereign state. This decision of the ruler of Kashmir antagonized a section of the Muslims of Kashmir as also the decision was viewed by Pakistan as the negation of the very basis of Pakistan, that is, the Two Nation Theory. Under the circumstances, the communal interests of a section of the frustrated Muslims converged with the nationo-emotional interests of Pakistan. Thus, the frustrated elements of the Muslims in connivance with the Pakistani regular armed forces resorted to revolt against the decision of the ruler of Kashmir. Unable to absorb the revolt and the resultant onslaught of the rebel forces, the King of Kashmir signed an accession treaty with India in 1948 and thus made Kashmir an integral part of

India. The changed situation was neither acceptable to the internal rebellion, nor to Pakistan. Further, the diplomatic blunder that India made in the United Nations by proposing for a plebiscite to legitimize the integration of Kashmir made the problem worse confounded. For obviously possible logical consequences of holding plebiscite, India could not hold it. This further antagonized the rebel forces in Kashmir and gave Pakistan an upper hand to exploit the Kashmir situation, embarrass India, and mobilize the Muslim countries and population throughout the world. As a result, the Muslims in Kashmir began to be mobilized against India through some indigenous moderate and militant organizations as well as Pakistan-based terrorist organizations. The mobilization was carried through the manipulative fear of the Kashmiri Muslims of cultural marginalization due to a process of state sponsored imposition of sanskritized pan-Indianness along with the manipulative politics of the ruling elites, impoverishments, unemployment, corruption and adhocism of the government. All these acted in favour of exclusivist interest and ideology.[51] Given the volatile atmosphere in the valley, a number of militant organizations have been mobilized and working for their demands of separate Kashmiri identity and these organizations receive constant material and moral support from Pakistan. In recent years, a large number of militant groups have proliferated in the region both endogamous and exogamous – and working to destabilize India and threaten the unity and integrity of the country. The recent proposal from the Sangh Parivar to divide Kashmir into three distinct parts on distinctive cleavages – the Ladakh region on Buddhism, the Jammu region on Hinduism and the Kashmir valley on Islam has further aggravated the problem by posing question mark to the so-called Kashmiri identity. Indeed, this has further widened the already existing gap between the Kashmiri communal identity on the one hand and the communal identities on the other along with the mainstream secular Indian identity.

Gorkhaland

Protest movements on ethnic considerations in the hilly

region of the northern part of West Bengal centering Darjeeling, the center of the Gorkhaland Movement, have a long history. But the history is not of a unilineal progress of these movements primarily because the leadership of the movement in different phases was shifting from this or that demand and experimenting with this or that strategy. However, the most notable aspect of their long history has been that they were absolutely non-violent until mid-1986.[52]

The first ever demand for a 'separate administrative set up' for the district of Darjeeling was placed before the Government by the leaders of the Hill people (Lepchas, Bhutias and Nepalis) in 1907. Even though the demand is thought of arisen due to the widespread idea of reforms and the anti-partition wave in Bengal, some other factors were there to which the root of the demand may be attributed. These were, in the main, the Bengali hegemony and the reluctance on the part of the British to concede to the demand for their strategic colonial interest.[53] In 1917, the representatives of the Darjeeling district submitted a memorandum to the Chief Secretary, Government of Bengal, demanding the 'creation of a separate unit' comprising the district of Darjeeling and the Dooars areas of Jalpaiguri district. They also suggested to the Government to consider the formation of a "North-Eastern Frontier Province (NEFP) consisting of the districts of Darjeeling, Dooars, Assam and Arunachal Pradesh. In 1929, they reiterated their demand for a separate unit in their memorandum to the Simon Commission. The Hill Men's Association, born sometimes between 1917 and 1919, in collaboration with other local associations, submitted a memorandum in 1930 to Sir Sammuel Hoare in which they demanded for exclusion from Bengal and the creation of an independent administrative unit. Subsequently, in 1947, the Darjeeling District Committee of the Communist Party of India (CPI) submitted a memorandum to Jawahar Lal Nehru and demanded for Gorkhastan for the Gorkhas that was to be comprised of the district of Darjeeling and Nepal to form an independent nation. But in 1954, the CPI leaders realized their stand and began to speak in terms of regional autonomy for the Darjeeling Hills. This demand for regional autonomy was jointly approved by the Congress, the CPI and the All India Gorkha League (AIGL) leaders and was placed before Nehru on his visit to Darjeeling.

Besides, the movement for the recognition of Nepali language had its impact on the Gorkhaland movement. The movement for Nepali language passed through three tentative phases. The first phase began in the early 20s and was characterized by the demand for the introduction of "Nepali" as a medium of instruction. The second phase that started in 1953, pressed for the recognition of "Nepali" as an official language in Darjeeling. During this phase the demand for inclusion of Nepali language in the Eighth Schedule of the Constitution was also articulated. The third phase began in 1972 and was exclusively concerned with the demand for its constitutional recognition.

More articulate and systematic demand for separate statehood for the district of Darjeeling and the adjoining Dooars areas of Jalpaiguri appeared after the appearance of the Pranta Parishad in April 1980 and the Gorkha National Liberation Front in July 1980. The Swatantra Morcha that was established in May 1985 also extended strong support for this demand. All these three organizations had other demands too but carving out a state from West Bengal was by all means the most important of them.

However, the movement was peaceful and democratic in nature for many years. The All India Gorkha League leaders joined hands with the Congress, the Communist Party of India (CPI) and the Communist Party of India (Marxist) [CPI (M)] at different points of time with the expectation that this would help them achieve their goal. Even the Gorkha National Liberation Front followed the same path for a long time until situation developed from ever increasing dissatisfaction and frustration and Subhas Ghising appeared in the scene, took the leadership and adopted the strategy of violence. It was due to the different strategy that Ghising used that helped him gain from the movement which his predecessors could not.[54] Thus, it was the change of leadership in the Gorkha National

Liberation Front and the consequent violent strategy that changed the complex of the movement and placed it on solid foundation to be reckoned with.

Rajbangshi (Kamtapuri) Movement

The northern part of West Bengal, particularly the districts of Cooch Behar and Jalpaiguri is witnessing a movement since the 1980s that is gradually gaining momentum and strength through a more organized and mobilized form and the emergence of some militant outfits operating terrorist activities in the region. The objectives of this movement range from mere assertion of cultural identity based on language and heritage to a separate state of 'Kamtapur'. The root of this movement may be traced back to the protest movement launched by Thakur Panchanan Barma, the ideological-spiritual saint of the Rahbangshis of this region. His basic objective was to bring up the Rajbangshis who were considered to be in the lower strata of the Hindu caste hierarchy by institutionalizing the use of sacred thread for them. This was indeed a symbolic protest against the domination and oppression of the upper castes. Later, in view of the perceived discrimination and marginalization in the face of socio-economic and political changes after the partition and the merger of Cooch Behar, the Rajbangshis got mobilized for redressing their imposed marginalization through a search for a separate cultural identity that they found in the Kamtapuri language – the colloquial language of the Rajbangshis in the region. As such, emerged in the scene the All Kamtapur Students Union (AKSU). The operation of the AKSU is, however, limited to specific pockets and among the younger generation of the folk. The Kamtapur Peoples' Party (KPP) which emerged in late 1980s is somewhat more organized and mobilizing the people for a separate state of Kamtapur comprising the districts of Cooch Behar, Jalpaiguri, Uttar Dinajpur, Dakshin Dinajpur and parts of Malda. However, the movement of the Kamtapur Peoples' Party under the leadership of Atul Roy is basically non-violent and thus the strategy that is being used is mostly democratic. But the militant outfit of the movement, the Kamtapur Liberation Organization

(KLO) is also gaining strength with the frustrated youth of the community being eluded to the promises of the leadership and thus attracted to the militant strategy of the organization. The KLO is operating in the remote areas of the Alipurduar subdivision of Jalpaiguri district that borders Assam and Bhutan. The organization also receives training from the militant organizations of Assam like the United Liberation Front of Assam (ULFA) and Bodoland Liberation Tigers (BLT) that run their training camps in the jungles of Bhutan. Information also reveal that these militant organizations maintain links with the militant Maoist group of Nepal. But, however, the KLO is found to be confined to few pockets only and it has not yet been able to penetrate into the common masses of the community in a big way. The community may be sympathetic to the organization but it does not approve in general the violent operations of the organization. This general apathy on the part of the Rajbangshi community towards the KLO may be attributed to the open and expressed disfavour of the Kamtapur Peoples' Party and its leadership to the KLO, partly to the passive, simple and innocent nature of Rajbangshi community and partly to the nature of operations of the KLO that is more found to be confined to forcible extortions, kidnappings for ransoms and killings for petty material and financial gains. Besides, there is also a women's organization that organize protest movements, sometimes in collaboration with the Kamtapur Peoples' Party for the cause of the Rajbangshi identity and the separate state of Kamtapur within the Union of India.

An observation of the Kamtapur movement shows that there is lack of coordination among the different groups. This may be the result of lack of able leadership with strong command over the masses. Besides, the creamy sections of the community – the educated, the established, and the intellectual class – have not yet shown their manifest support and solidarity to the movement, not to speak of coming forward to provide the leadership of the overall weak nature of the movement with less penetrating capability. However, it cannot be denied that it is the onset of this movement that aroused awareness among the people of North Bengal about the lopsided development in the state and made all the political parties realize the immediate need to redress the frustration that resulted from the uneven development in the state through a formal institutional mechanism. This may be the precise background for the establishment of the 'Uttar Banga Unnayan Parishad (North Bengal Development Council)" for the development of North Bengal. This is definitely a positive aspect of the protests spearheaded by the Rajbangshi community.

Protest Movements on Castes

Since the Indian society has been hierarchically organized on caste and since the society has also been characterized by oppression on caste line, there has been a number of protest movements on castes. One of the important features of the caste movements in India is the opposition, conflict and protest that marks the relationship of the lower castes with the upper castes. The logic of the hierarchical social structure makes the backward caste generally occupy a lower status and position in the society, characterized by social, ritual, cultural, economic and political disadvantages, discriminations and disabilities of several kinds and of different degrees which go under the general level of relative deprivation.

However, all the backward castes do not enjoy a uniform socio-economic status and there is a marked overlapping of caste and class in the Indian society. In his study on caste movements, M.S.A. Rao[55] divided non-upper castes into three categories. The upper most category of the backward castes consists mostly of the landowners. These castes operate with relatively substantial presence in different parts of the country, such as the Jat, the Ahir, the Gujjar in Punjab, the Maratha in Maharastra, the Vellata in Tamil Nadu, the Kamma, the Kapu and the Reddi in Andhra Pradesh, the Vokkaliga and the Bant and the Lingayats in Karnataka. Ranking below them are the tenant cultivators, artisans and other service castes. They include the Ahir and Kahar in Bihar, the Koli in Gujarat and the Vaddar in South India. They are considered as caste Hindus above the pollution line. At the bottom are the untouchable castes who are designated as the Scheduled Castes under the Constitution of India.

Backward caste movements in India has been classified into four broad types on the basis of structural cleavages and manifest conflicts.[56] The first type is that of the movements led by upper non-Brahmin castes such as the Vellata, the Reddi, and the Kammah of Tamil Nadu, the Vokkaliga and the Lingayat in Karnataka and the Maratha of Maharastra. Ramaswami Naikar of Tamil Nadu launched the 'Self-Respect' movement in Madras in the late 1920s to perform marriage ceremonies without Brahmin priests. Similarly, Thakur Panchanan Barma launched the movement in undivided Bengal against the material and psychological oppression of the Rajbangshis by the upper castes and classes in Bengal and declared that neglected and oppressed Rajbangshis as the 'Khatriyas'. As a mark of symbolic protest he institutionalized the use of sacred thread for the Rajbangshis thus making a state of mind that symbolized no difference between the upper caste Brahmins and the Rajbangshis. The non-Brahmin movements in Maharastra and Tamil Nadu raised cultural issues and the leaders of the backward caste movement attacked caste and condemned it as a tool of Brahmin oppression.[57] The second type of the backward caste movement hinges on the cleavages within the non-Brahmin castes, mainly led by the intermediate and low castes such as the Ahir and the Kurmis in Bihar, the Mania in Punjab, the Koli in Gujarat and the Mali in Maharastra. The movements by depressed classes or untouchables against other backward castes are the third type of backward caste protests. The fourth type is that of tribal protest movements.

The typology of backward caste protests is not and cannot be exclusive. Mere structural cleavages cannot explain the whole gamut of the origin and development of the protest movements by the backward castes. In fact, the structural cleavages along with the manifest conflicts are the manifestation of other important and overlapping factors that result the mobilization in the form of protest movements. Indeed, oppression of different types, dimensions and degrees – social, cultural, economic and political – is the root cause of mobilization but unless there is the perception and feeling of oppression among the so-called oppressed, mobilization for protest may not be so manifest as to result in movements. Structural cleavages and manifest conflicts are thus to be considered as dependent variables, the primary or independent variable being the elites of the backward castes who want to retain their elite status in the face of the lose or threat of lose of the same and as such, resort to mobilizations by feeding the generally passive and innocent masses that they are deprived of their due share and thus oppressed and hence, need to protest against. Under the circumstances, in order to understand and explain the backward caste movements too, the leadership issue is to be taken into consideration.

The non-Brahmin caste movement in Maharastra tends to include both an elite-based conservative trend and more genuine mass-based radicalism. It has attained the conservative goals but radical goals are yet to be attained. As Gail Omvedt observes, "The Maharastrian Brahman intelligentsia, though still dominant in educational and cultural institutions, has been swept from political power by a rich peasant non-Brahman elite, with strong roots in villages and with an institutional basis in rural cooperatives and educational societies".[58] Rudolph and Rudolph consider the backward castes of Northern, Western and upper Southern states "bullock capitalists". The mobilization of 'bullock capitalists' in the 60s and 70s as an economic class has been reinforced by the simultaneous mobilization as a status order of other backward classes, a eupheism for castes who by their own and states' reckoning are socially "depressed" or "backward". This layering of status and class interest enhances the political significance of both.[59]

As a first step to fulfill their aspiration to rise in the caste hierarchy and resist oppression, the backward castes followed the path of 'sanskritization' adopting the rituals and the life style of the upper castes. They invented legends about their ancestors and as such, demanded higher social status. However, the backward castes rarely resorted to large scale protest and direct action for asserting their demands till very recently as is found in Bihar where the backward castes under the ideological and organizational umbrella of Marxist-Leninist-Maoist extremism often resort to violence and direct action against the "Ranabir Sena", an upper caste private army, constituted by the upper castes to counter and oppress the backward castes. Thus, many of them undertook social reform which generally did not evolve confrontation with the higher castes. This is also due to the relatively disadvantageous social, economic and political position of backward castes that gets reinforced further by the fear of oppression by the upper castes with the help of the state machinery. The non-Brahmins of South India formed political parties to capture political power as did B.R. Ambedkar in Maharastra. The Bahujan Samaj Party of Kansiram and Mayavati is also an example of this sort of assertion.

Women's Movement

Women's protest to male domination is the product of western culture and education. British women took the initiative in forming organizations and defining their objectives. However, scholars and activists have started to raise issues relevant to the Indian context. Liddle and Joshi feel that the nature of male domination is different in India from that in western society and hence, the demands and protests of women against males are also different.[60] They argue that ideologically, cultural imperialism has introduced the notion of female inferiority which had no part in Indian culture and although females were segregated in the upper castes into the domestic sphere. This separation did not imply an inferior evaluation of the domestic, since the area was considered crucial to the maintenance of caste purity.[61]

There is dearth of agreement among the scholars on the classification of women's movements. Gail Omvedt[62] classifies women's movements into two types: (a) women's equality movements; and (b) women's liberation movements. While the former do not challenge directly the political or economic or family structure but rather aims at attaining an equal place for women in it and at abolishing the most open remnants of feudal patriarchy, the latter, that is, the women's liberation movements directly challenge the sexual division of labor itself. Jana Everette[63] classifies women's movements on the basis of two different ideologies of feminism. They are 'Corporate Feminism' that claims a larger role in politics for women on the ground that they have a special contribution to make as 'women', and 'Liberal Feminism' that rests on the claim that the rights of men should be extended to women on the grounds that women are equal to men and thus should have the same rights. The discourse on women's movements is thus replete with liberalism within liberalism and radicalism within radicalism. In order to avoid the inherent complexities in the process of classifying women's movements along the different variants of liberalism and radicalism it would be wise to make a broad classification of women's movements. Reformist women's movements are those that aim at bringing about change in the existing position of women without challenging the existing social, economic and political system as such while radical women's movements are those that are directed towards the root of gender discrimination.

Women's movements in India began as a part of the broad social reform movement in the 19th century. Social reformers like Rammohun Roy, Iswarchandra Vidyasagar, Mahadev Gobind Ranade, Behramji Malbari raised their voices against the prevailing religious and social customs that subjugated women. Under the influence of the movements the British government in India was encouraged to enact certain laws against the 'Sati' system, permitting women to remarry, abolishing the custom of child marriage etc. During the period, efforts were also made to spread education among the girls. Mahatma Gandhi made efforts to bring women out of the traditional confinement in the kitchens. However, the role of Gandhi in the protest against the subordinate position and in raising the status of women has been interpreted differently by different scholars. Vina Majumdar[64] and Devaki Jain[65] see

Gandhi as a greater liberator who adopted a revolutionary approach in raising the status of women while Madhu Kishwar[66], Kalpana Shah[67] and Sujata Patel[68] are the critics of Gandhi in regard to his role for the cause of the liberation women.

Women's organizations such as the Women's Indian Association and the All Indian Women's Conference (AIWC) came into existence in the 1920s to spread education among women and thereby to implant in them the feeling and strength of equality. However, Kalpana Shah argues that the role of AIWC in the struggle for the liberation of women is negative. To her, the Conference, through its programs, strengthened the traditional role of woman as a wife, housekeeper and mother. She goes on to argue that such organizations have been the instruments in spreading an ideology that assigns an inferior role to women and as such, they strengthen the revivalist values that are oppressive to women.[69] Similarly, Jana Everett identifies five factors that tended to shape and condition such reformist type of Indian women's movements. These are: (i) the hierarchical caste system; (ii) the Hindu religion; (iii) the joint family system; (iv) Islamic rule, and (v) British colonialism.[70] Besides, the 'purdah' system kept women secluded from men and discouraged them from public participation. It, therefore, gave women a certain sense of solidarity. The ideological implication of this 'purdah' system tended to shape the goals of early women's movement leaders toward corporate ideals, that is, improving women's performance of traditional female roles and away from liberal ideals, that is, achieving identical rights for men and women.[71]

Histories of various protest movements, such as, the freedom movement, the peasant movement, the tribal movement, the student movement and the like show and analyze the role and participation of women in these struggles. But most of the studies do not examine the role of women in the movements specifically. It is the assumption that these were led and dominated by males and as such, women had either no role or an insignificant one in these movements. However, this is a blatant misconception and misrecognition of the role of women in these movements. Govind Kelkar argues that "women have had a distinctive active role in the area of social and political movement that has not been fully described and explained".[72]

However, a close look at the operational part of these movements show that such conclusions are arrived at on the basis of stray instances rather than being based on adequate evidence. Kelkar herself observed that women were mobilized in the freedom movement because they were suited to carry out the non-violent struggle. She asserts that women's role in the freedom movement was that of "helpers" rather than that of "comrades".[73] Rajani Alexander observes that "women's participation in the independence movement took diverse forms and was not always organized and orchestrated political protests...."[74]

Some scholars[75] show that women were an integral part of the various tribal movements in the 19th century in Bihar and Maharastra. They were found using weapons skillfully. Some of them were arrested, beaten, molested and imprisoned by the police. Manashi Mitra observes that all the contemporary accounts demonstrate the role played by women in protest movements, both in militant attacks and confrontations with the authorities when they were not behind others in wielding the traditional weapons with skill and courage, as well as in maintaining links of supplies to the rebels in their hidden fortresses.[76] Women were also found participating actively in large numbers in the Telengana, Tebhaga, Naxalite and such other movements. Sunil Sen shows the active participation of women in various peasant movements from the twenties to the seventies in West Bengal.[77] Peter Custers demonstrates women's role in the Tebhaga movement and shows how the women from laboring and poor peasant classes provided effective leasership.[78] Shetkari Sangathana had also mobilized women in farmers' agitations.[79] Similarly, women also played a leading militant role in the Chipko movement resisting the cutting of trees from forests. In fact, women never had any contact with government officials or other outsiders and had no model of interaction with them but they only understood that cutting of trees was harmful for their well being and as such they acted according to their convictions.[80] However, it must be noted that the feeling of the negative impact of deforestation was indeed there across the males and females but that was implanted, nourished, strengthened and characterized in the form of protests and movements. In the course of the Bodh Gaya protests and struggles against the absentee landlords, women were found asserting their rights on the land. They collectively insisted that land should be given in their names and in some area they were successful in realizing their demands.[81]

Women in India also played a significant role by actively participating in the Communist-led movements and they are still an organized force to be reckoned with. In Kerala, women participated on a large-scale in the 1938 protests and formed the base of a crucial communication network.[82] Later on, the women workers launched protest movements on varied issues such as maternity benefit and retrenchment of women workers and participated in the armed struggle led by the Communist Party in the late 1940s.[83] Thus, the role of Kishan Sabha and Communist Party in mobilizing women in various peasant struggle is worth-mentioning. Renu Chakraborty, a Communist leader, who herself participated in several protest movements, highlights the role played by the communists in mobilizing women in various movements. According to her, the communist women identified themselves with the toiling masses of women and gave a new turn and outlook to entire women's movement.[84] However, other scholars, though recognize that the Communist Party did play an important role in women's mobilization, are critical that it did not play the role that was expected of it. Indra Munshi Saldanha argues that "women were not involved by the Kishan Sabha in the struggle in the same way or to the same extent as their male counterparts even in the most intensive phase of the struggle. The militancy, commitment and integrity of women, of which there was ample proof, were neither fully absorbed nor developed, and women were, by and large, assigned a mere supportive role".[85] Taking Kerala as the reference state, Kannan observes, "In varying degrees, the absence of any real participation by women at all levels of leadership has continued to this day. While their "help" was actively sought and secured during the early stages of mobilization and organization, they were not incorporated into the important levels of leadership and decision-making".[86] The observations made by Saldanha and Kannan thus point to the trend that the leadership allowed the involvement of women in the communist-led movements to that extent their leadership remained secured and also served the interests of the leadership.

Women's organizations also raise issues affecting them as women. They protest and fight around issues such as atrocities against women in the form of rape, alcoholism and wife-beating, sati, harassment and murder, violence in the family, common civil code, problems of working women, trafficking on women, oppression and exploitation of women belonging to 'dalit' and minority communities, problem of women in slums, communalism, obscene posters, problems of maid servants, the system of temple prostitution, superstition and witchcraft, deforestation etc. The frontal organizations of different political parties in West Bengal, the Mahila Samity of the CPI (M) in particular and the NGOs are doing significant influential work in organizing and mobilizing women along the common issues confronted by the women.

Women's movements in India are found to be ones focusing on women's issues rather than against the males and hence, not anti-men and extreme feminist. They are basically oriented towards development and empowerment and as such, cannot be of extreme feminist nature of the west. One of the important explanations for this Indian variant of feminist protests and movements is the homogeneous patriarchal socio-cultural ideology and its impact on the collectivity, mobilization and leadership of these movements.

Political Protests

It is true that all the protest movements are, in some way

or other, political protests because of their manifest or latent purpose of influencing the political system in a desired way. But in terms of the primary objective(s), pattern, collectivity of the mobilization and the character of the leadership, not all the movements can be designated as political protests aiming exclusively to political change. In Indian politics, there took place a number of protests of this type that shook the entire Indian polity.

In the mid 1970s, there was an unprecedented turmoil in the history of post independence India. The continuing and deepening economic crises and the eroding legitimacy of political institutions due mainly to an authoritarian trend of governance and the extra-constitutional centers of powers degenerating the process of governance in a big way resulted in a situation that was characterized by disturbances and conflicts, even spreading rioting in several parts of the country. This has its culmination in Gujarat and Bihar. The Gujarat agitational protest of 1974 ended with the dissolution of Gujarat Assembly - the specific goal of the agitation. In Bihar, the movement began in 1974 and spilled over to 1975. Unlike the Gujarat agitation, the Bihar movement had an organization with mobilized collectivity, a central guiding authority of Bihar Chhatra Sangarsh Samity, planned programmes, a cadre and the leadership of the charismatic Jayaprakash Narayan. Indeed, these two protests had far reaching consequences for the Indian political system as they had raised certain basic questions regarding the politics and society of India.

Since the beginning of the seventies, hopes among the urban and rural poor in Gujarat had been aroused with the populist promises and programmes of the central and the state government. But the big businessmen and rich peasants became alarmed and apprehensive with the 'Garibi Hatao' slogan of the Congress. As such, they organized and mobilized themselves and pressurized the government to look after their interests. The party in power, dominated by the rich, thus succumbed to their pressures both at the policy and implementation levels.[87] As a result, artificial scarcity, hording and black-marketing, rising prices loomed large throughout the state. Given this state affairs, people in general and the middle class in particular had found themselves disempowered, neglected, left to the uncertainties resulting thus in the alienation of this section of the people from the political regime. Under the circumstances, the protest movement that resulted and the consequent political upheaval that shook Gujarat during January-March, 1974 was an unprecedented phenomenon in the history of India after independence. The intensity of the movement was so widespread that no town in the state remained untouched by the upsurge and tensions even spread to some parts of the countryside also.[88] In fact, spiraling prices and scarcity of essential commodities and inadequacy of basic amenities in urban areas provided the breeding grounds for the intense protest in Gujarat that were used by the disgruntled sections for their political mileage.

In this situation, the students, one of the most organized sections of the middle class, spearheaded the protest. In Ahmedabad, it had begun with the formation of the Yuvak Lagni Samity, which later transformed itself into the Navanirman Yuvak Samity (NYS). As the protest movement gained momentum, particularly after the resignation of Chiman Bhai Patel as the Chief Minister, such organization proliferated throughout the state. Several other organizations such as the Gujarat Student Circle in Ahmedabad, Study and Struggle Alliance in Boroda, Akhil Bharatiya Vidyarthi Parishad, and Tarun Shanti Sena of Sarvodaya Mandal also took active part in the movement. However, each of these organizations functioned independently of the city level Navanirman Yuvak Samity and no coordination was noticed among them.

Observation of the Gujarat political protest shows that the movement was rooted to the issue of price rise and scarcity of essential commodities but got strengthened and succeeded under the shrewed guidance of organized interest groups and parties in general and the disgruntled elite in particular in ousting Chiman Bhai Patel as the Chief Minister and dissolving the State Assembly. The movement also shows that though the students had an immediate sense of purpose and direction, spontaneous mobilization and support base, they lacked well-defined organization and cadre and as such, they were confused and suffered from lack of agreement as to their immediate and future programmes. Indeed, under the influence of some radical leaders, the Navanirman and other Samities tied in the beginning to link up their problems with those of the larger society. But because of their adhoc approach, lack of organization, coordination and well articulated direction and above all, because of the movement being garbed by the disgruntled but organized elites, they merely became the instruments of organized groups and hence, lost track of their own objectives. Thus, the political protest launched by the students in Gujarat suggests that "students can overthrow a government and yet be unable to become an independent force for political change"[89] perhaps because the vested interests of the organized groups of which they became the victims would not allow them to be so.

The Bihar protest movement of 1974 was the culmination of a number of developments in different parts of rural and urban Bihar. Since the late sixties, agrarian tensions had been mounting and in the year 1970 alone, there were as many as 649 agrarian agitations.[90] The Naxalites and other left political parties had made inroads among the poor and oppressed peasants and landless laborers and had mobilized them against the oppression of the landlords. Under the circumstances, clashes between them were frequent. In the urban areas, government employees, teachers and other sections of the vocal middle class raised their voices against spiraling prices and increasing hardships. The imposition of professional tax by the government in 1973 added fuel to the fire. The opposition parties and trade unions formed an organization known as 'Bihar Rajya Mahgai Abhab Pesha kar Virodhi Mazdoor Wa Karmachari Sangharsh Samity' (the Bihar State Struggle Committee of Labourers and Employees to oppose price and professional tax) under the dominated influence of the Communist Party of India and other left political parties to protest against the hardship caused by the increasing price rise and the imposition of the professional tax and as such, a struggle was launched for the same. Simultaneously, students too joined the movement in Patna and some other towns with their demands relating to amenities in the campuses, reduction in fees, concession in cinema tickets etc. Meanwhile, the leaders of the Akhil Bharitya Vidyarthi Parishad (ABVP) of Bihar wanted to launch a state-wide agitation excluding the communists. For the purpose, they considered Jayaprakash Narayan as the acceptable leader to guide their non-communist movement. Jayaprakash Narayan also took the opportunity to streamline the protest against the authoritarian Congress rule both at the centre and the state and as such, appealed to the students to sacrifice their studies for a year to "save democracy". During the period, the left-oriented students formed the Bihar Chhatra Naujawan Sangharsh Morcha (BCNSM) and organized protests against price rise under the banner of BCNSM in Patna, Muzaffarpur, Begusarai, Sahebganj, Motihari and many other places. Besides other demands, they pressed for the closure of universities and colleges for one year, implementation for land reforms and take over of the universities by the state. The nature of the demands and subsequent political protest show as to how the organized groups and parties grabbed the movement for political gains. The student leaders felt that there was no way out for them to organize a militant struggle for the removal of the "present anti-people government".[91] As a fall out of a highly politicized movement, several hundred students assembled near the Raj Bhavan and the State Assembly on March 18 to prevent the Governor from attending the Assembly for his address. As such, a direct confrontation between the police and students took place near the Assembly and then onwards, the protest movement centred around political demand, that is, the resignation of Abdul Gafoor as the Chief Minister and the dissolution of the State Assembly.

As the movement got momentum with the direct clash between the police and the students, different sections of the urban middle class joined the movement. In April, J.P. Narayan assumed the leadership of the movement and it was declared as the revolutionary movement aiming at bringing about 'total revolution' in the society. After June 5, 1975, Jayaprakash Narayan himself announced "total revolution" as the ultimate objective of the movement.[92] It was declared that "the crux of the matter is that the movement is basically one against the existing system".[93]

However, like the Gujarat movement, the Bihar movement was not free from in-built limitations, particularly in terms of ideology, leadership and participation. The ideology that guided the Bihar movement had come to be the Sarvodaya ideology. But it has been observed that the ideology had produced results exactly the opposite of those expected by the Sarvodayaists themselves and it was primarily because of the deficiencies of the ideology itself.[94] Similarly, not all the constituent parts of the Bihar movement did share the Sarvodaya ideology but most of them were primarily interested in dethroning the Congress regime and seizing political power for themselves. It was due to the inadequacy of the ideology coupled with the narrow outlook of the leadership that resulted in putting the economic issues in second fiddle and despite all denials, the dissolution of the State Assembly became the ultimate end in itself. It is argued that "the beginning and the end of every revolution is characteristically political, in the sense that it begins with a political crisis and ends with political settlement".[95] Indeed, it may be true but the question that can be raised in this connection is what kind of political settlement and in whose favour. It appears that the Bihar movement led to the settlement for status quo in favor of the already privileged sections.[96] Thus, the Bihar movement was a protest movement protesting against the alleged misrule of the Congress and for replacing the Congress regime by other non-Congress aspirants within the existing systemic boundaries.

Another example of equally interesting political protest movement has been the one that was launched against the decision of the Government at the centre to divide railway zones. Alleging that the decision was the outcome of narrow political considerations of Nitish Kumar, the Railway Minister, Mrs. Mamata Banerjee, former Railway Minister and her

Trinamul Congress Party launched the protest against the decision, particularly of the division of the Eastern Zone. The protest was also supported by other political parties in West Bengal including the left political parties that are in power. Similarly, a protest was organized in Bihar, the state of the Railway Minister, Nitish Kumar but that was in favor of the decision to divide the Railway Zone and the protest was organized by the Samata Party and Rashtriya Janata Dal of Laloo Prasad Yadav, the political rival of Nitish Kumar's Samata Party. These protests in two States show that the leaders of these protests were guided by their narrow political gains in two different political settings that were thought to provide legitimacy to their leadership and also their grip over the passive means.

Environmental Movements

Besides the typical varieties of protest movements outlined above, there is also noticeable in India in recent years what is called 'new social movements' supposedly based on non-class issues, such as environmental movements that are generally neglected by established and mainline political parties. Ideally, an environmental movement is a people's protest for protecting the natural environment from degradation, decay and destruction by various activities of human beings and for promoting the development of the fragile ecosystem which is required for human development.[97] The protest movement for environmental protection may be against an individual act of environmental degradation or against the enforcement of environmentally destructive or harmful policies by the government. Thus, concern for environmental protection may take the form of localized movement or become a sub-national, national or a global movement. At the global level, concern for environmental protection was initiated with the United Nations sponsored World Conference on Environment and Development held in Stockholm in 1975. The Brundtland Commission, 1987 came out with the emphatic assertion that sustainable development was development that met the needs of the present without jeopardizing the ability of the future generations to meet their own need. The Rio Earth Summit 1992 also reiterated the synergic relationship between environment and development. M.S. Swaminathan has aptly stressed that 'development which is not equitable is not sustainable; which is not economically viable is not replicable and which is not ecologically sound will be self-destructive. Integration of the principles of economics, equity, ecology and employment in a development project can be achieved only through a pro-nature and pro-poor orientation to technology development and dissemination'.[98]

In India, the most highlighted environmental movements are those relating to the Sardar Sarovar Project and the Tehri Hydro-Electric Project under the inspiring and able leadership of Mrs. Medha Patekar and Mr. Sundarlal Bahugana, respectively. These two leaders have been found successful in mobilizing the affected people for opposing the government's policy of constructing dams at a huge social and environmental cost. Through their intense movements, these leaders have shown the hollowness of the government's policy, lack of national rehabilitation policy and have espoused the cause of the tribals whose villages are apprehended to be submerged under the dams. With utmost dedication and personal sacrifice these two leaders resorted to different methods of protests like courting arrests, organizing dharnas, fasts unto death and thus have earned the sympathy of large number of people throughout the country. As such, the government has been pushed to the defensive as to the viability of these projects.

NOTES & REFERENCES

1. Rao, M.S.A.: *Social Movements and Social Transformation: A Study of Two Backward Class Movements in India*, Delhi: Macmillan, 1979, p. 6.
2. O'Malley, L.S.S. (ed.): *Modern India and the West: A Study of the Interaction of their Civilizations*, London: Oxford University Press, 1941, pp. 67-68.
3. Jones, Kenneth N.: "Communalism in the Punjab: The Arya

Samaj Contribution", in *The Journal of Asian Studies*, Vol. 28, No. 1, 1968, pp. 39-54.

4. Rao, M.S.A.: *op. cit.*, p. 7.
5. Singh, Dalip: "Protest Movements in India", in *Indian Journal of Political Science*, Vo. 52, No. 4, 1991, pp. 448-457.
6. *Ibid.*
7. *Ibid.*
8. *Ibid.*
9. Wolf, Eric R.: "Types of Latin American Peasantry: A Preliminary Discussion", in *American Anthropologist*, Vol. 57, No. 3, 1955.
10. Wolf, Eric R.: *Peasants*, Englewood Chiffs, N.J.: Prentice Hall, 1966.
11. Wolf, Eric R.: *Peasant Wars in the 20th Century*, New York: Harper and Row, 1970. also

    Landsberger, Henri A.: "Peasant Unrest: Themes and Variations", in Landburger, Henri A. (ed.): *Rural Protest: Peasant Movements and Social Change*, London: Macmillan, 1974.
12. Thorner, Daniel: *The Shaping of Modern India*, Bombay: Allied Publishers, 1980.
13. Beteille, Andre: *Studies in Agrarian Social Structure*, Delhi: Oxford University Press, 1974.
14. Habib, Irfan: "The Peasant in Indian History", in *Social Scientist*, Vol. II, No. 3, 1983. Also

    Kannan, K.P.: *Of Rural Proletarian Struggles: Mobilization and Organization of Rural Workers in South-West India*, Delhi: Oxford University Press, 1988.
15. Rudolph, Lloyd I. and Susanne, H. Rudolph: *In Pursuit of Lakshmi: The Political Economy of the Indian State*, Hyderabad: Orient Longman, 1987, p. 53.
16. Shah, Ghanshyam: *Social Movements in India: A Review of Literature*, New Delhi: Sage Publications, 1990, p. 33.
17. Moore, Barrington Jr.: *Social Origins of Dictatorship and Democracy: Lord and Peasant in the Making of the Modern World*, London: Allen Lane, 1967, p. 202.
18. *Ibid.*
19. Stokes, Eric: *The Peasants and the Raj: Studies in Agrarian Society*

and Peasant Rebellion in Colonial India, Delhi: Vikas Publications House, 1978, p. 315.

20. Gough, Kathleen: "Indian Peasant Uprising", in *Economic and Political Weekly*, Vol. 9, Nos. 32-34 (special number), August 1974, p. 1319.

21. Desai, A.R. (ed.): *Peasant Struggles in India*, Delhi: Oxford University Press, 1979, p. XII.

22. Guha, Ranjit: *Elementary Aspects of Peasant Insurgency in Colonial India*, Delhi: Oxford University Press, 1983, p. 51.

23. Dhanagare, D.N.: *Peasant Movements in India, 1920-50*, Delhi: Oxford University Press, 1983, p. 5.

24. Gough, Kathleen: "Indian Peasant Uprising", in *Economic and Political Weekly*, Vol. 9, Nos. 32-34 (special number), August 1974, p. 1406.

25. Beteille, Andre: *Studies in Agrarian Social Structure*, Delhi: Oxford University Press, 1974, p. 6.

26. Weiner, Myron: *The Politics of Scarcity: Public Pressure and Political Response in India*, Bombay: Asia Publishing House, 1963, p. 140.

27. Dev, Acharya Narendra: *Presidential Address*, Gaya: All India Kissan Conference, 1939.

28. Ranga, N.G. and Saraswati, Swami Sahajanand: *History of the Kisan Movement*, Madras: All India Kishan Publications, 1939.

29. Ram, Mohan: "The Telengana Peasant Armed Struggle 1946-51", in *Economic and Political Weekly*, Vol. 8, No. 23, (January 9) 1973. Also Pavier, B.: *The Telengana Movement, 1944-51*, Delhi: Vikas, 1981, and Dhanagare, D.: *Peasant Movements in India, op. cit.*

30. Mukherjee, Partho N.: "Naxalbari Movement and the Peasant Revolt in North Bengal", in Rao, M.S.A. (ed.): *Social Movements in India*, Vol. I, Delhi: Manohar, 1979.

31. Hamja Alavi argues that the middle peasants, who are economically somewhat more independent have greater potential that other peasant classes to play a revolutionary role. The poor peasants are initially the least militant class because of their dependence on landlords or rich peasants. Alavi, Hamza: "Peasants and Revolutions", in Gough, Katheleen and H.P. Sharma (eds.): *Imperialism and Revolution in South Asia*, New York: Monthly Review Press, 1973. But Sarkar, Pavier and Dhanagare do not support Alavi's thesis.

32. Sarkar, Krishna Kanta: "Kakdwip Tebhaga Movement", in A.R. Desai (ed.): *op. cit.*
33. Pavier, Barry: *The Tebhaga Movement, 1944-51, op. cit.*
34. Dhanagare, D.N.: *Peasant Movements in India 1920-25*, op. cit.
35. Dutta, Prabhat K.: "Secessionist Movements in North East India", in *Indian Journal of Political Science*, Vol. 53, No. 4, 1992.
36. Sarkar, Ajeya: "Regionalism, State and the Emerging Political Pattern in India", in *Indian Journal of Political Science*, Vol. 51, No. 4, 1990.
37. Raj, A.L.: "Ideology and Hegemony in Jharkhand Movement", in *Economic and Political Weekly*, Vol. XXVII, No. 5, 1992.
38. Sengupta, Nirmal: "The Social and Economic Basis of Current Tribal Movements", in *Social Action*, October-December, 1990.
39. Sharma, K.L.: "Jharkhand Movement in Bihar", in *Economic and Political Weekly*, Vol. XI, No. 2, 1976.
40. Raj, A.L.: *op. cit.*
41. Sengupta, Nirmal: "Background of the Jharkhand Question", in Sengupta, Nirmal (ed.): *Fourth World Dynamics: Jharkhand*, Delhi: Shankar Printing Service, 1982.
42. Sharma, K.L.: *op. cit.*
43. Raj, A.L.: *op. cit.*
44. Brass, Paul: *Language, Religion and Politics in North India*, Delhi: Vikas Publishing House, 1974, p. 274.
45. Sahni, Ruchi Ram: *Struggle for Reform in Sikh Shrines*, Amritsar: SGPC, undated, p. 12.
46. Puri, Harish K.: "The Akali Agitation: An Analysis of Socio-Economic Bases of Protest", in *Economic and Political Weekly*, January 22, 1988, pp. 113-118.
47. Brass, Paul R.: *op. cit.*, p. 280. Also Uperti, P.N.: *Religion and Politics in Punjab in 1920's*, Delhi: Sterling, 1982.
48. Dhami, M.S.: "Political Parties and State-Autonomy Issue: A Case Study of Akali Party", in Bombwall, K.R. (ed.): *National Power and State Autonomy*, Meerut: Meenakshi Publications, 1978, p. 147.
49. Sarkar, Ajeya: *op. cit., p.* 483.
50. *Ibid.*

51. Sarkar, Ajeya: "Regionalism, State and the Emerging Political Pattern in India", in *Indian Journal of Political Science*, 51, 4, 1990, pp. 477-490.

52. Subba, Tanka B.: *Ethnicity, State and Development: A Case Study of the Gorkhaland Movement in Darjeeling*, New Delhi: Vikas Publishing House, 1992, p. 75.

53. *Ibid.*, pp. 76-77.

54. *Ibid.*, p. 101.

55. Rao, M.S.A.: "Social Movements among the Backward Classes and Blacks: Homology in the Sources of Identity", in Rao, M.S.A. (ed.): *Social Movement in India*, Vol. I, Delhi: Manohar, 1979, pp. 191-218.

56. *Ibid.*

57. Hardgrave, R.L.: *The Dravidian Movement*, Bombay: Popular Prakashan, 1965, p. 6.

58. Omvedt, Gail: *Cultural Revolt in a Colonial Society: The Non-Brahmin Movement in Western India 1879-1930*, Bombay: Scientific Socialist Education, 1976, p. 2.

59. Rudolph, Lloyd and Rudolph, Susanne: "Determinants and varieties of Agrarian Mobilization", in Desai, Meghnad *et al.* (eds.): *Agrarian Power and Agricultural Productivity in South Asia*, Delhi: Oxford University Press, 1984, p. 323.

60. Liddle, Joanna and Joshi, Rama: *Daughters of Independence: Gender, Caste and Class in India*, New Delhi: Kali for Women, 1986, p. 31. Also, Kaushik, Susheela: "Women Movements in India", in Chaube, S.K. and Chakraborty (eds.): *Social Movements in Contemporary India*, Calcutta: K.P. Bagchi, 1999, pp. 77-94.

61. *Ibid.*

62. Omvedt, Gail: "Women and Rural Revolt in India", in *The Journal of Peasant Studies*, Vol. V, No. 3, April, 1978.

63. Everett, Jana Matson: *Women and Social Change in India*, Delhi: Heritage, 1979, p. 3.

64. Majumdar, Vina: "The Social Reform Movement in India: From Ranade to Nehru", in Nanda, B.R. (ed.): *Indian Women from Purdah to Modernity*, Delhi: Vikas Publishing House, 1976, pp. 38-52.

65. Jain, Devaki: "Gandhian Contribution towards a Theory of Feminist Ethic", in Jain, Devaki and Diana Eck (eds.): *Speaking*

of Faith: Cross-Cultural Perspectives in Women, Religious and Social Change, Delhi: Kali for Women, 1986.

66. Kishwar, Madhu: "Gandhi on Women", in *Economic and Political Weekly*, Vol. XX< Np. 40, October 5, 1985.

67. Shah, Kalpana: *Women's Liberation and Voluntary Action*, Delhi: Ajanta Publishers, 1984.

68. Patel, Sujata: "Construction and Reconstruction of Women in Gandhi" in *Economic and Political Weekly*, Vol. 20 XXIII, No. 8, February 20, 1988.

69. Shah, Kalpana: *op. cit.*, p. 145.

70. Everett, Jana: *op. cit.*, p. 37.

71. *Ibid.*, p. 41.

72. Kelkar, Govind: "Women's Movement Studies: A Critique of the Historiography", in *Samya-Sakti – A Journal of Women's Studies*, Vol. 1, No. 2, 1984.

73. *Ibid.*

74. Alexander, Rajani: "Participants and Perceptions: Women and the Indian Independence Movements", in *Samya-Sakti – A Journal of Women's Studies*, Vol. 1, No. 2, 1984.

75. Mitra, Manoshi: "Tribal Women and Tribal Movements", in *Samya-Sakti – A Journal of Women's Studies*, Vol. 1, No. 2, 1984.

    Munshi, Saldanha, Indra: "Tribal Women in the Warli Revolt of 1945-47: Class and Gender in the Left Perspective", in *Economic and Political Weekly*, Vol. XXI, No. 17, April 26, 1986.

76. Mitra, Manoshi: *op. cit.*, p. 90.

77. Sen, Sunil: *Peasant Movements in India – Mid-19th and 20th Centuries*, Calcutta: K.P. Bagchi, 1982.

78. Custers, Peter: "Women's Role in Tebhaga Movement", in *Economic and Political Weekly*, Vol. XXI, No. 43, October 25, 1986.

79. Bahuguna, Sundar Lal: "Women's Non-Violent Power in the Chipko Movement", in Kishwar, Madhu and Vanitha Ruth (eds.): *In Search of Answers*, London: Zed Books, 1984. Also,

    Dogra, Bharat: *Forests and People*, Rishikesh: Himalaya Darshan Prakashan Samity, 1980.

80. Jain, Shobhita: "Women and Peoples Ecological Movements: A Case Study of Women's Role in the Chipko Movement in Uttar

Pradesh", in *Economic and Political Weekly*, Vol. XIX, No. 4, October 13, 1984.

81. Manimala: "Zamen Kenkar" and Jote Onkar? The Story of Women's Participation in Bodhgaya Struggle", in *Manushi*, Vol. 3, No. 2, January-February, 1983.

82. Velayudhan, Meera: "Women Workers and Struggle in Alleppey", in *Samya-Sakti – A Journal of Women's Studies*, Vol. 1, No. 2, 1984.

83. Kannan, K.P.: *Of Rural Proletarian Struggles: Mobilization and Organization of Rural Workers in South-West India*, Delhi: Oxford University Press, 1988.

84. Chakraborty, Renu: *Communists in India's Women's Movement*, Delhi: Peoples Publishing House, 1980.

85. Munshi, Saldanha Indra: *op. cit.*, p. 51.

86. Kannan, K.P.: *op. cit.*, pp. 138-139.

87. *Ibid.*

88. Shah, Ghanshyam: *Protest Movements in Two Indian States: A Study of the Gujarat and Bihar Movements*, Delhi: Ajanta Publications, 1977, pp. 29-30.

89. *Ibid.*

90. Pant, K.C.: "Violence in a Period of Social Change", in *Young India*, Vol. III, Nos. 29-30, 1973.

91. *The Indian Nation*, March 16, 1974.

92. *Everyman's*, July 20, 1974.

93. *Everyman's*, November 9, 1974.

94. Shah, Ghanshyam: *op. cit.*, p. 159.

95. Sethi, J.D.: "Jayaprakash Narayan and His Revolution", in *Gandhi Marg*, January, 1975.

96. Shah, Ghanshyam: *op. cit.*, p. 162.

97. Bava, Noorjahan: "Environmental Movements for Sustainable Development", in Chaube, S.K. and B. Chakraborty (eds.): *op. cit.*, pp. 169-181.

98. Swaminathan, M.S.: "Foreword" to Ismail Seragaldin: *Promoting Sustainable Development: Towards a New Paradigm*, Rajiv Gandhi Institution for Contemporary Studies, Paper 12, 1994.

Chapter – 4

Protests and Movements in India: Issues, Types, Leadership and Ideology

One of the important legacies that India inherited from the past was the existing order, social structure and social conflicts that influenced to a significant extent the subsequent ideas, practices and movements. The contradictions that are abundant at different levels of the society actually thus provide the breeding grounds for antagonism that is being manipulated by leaders giving them shape of protests. In fact, there is no denial of the fact that India's legitiuistic, religious, ethnic and cultural diversities are proverbial. So also are the socio-political mobilizations, protests, violent conflicts and antagonisms that arise from time to time among and between persons from distinctive groups. But it is equally important to note that neither socio-political mobilizations and protests nor social, cultural, religious and ethnic antagonisms flow naturally of India's diversities.[1] They are, indeed, made to flow.

Issues

The independent India, in line with the logic of pluralism, witnessed as many as thirty-three languages with speakers of more than one million but only fifteen of them achieved any form of significant political recognition (1971 Census). Similarly, the 1981 Census enumerated a tribal population of more than fifty million divided into hundreds of distinct groups. Among these tribals, a large number of socio-political mobilizations took place, a number of which developed into bitter, violent and secessionist protests and movements directed against the non-tribals – the movement of the tribals in the State of Jharkhand in favour of the Domicile Policy of the State; against particular state government – the movement of the Jharkhandis against the State of Bihar and West Bengal and the movement by the Rajbangshis against the State of West Bengal; or against the Government of India itself – the movement by the tribals in the North-East. These tribal mobilizations thus took diverse forms·focusing on economic grievances on being class-based and drawing support from Marxist and radical political organizations while others focusing on political demands being organized and led by tribal leaders and exclusively by tribal organizations.

Again, the whole modern history of India has been deeply affected by the conflict between Hindu and Muslim communal violence. However, these conflicts, protests and associated violence may also be contrasted with periods of marked cooperation between the two communities. Similarly, such communal protests and resultant conflicts have been more intense in some parts of the country while less or non-existent in other parts where Hindus and Muslims also live side by side.

In the 1980s and 1990s, India has found an extremely violent protest movement by the militant Sikhs, some of whom were secessionist too. Punjab where most Sikhs live became an unfortunate battle ground in which a violent guerilla war was waged between the Sikh militants and the Indian police. But in spite of this situation, the Sikhs and Hindus have shown gesture of cooperation in social and political fields and were never before considered to be hostile communal groups.

Plural character of Indian society is also manifest as a society divided on caste and caste antagonism and thus protest movements, sometimes assuming violent, emanate from these caste considerations and caste antagonisms. Various census reports reveal that there have been, as in the past, thousands of castes and dozens of caste clusters in each linguistic region. In view of this, caste mobilizations and inter-caste conflicts have been rampant in India among many such groups. In the 1970s and 80s, inter-caste conflicts between so-called backward and upper caste groups became intense in several states because mainly of the erosion of Congress as a dominant political party in Indian politics and the increasing politicization of caste by several political parties. But, however, it needs to be stressed that such mobilizations and protests have occurred among specific groups in specific regions at particular times and not others and hence, no regular pattern should be drawn in this respect. The State of West Bengal may be cited in this connection as an example that comes in the way of drawing a common pattern of caste in Indian politics.

Migration of persons from one linguistic region and country to another, particularly to the relatively less densely populated tribal regions of the country and to North-Eastern part of the country and also to the metropolitan centres has produced situations which have sometimes led to migrant-nativist political conflicts. Similarly, women in India have been found mobilizing themselves and resorting to protest movements against male chauvinism, and other issues affecting them directly and some others relating to politics, society and the environment. But these mobilizations and protests too do not constitute a regular pattern and hence, not frequent. The students' community also mobilizes them and protest against issues ranging from the direct concern to those relating to social, economic and political change. Here also the mobilization and consequent protests are not permanent and frequent.

It follows, therefore, that mobilizations, protests and resultant conflicts in India are not natural flowing naturally. If it would have been natural, it would have occurred frequently with regular patterns of its own. But there is no such regular pattern in the mobilizations and protest movements in India. However, the sources of these linguistic, tribal, religious, caste migrant-non-migrant mobilizations, protests and conflicts may be identified and stressed.

In both the pre and post-independence periods, the nature and way of extending recognition by the state itself has been a critical factor in causing the rise of some ethnic and cultural protests and movements.[2] The British, for their own colonial interest, extended official preference to the Bengali language in the east rather than to Assamese and Oriya and to Urdu in the North rather than Hindi. Similarly, they provided for separate electorates and other political concessions to Muslims and Sikhs. They also allowed migration of plain's people into tribal areas in central India and tribal people in the plantations areas of the east while forbad it in some parts of the North East. Again, it was their colonial strategy to patronize non-Brahmin movements, particularly in the southern part of the country when Brahmins were found leading the Indian national Congress there. Indeed, the British resorted to these partisan policies to widen the divide among the Indians, so that any concerted effort to oppose the British regime could be averted. As such, the requirement of colonial interest led the British to adopt discriminatory treatment for the Indians that, in the long run, became the issues for collective mobilization and protests on respective lines of discrimination.

In the post-independence period too, the Government of India and the state governments were found seeking to change the balance of recognition among some groups. Hindi was adopted as the official language of the country and of the north Indian states thus displacing Urdu from the remaining bastion in Punjab and Uttar Pradesh. Assamese was adopted as sole official language of Assam against the wishes of the large Bengali-speaking minority and many other tribal groups. Provisions for separate electorates for Muslims and Sikhs were done away with but provisions for reservation of legislative seats and administrative and educational places for Scheduled Castes and Tribes were retained or introduced. All these caused a sense of alienation to some of the target groups of governments' discrimination thus leaving the ground for mobilization and movements.

Thus, recognition extended by the state sometimes worked in contrary ways. On the one hand, it strengthened some of the groups so recognized while weakening the others. On the other hand, in some cases, it contributed to the origin and development of counter-movements by the groups that were denied recognition. The best examples of this type are the numerous movements and protests among the unorganized "backward castes" who sought systems of reservations equivalent to those granted to Scheduled Castes and Tribes.[3] Again, state recognition has often been extended on political considerations and on political expediency. This acts as pacifiers to some protests while making room for the other protests and movements.

Besides, there are other factors that concern the specific policies and political strategies pursued by the central and state governments in relation to regional and sub-regional ethno-cultural entities. It is argued that the state policy of India towards varied minorities has differed in the Nehru and post-Nehru periods. In the Nehru period, the central government pursued pluralist policies in relation to major language and ethno-cultural movements, recognizing especially most of the large language groups among whom major mobilizations developed for the creation of separate linguistic states. But at the same time, the centre wanted to avoid direct involvement in regional conflicts among different ethnic and linguistic groups.[4] But in the post-Nehru period, the centre has played a more interventionist role in regional conflicts between opposed ethnic, communal and caste groups. It is found on analysis that the central government tolerated the disruptive and allegedly murderous and terrorist activities of Bhindranwale in Punjab in order to embarrass its main political rival in the state, the Akali Dal. Similarly, it followed inconsistent policies in Kashmir, Assam and other norti-eastern states. Moreover, during the succession struggle between Mrs. Indira Gandhi and her rivals after 1965, the central Congress leadership took initiatives in several states to displace upper caste leaders from state Congress organizations and replace them with backward caste persons and to mobilize the votes of the latter castes to defeat its rivals in the state Congress and in the opposition. The consequences of these interventions, some of which may justly appear as socially progressive, had often had the consequences of intensifying inter-ethnic regional conflicts.[5]

Thirdly, the uneven social change among different social groups leading, in turn, to imbalances in their relative access to economic opportunities, educational advantages and political power has often been contributory to the mobilization of some groups for protests. In view of the plural character of Indian society, each region of India presents a dominant language and/or particular caste group who have long held disproportionate shares of social, economic and political opportunities. As such, a sense of self-consciousness and identity has been articulated in the groups so dominated particularly among the elites of the disadvantaged groups that disparities exist and are made to continue between the life chances of persons from their own groups and hence, the disadvantaged groups are mobilized for challenging the preponderant shares of the dominant groups in the process of social change.[6] The recent introduction of the domicile policy in the State of Jharkhand and the protests and movements against the said policy by the dominant groups and the consequent counter movements by the hitherto disadvantaged groups is a case in point.

Fourth, the extent to which persons from different ethnic, language and cultural groups actually find themselves in competition for the same positions in the division of labour in the society is another related factor responsible for different mobilizations and protests. It has been a common pattern and getting intensified in recent times that educated persons from religious, language, caste and other ethnic and social categories compete for the prestigious and secure jobs in public services and for the educational opportunities to gain access to them. As such, conflict between and among competing educated classes in search of scarce jobs has been among the most prevalent sources of ethnic conflict in India.[7]

Another factor influencing and conditioning the types of mobilization, protest and conflict that are prevalent in India concerns the levels of political action and the levels of ethno-cultural loyalties. Indian society, in view of the logic of plurality, continues both multiple levels of political arenas and hierarchies of loyalties to ethno-cultural categories. At the village level and its surroundings, 'Jati', the local version of caste, provides a basis for economic action, political organization and social conflict. However, this phenomenon depends on the configuration of the village as a unit and the kind of environment that it presents. Thus, there may not be rare cases where mobilization at the village level may be a combination of caste and religion, religion and class and caste and class. In a unit larger than the village and corresponding to a district, correspondingly larger units of political activities or political coalitions across 'jati' boundaries become necessary for effective political action. The unit of loyalty and political action may then become the caste category or caste cluster or a coalition of related castes. At the state level, only the largest caste categories with wide representation throughout large parts of a state may be able to act in solidarity and politically effective ways. In many cases, such actions at the state level become impossible and other kinds of loyalties to factions and parts become predominant. At the national level, it is argued by a serious observer of Indian politics, caste becomes virtually ineffective as a basis for sustained political mobilization for the available caste categories at this level lack appropriate social or economic content. Thus, alternatives to caste as an organizing principle for political conflict exist at every level in Indian politics, particularly from the district upwards. At those levels, categories such as Hindu and Muslim become more prominent, language loyalties become critical, ones identity as a migrant or a "son of the soil" may be decisive, or factional, party and ideological bases for political divisions may prevail.[8]

In fine, issues around which mobilizations and resultant protest movements seem to centre are the manifest form of the perceived deprivations emanating from the contradictions prevailing at different levels of the society. Thus, some issues tend to make mobilizations and protests stronger with lasting implications while others do not. In fact, the issues that are basically primordial in nature tend to have lasting effect. The mobilizations and protests around the issue of language in the 50s has a considerable impact on the stability and integrity of the political system. Similarly, caste factor, particularly the protests for and against 'reservations' in the wake of Mandal Commission Report left a seemingly unbearable jerk on the political system. The protest around the 'domicile policy' in Jharkhand state in recent times reveals the deep impact of the primordial issues that appear to and bring together a large sections of the population across the social, economic and political boundaries. The sweeping victory of the BJP and Narendra Modi in Gujarat in the recent Assembly polls vindicates how strong the bond of 'Hindutwa' could be for the cross-section of the people at large. On the other hand, secular issues like protest against price rise, privatization, unemployment, fee-hike in educational institutions, economic reforms, educational policy – though do not draw blank, are the issues which leave comparatively absorbable impact on the system as a whole. Besides, these issues get confounded or are artificially confounded because of their susceptibility to political maneuvering. This indicates the limited mobilizing capability of the secular issues in Indian socio-political system. This phenomenon of Indian socio-political system may be conceptualized as the "indigenization of secularism" – a phenomenon whereby secular forms of protests are indigenized by Indian primordiality. In the face of indigenization of secularism, the phenomenon of 'secularization of 'indigenous primordiality' that should have outweighed the former over the long fifty years journey of the Indian political system, has been inwardly passive, or has been made to be passive for parochial political gains. This phenomenon speaks of the secular use of the primordial means.

Types

Given the social, economic, political, religious, ethnic and cultural contradictions of the Indian society and the factors being contributory to the mobilizations, protests and conflicts as outlined above, protest movements in India assume different types, with varied content, leadership and ideology. Thus, some protest movements take the form of merely seeking to reform the existing arrangements – regions, social, cultural, political and economic – while others go to the extent of threatening the system itself to break down or collapse. An analysis of protest movements in India thus suggests that they may take any form – from a slow and gradual reform movement to a radical and revolutionary one.

Protest movements may be classified on the basis of one or the other criterion.[9] These criteria may be directions of the movement, quantum of change sought for, mobilization pattern, configuration of the collectivity, ideological orientation, place in the continuum of tradition and modernity, etc. M.S.A. Rao[10] suggests the possibility of classifying movements on the basis of their consequences. Thus, movements may aim at reforming in one or another aspect of social life, or oriented to bring about changes in the super-ordinate or subordinate relationships and finally, those oriented towards bringing about revolutionary change in every sphere of life and in basic values. Accordingly, these movements are referred to as reformative, transformative and revolutionary. Emphasizing on the means adopted by change oriented movements reform movements are described as those movements, that utilize legitimate means. In these movements, changes are sought to be brought about within the given framework of a society and the means adopted are consistent with the social norms and values of the society. Radical or revolutionary movements are characterized by the rejection of existing legitimate means and by the adoption of means that are considered improper by the establishment in their attempt to achieve change in all spheres of life, including basic values. Basically, then, Rao classifies protest movements on the system. While the former two types aim at the intensity of consequences of movements on, by maintaining the basic ingredients of the system, seeking changes within the system, the last category aims at changing the system itself. Besides, these movements may also vary in terms of conflicts embedded in them. Conflict is least in reform movements; it acquires a sharper focus in transformative movements, and in the case of revolutionary movements conflict is based on the Marxist ideology of class struggle.

However, there are a number of ambiguities and imperfections in Rao's typology of social movements. Reform and revolutionary movements are differentiated in terms of the quantum of change – partial and total. While in the former, the desired change is thought to be partial, in the latter, it is total. Similarly, reform or transformative movements are distinguished on the basis of where the change takes place. In reform movements, change occurs in the value system and in the case of the transformative movements, it takes place at the middle level of the structure. The twin basic principles of any classification are exclusiveness and exhaustiveness and Rao violates the principle of exclusiveness by shifting the criteria of classification used in three types of movements.[11] This shifting criteria brings in a number of questions. For instance, the questions may be as to which type of social movement and protest pursues either partial – middle level structural change or total middle level structural change; how we should classify a movement that aims at partial as against total change in the value system; where we should place a movement which pursues revolutionary changes through non-violent means; how we should account for frequent and intensely violent conflicts that occur in the course of movements that have primordial collectivities rather than class as their locus. These and several other equally important issues are not properly covered in the classificatory scheme proposed by Rao. Indeed, this is a broad classification made on the direction and quantum of change and as such, may be treated as an analytical tool for evaluating the consequences of protest movements in general.

Partha Mukherjee[12] classifies movements on the basis of the quality of change sought to be brought about – 'accumulative', 'alternative' and 'transformative'. While accumulative changes are intra-systemic, the other two are systemic changes. Alternative change is geared to create new structures and by implication, to destroy the existing ones; transformative change aims at replacing the existing structure and substituting it by another. This characterization is also problematic in that unless one creates new structures one cannot replace and substitute the existing ones and, hence, the distinction between alternative and transformative change becomes pointless. Again, Mukherjee's analysis implies that revolutionary means suit only movements which pursue systemic change, and revolutionary movements should not only aim at far-reaching systemic changes but should necessarily pursue them through revolutionary means. Such a position is untenable because it cannot explain the lack of it between means and ends in the case of several movements. For example, which type of movement it will be which has intra-systemic change as its goal but adopts revolutionary means to achieve it. Again, if a movement pursues systemic changes through institutionalized and even non-violent means how we will characterize it.

T.K. Oommen[13] has suggested that a situation of strain in a society may be met through one or another of the following response patterns depending upon the system characteristics: (a) emergence of a charismatic leader who promises to mitigate the evils at hand and lead the people to a future utopia; (b) crystallization of a new ideology which champions the cause of the deprived; and (c) establishment of a new organization to deal with the problem at hand. As such, each of these developments give rise to the emergence of three distinct types of movements – charismatic, ideological and organizational. An analysis of this categorization reveals that the main focus of this typology is on the process of movement crystallization, the life-cycle and phases of the movements. Unlike other typologies, it does not insist on that movements are necessarily oriented to change. Rather, they may not only lead to system stability but may pursue it as a goal. One of the important limitations of this typology is that it is based on a componential analysis of movements in that it gives primacy to one or another component of the movement – leadership, ideology, organization. Indeed, these components determine the shape and impact of a movement to a substantial extent but these cannot be considered exclusive. In fact, this way of looking at the movements tends to blur the relevance of other components which are equally important for the sustenance of movements.

Thus, it is important to note that the characteristics of a society shape the direction, content, idioms and styles of its movements. The relative tolerance of a society will inevitably be reflected in its style of protests. Thus, tribal societies in northern part of India exhibit a type of mobilization and protest completely different from those in the tribal societies in the north-east. In other words, every social structure creates its own style of protests and modes of expressing these protests.[14] Therefore, an adequate framework for the study of protest movements should take into account the historicity of the elements of social structure and the future vision of the society in which they originate and operate, and it is the dialectics between these which provides the focal points for the analysis of social movements in general and protest movements in particular.[15] Thus, what needs to be investigated is the nature and types of movements in a particular society and the characteristics they partake and exhibit.

An inadequate perception of the importance of the historical context in shaping protest movements has also given birth to some misconceptions about the nature of movements.[16] The predominant orientation of protests and movements in ancient and even in medieval India was religious and this was for two reasons: the absence of a centralized political authority, and the nature of the authority challenged was inevitably legitimized by religion.[17] However, this aspect of the analysis does not suggest that non-religious, that is, political or economic context was absent in those movements. In fact, often religious symbols and styles of protest were invoked, as is done now too, to achieve non-religious goals. However, an exception to this way of looking at the general pattern of protests may be that some religious movements in India appear to be independent of political involvements and do not pursue any structural reforms or political changes, as may be the case of the movement by the Ramkrishna Mission. But the motivation involved in preventing conversion from Hinduism to other religions or the political activities of the 'Sangh Parivar' and the Rashtriya Swayam Sevak Sangh in particular do not support this position. Similarly, there are those who proceed exclusively along 'class-conflicts' characterize all these mobilizations as predominantly economic in orientation.[18]

During the period of national liberation movements in India, most of the mobilizations and protests were directly against the forces of imperialism and colonialism irrespective of their categories, namely, students, peasants, women, workers, etc. or underlying motivations involved. But after independence, the absence of an over-arching enemy like the British colonial power, and the differing perceptions about the 'enemy' to be attacked necessarily led to (a) divergence in the targets of attack, that is, political authority, economic exploitation, cultural domination, and (b) varying perceptions about the immediate targets of attack. This led to diversification in the nature and proliferation of protest movements in India.[19]

Again, the change in the historical context also leads to changes in perspectives of analyzing protest movements. What were earlier perceived to be religious or reform movements[20] later came to be viewed as socio-political in orientation.[21] That is, the changing historical context shapes the attitude of the people towards protest movements and hence, changes their typology in view of change in their orientation. Movements are also labelled on the basis of a particular identity of participants even when the goals pursued are innate to the interests of the specific identity. The movements are named after primordial collectivities such as religious, caste, or linguistic groups and civil collectivities such as peasants, students and workers. Similarly, labelling of movements is also done on the basis of the nature of collectivities against whom they are targeted – the anti-Brahmin movement, anti-Congress movement etc. This way of labelling movements can be highly misleading for a number of reasons. The individuals and groups involved in these movements may have several identities and the specific identity invoked may not have any relevance for the movement concerned. Moreover, a particular identity may be invoked by the enemies of the movement to discredit it. Similarly, several social groups or categories may be participating together in a protest movement and to designate it after one of the categories would be misleading even if that category constitutes the bulk of the participants who have initiated it.

Another frequent tendency is to classify and name movements on the basis of their territorial coverage, particularly the locality in which they originate and operate. Examples of these designations are Bihar, Telangana, Assam, Vidharva, Jharkhand, Naxalbari movements and the like. Such designation of movements does not reveal the nature of these movements at all – the background of the participants, the goals pursued, the means employed, the ideology followed etc. This mode of designating protest movements places, for instance, the Assam movement and the Naxalbari movements on the same footing which is utterly inappropriate. Further, if the movements subsequently spread to a wider territorial area, the initial labelling becomes obsolete, as illustrated by the case of the Naxalbari movement. In fact, the Naxalbari movement is known more for its ideological radicalism, the goal of systemic change and the violent means than the geographical territorial designation attached to it.

Protest movements are also named after the issues they pursue. Examples of these protest movements are the Tebhaga movement, Narmada Bachao movement, anti-Hindi movement and the like. There are likewise limitations in designating protest movements by the apparent issues they seek to pursue. One of the important limitations of this designation is that since protest movements are likely to undergo goal transformations, the initial focus of the movement may change, making the name redundant. Besides, these issues may be too narrow in their orientation and may be but one of the several issues pursued by the movement. Hence, there is the possibility of mistaking the part for the whole.

Finally, there is the tendency to name movements after their initial or top leadership. The Ramkrishna Mission movement, the Gandhian movement, the J.P. movement may be the examples of this type of designation. But this mode of naming the movements too is inappropriate in view of the possibility of the movements transcending the physical-biological life-span of the specific individual leaders. Similarly, the mode of labelling movements in the name of their leaders smacks of the personality-centredness of the movements as against the systemic orientation. Actually, it tends to ignore and relegate the role of the collectivity, which is so critical in any movement, to the background.

Given the above discussion, it can be said that none of the attempts to classify protest movements is comprehensive to encapsulate all varieties of protest movements found in India.[22] Thus, for convenience, protest movements in India may be classified on the basis of the socio-economic characteristics of the participants and the issues involved. Such as, the peasant protests, tribal protests, backward caste protests, Dalit protests, women's protests, students' protests, middle class protests, working class protests and the like.[23] However, the way Shah classifies protest movements is not free from limitations. There may be, and are, protests which comprise collectivities across the typologies suggested by Shah. The Assam movement, the Bodoland movement, the Gorkhaland movement, the Jharkhand movement, the Kamtapur movement cannot be put exclusively in either of the categories suggested by Shah because these movements tend to exhibit collectivities from the categories of peasants, workers, students, women, intellectuals etc. simultaneously. Similar is the case with broad ethnic or secular protest movements.

Under the circumstances, it appears to be very difficult to classify protest movements into exclusive typologies in view of their being of diverse nature with diverse issues, collectivities, ideologies, goals and means. Thus, for convenience as useful analytical tools to measure and evaluate the impact on the society, economy and polity, protest movements may broadly be classified into primordial protest movements and the secular protest movements. Here, the important parameters for classification have been the goals and means of the protest movements. Thus, when a movement aims at achieving goal on primordial considerations like identity formation, cultural revitalization or upliftment in the social hierarchy, it is indeed primordial. Similarly, when a movement is directed towards achieving a secular goal devoid of traditional consideration and is based on modern means it may be called a secular movement. Though there is the possibility of overlapping of the primordial and secular movements – a primordial movement seeking to achieve a secular goal, as for instance, the Kamtapur movement or the Jharkhand movement where the mobilization is on primordial considerations but the goal is secular, that is, separate state within Indian Union or even a separate sovereign state implying right of self-determination. Conversely, there may be movements where the mobilization may be on secular consideration but the goal sought to be achieved is primordial. Despite these limitations, the broad typology of primordial and secular protest movements avoids many other limitations and drawbacks of other classificatory schemes and hence, appears to be more useful as an analytical tool than the others.

Leadership

Leadership occupies an important place in the protest movements as the leaders are responsible for and instrumental in translating objective causes into subjective consciousness articulating causes of deprivation of which the common people may have little or no knowledge, and thus mobilizing the participants. Hardly there can be any situation when the participants by themselves can organize and lead a movement, nor can they mobilize themselves into a collectivity fit for a protest and movement. However, the leadership pattern in different protest movements in India has been different.

As far as the pre-independence peasant protests are concerned, peasant struggles that came into being in rural India could never assume a genuinely political character unless they were taken over by leaders belonging to politically advanced social groups than the peasant themselves. In fact, the relatively educated intelligentsia provided the leadership to most of the peasant movements during the nationalist period. The 'Babas', 'Fakirs', and 'Sadhus' played the role of militant rural intelligentsia in peasant movements. They organized the peasants against the British rulers. Indeed, they were not revolutionaries of any accepted description belonging to any defined revolutionary social class; nor did they have any well-founded ideology; nor did they conform to the behavior pattern or articulation style of the recognized leadership. They had mobility and utmost dedication for the cause of the deprived and the exploited peasants, were the full timers but lacked the sophistication of the urban, educated and propagandist leaders. Their exercise rested on a precise understanding of the situation and a detailed diagnosis of contemporary social ills[24]. Some of these movements are thus called the "Sanyasi' rebellion.[25]

It is found on observation that the educated middle-class which had lost its ties of material interest with land provided the organized cadres of the new parties of mass mobilization. Their intervention provided a radical edge to the anti-landlord demands of the mass of the tenancy, but it continued to display an ambivalent attitude towards the progressive historical potentiality of the new contradiction.[26] Similarly, it is also found vindicating the theoretical framework suggested in the introductory chapter that the urban leadership actually exploited the peasant discontent to further its own political party and personal ends. The leadership of the Naxalite movement rested basically with the urban educated middle class with the exception being Jangal Santhal. In the land grab movement, the leadership came from the urban better-off section of the society.[27] It is held that the urban-based leadership used a relatively more sophisticated and often camouflaged ideology commensurate with the goal and claimed superior knowledge and status with regard to the manner in which the movement should be conducted. They would insist that the others follow the direction that they give and would assume that the predicted outcome would ensue.[28] The urban based middle class leadership had the capability, by virtue of their knowledge, position and relative deprivation, to convice the target groups and as such, mobilize on a systematic formulation of ideas – an ideology – promising an utopia. Even the protest movements organized by the Kisan Sabha, the frontal organization of the Communist Party of India (CPI) were dominated by the urban-based middle class leadership. The exception to this is, besides Jangal Santhal as mentioned above, has been Mahendra Singh Tikayet, leading the protests for the farmers in northern India, but he too comes from a rich upper class peasant and representing 'bullock capitalism'. However, of late, with the revitalization of the Panchayati Raj in West Bengal after the Left Front came to power in 1977, the leadership in rural West Bengal, particularly in the peasant front has been decentralized and descended to the grassroots level. But here too, the picture has substantially changed since early 1990s and the privileged sections of the rural West Bengal has replaced the leadership from the poor and has been, for their narrow and immediate interests, the handmaide of the urban middle class leadership that has been controlling the overall structural, organizational and functional aspects of the political parties.

So far as the tribal protests are concerned, the leadership of the Santhal, the Kol, and the Munda rebellions came mostly from religious leaders or leaders who proclaimed themselves, or were seen as, the incarnation of God. Birsa Munda is an example of this type of leadership.[29] A similar case is that of Sido and Kanhu, the leaders of the Santhal rebellion who claimed that they received messages from supernatural powers. These leaders had powerful command and influence over their followers. Their leadership capability gained further strength by taking resort to their being representatives of God. Given this background, "all leaders of the messianic movements in India have demanded great and often heroic sacrifices from their followers not only for admission into their movements but also as a condition for staying on in them".[30] On the socio-economic background of the tribal leadership, it has been observed that while the leadership of the first phase (1795-1860) emerged from the upper section of the tribal society, that of the second phase rose from the lowest strata of the society. Sido and Kanu were the landless, Birsa Munda was a 'raiyat' or 'proja' (sharecropper) and Gobind Giri who led the Bhil movement in the Rajasthan-Gujarat border was a 'hali' (labor).[31]

The leadership of the tribal movements in the post-independence era is found to come, in most cases, from the educated elite tribals. The tribal solidarity movements of the recent periods are primarily the product of the initiative and interest of a limited coterie of the educated tribal elite, and there is considerable communication gap between the interests and ideas of the elite leaders and the tribal masses.[32] The leadership of some of the tribal peasant movements such as those of the Telengana, the Warli, the Sahada, the Bhumisena and the Naxalbari, was provided by the non-tribals coming from different political groups.[33] At the same time local leadership among the common tribals has also emerged. Amar Singh in Dhulia, Kalu Ram in Thana[34] and Jangal Santhal in Naxalbari are the examples. Thus, in the main, it may be observed that leadership in the tribal protests and movements has come from the upper sections of the tribal society. May be it was their education and resultant awareness of the subdued position of their community that led them to come forward and lead the community for a better world. But it will be equally relevant to mention here that they were more concerned about the deprived and unprivileged position of their own than their community and as such, to redress, in main, their own position in the society in the name of redressing the overall position of their community aroused and mobilized the respective uneducated, unaware, passive communities. The leadership of Shibu Soren, Simon Marandi, Suraj Mandal of the Jharkhand movement may be cited in this connection. They have been found to compromise the interest of the community with their narrow interest when they decided to support the P.V. Narasimha Rao government at the centre for a huge amount of money.

As far as other cultural movements are concerned, it is noticed that in most cases the leadership comes from the educated upper and upper-middle class of the society. In the

Assam movement, the Bodo movement, the Akali movement, the Gorkhaland movement, the movements in the North-East, the Jharkhand movement and the Kamtapur movement in the northern part of West Bengal, the leadership is provided by the educated elite section of the society which perceives of deprivation from the share of power and privilege in the mainstream of society.

In the Dalit protests, one finds the undisputed and the most important leader in Dr. B.R. Ambedkar. By his inherent foresight, he integrated modernity with tradition in mobilizing the dalits. Ambedkar planned his programme to bring the untouchables from a state of 'dehumanization' and 'slavery' into one of equality through the use of modern methods based on education and the exercise of legal and political rights. At the same time, Ambedkar's modernizing ideology was tempered in practice by a clear perception of the tenacity of caste and tradition. Thus, he advocated for a separatist policy accentuating caste distinctions as an initial stage in creating a society in which identities would be unimportant.[35] Besides Ambedkar, the dalits found a leader in Mangoo Ram who "was something of a broker, making religious symbols and ideas accessible to ordinary people".[36] But here too, the leadership of the protests of the dalits has come from those sections of the dalits who had improved their economic conditions, were relatively educated and became aware of the consequence of the social stratification. The modern contemporary leadership of the dalits in the form of Kansi Ram and Miss Mayabati reflects a clear hierarchy in the dalit community and these leaders are found to use the dalit identity for mobilization but for interests other than those subserving the dalits.

Besides the dalit protests, there were a number of backward caste and/or class protests in India. Like Ambedkar in the dalit movement, Jatirao Phule was the ideologue of the non-Brahmin movement in Maharashtra. Phule rejected the Hindu scriptures in caste system and believed that the Hindu religion, as interpreted by the Brahmins, was both the ideological means of supervision and the cause of the poverty of the low castes.[37]

However, Phule's theory of exploitation was focused on cultural and ethnic factors rather than on economic and political ones.[38] Shahu Chhatrapati, the Maharaja of Kolhapur, was also an important leader of the non-Brahmin movement in Maharashtra. Ramaswami Naikar founded the Dravidian movement to fight Aryan 'domination' which, to him, was synonymous with Brahmin domination and Brahminism.[39]

In other secular protest movements too, it is found that the leadership comes from the upper caste middle class section of the society. So far as Gujarati Nav Nirman movement and Bihar's movement for total revolution are concerned, one notices that at the initial stage, the leadership came from the students and the students' leaders belonged to the middle class section of the society. It has been observed that students who are protected by the wealth or influence of their families participate in agitation.[40] Similarly, the leadership that mobilized the students in the movements in Gujarat and Bihar represented the middle class and the upper class of the society. However, exception to this general trend is said to be Laloo Prasad Yadav, the ex-Chief Minister of Bihar, who provided the leadership in the Bihar movement for total revolution in 1974 as the President of the Students' Association of Patna University and he belonged to the backward caste and lower class. But these types of exceptions are bound to be exceptions only. Given the level of socio-economic development of the Indian society, leadership has been, and will continue to be, poured in from the upper caste middle class and upper class of the society.

Ideology

Ideology is considered to be one of the most important components of any protest movement. It is the ideology that legitimizes the goal of the protest and the means to be adopted to reach the goal so defined. Marx located ideology within the frame of class structure[41] and Mannheim considered it a means of discrediting an adversary.[42] Clifford Geertz, emphasizing its symbolic aspects, observes that ideology is no merely an occurrence in the head but an interworking of images to grasp reality in the actual behaviour and activities of people and this ideology names the structure of situations in such a way that the attitude contained towards them is one of the commitment. Its style is ornate, vivid, deliberately suggestive and it seeks to motivate action.[43] In this sense, ideology interprets the environment and projects self-image. It codifies and organizes beliefs, myths, outlook and values, defines aspirations and interests and directs responses to specific social situations. Thus, it is not only a "framework of consciousness" but also a source of legitimizing action.[44]

As such, ideology has been an important component of all protest movements either in tacit or manifest form. Protest movements of all forms and types develop a protest ideology based on their conditions and perceptions of relative deprivation. However, there are variations in the themes of protest ideology that are formulated by the leaders of the protest movements to serve their material and subjective interests and also to gain prestige, honor, self-respect and worth. To legitimize their acclaimed status and to work a programme of action for collective mobilization, they use both religious and secular elements in building up the symbolic belief system – ideology. Protest ideology, based on relative deprivation, thus helps establish the identity and draw boundaries between the protesting and dominant groups. This means that the members of the concerned groups want to challenge and wrest away the monopoly of the dominant groups in the use of religious, economic, social, educational and political goods and services along the line of the belief system that legitimizes and justifies their action in this regard.

The tribal, ethno-cultural, caste, women and all other secular protests centre around the ideology, that is characterized by protest against the participants' conditions of relative deprivation. The assertion of rights of equality of opportunities in the sphere of education, employment and in the overall social, economic and political domain formed part of the ideology of the protest movements in India. Indeed, systematic belief system in the form of ideology might not have been explicit and manifest in all the protest movements but it was there, may be sometimes in the latent form, to lead and direct the movement as also to mobilize for the movement. However, in these protest movements, ideology was not merely the rationalization of material interests only. Rather, ideology of these movements, included religious, economic, educational and political interests. In fact, the religious and secular interests are seen as parts of the protest ideology to equalize by attacking the monopoly of the dominant sections of the society.[45] Further, the ideology of these movements, far from being fixed, tends to be a flexible one, for it is amenable to diverse interpretations, responding to the issues and interests that crop up from time to time. Thus, ideology is seen as a force that is continuously shaped and reshaped by the emerging interests, which are manifested in situational contexts. Ideology and interests thus interact with each other – the former rationalizing and justifying the latter while the latter articulating and systematizing the former.

The primordial elements form an essential part of protest ideology. This is so because the primordial components provide the chief mechanism to improve self-image and self-respect and helps to establish an identity. Thus, the primordial aspect is as important as the economic, social, educational and political one. All these aspects form parts of the syndrome of protest ideology guiding most of the protest movements in India. It is this form of ideology that provides the motive force in most of the protest movements in India and is believed to be transformed into actuality by collective mobilization through an organizational framework and leadership.

In all the ethno-sectarian protest movements in India, like that of Punjab, Kashmir, Assam and other parts of North-East, Gorkhaland, Jharkhand, Kamtapur, as the preceding chapters show, the ideological source is perceived to be rooted in the deprivation of the protesting groups against the dominant groups and/or the state machinery thought to be the protector and guarantor of the interests of the dominant groups. However, it is also found that in many such protest movements, the leaders who are, for one reason or other, out of the helms of power or far from the power centre but wants to be around the power centre articulate such deprivations which might have been under surface, and mobilize the innocent passive masses with an ideology – latent or manifest – highlighting and magnifying the deprivation and promising a better world – an utopia. The motive here is basically to come near to power. The Assam movement and the Assam Gana Parishad's coming to power, the Gorkhaland movement and the Gorkha National Liberation Front (GNLF) leadership's changing postures, the Jharkhand movement and the proliferation of organizations within the movement and the episode of the leadership of Jharkhand Mukti Morcha's (Soren) involvement in bribery scandal explain this mode of looking at the ideological theoretical aspects of the protest movements in India. Even the politico-secular protest movements in 1974 in Gujarat and Bihar were finally grabbed by the frustrated leaders for their own parochial interests. However, exceptions to this apparent general trend are noticeable. The protests of Medha Patekar and Sundarlal Bahuguna do not seem to fit in the dominant framework of analysis. But exceptions cannot and should not be invoked to undo the dominant framework and its explanatory potential.

Besides, there are two other themes based on related deprivation that are talked about. They are the Marxian ideology of class struggle devoid of ethnic component and the Millenarian ideology. Many peasant protests such as the Tebhaga, Telangana and the Naxalite had class struggle as their basis of ideology. However, within this too, one can identify several variations ranging from radicalism to the extreme left position. Peasant movements, like trade union movements, tend to be affiliated to or involved in sharply defined political movements or parties, in most cases, left political parties and as such, call for continuous adjustment and adaptation of ideology to suit the political interests of the movement or the party and its leadership. Similarly, the Millenarian ideology has been the dominant manifestation of relative deprivation among many tribal movements in India. Here, the future state of affairs to come which is thought to be the complete reverse of the present state of deprivation, acts as the motivating force to act in the present to prepare for the millennium. It is characteristic of colonial-like situations where the concerned sections or the deprived groups feel helpless with regard to their perceived capabilities in altering the existing situation.[46] But this Millenarian ideology also cannot be conceived to be linear and hence, dependent to and conditioned by the contemporary socio-economic situation and the socio-economic background of the leadership. Given this, it is very difficult to identify a pattern in the protest movements under the Millenarian ideology.

Thus, it is to be noted that ideology which motivates action is, in most of the protest movements in India, formulated, shaped and reshaped in accordance with the requirements of environment in which the movement takes place as well as the desires and interests of the dominant leaders of the concerned movements. For the purpose, ideology is often adjusted and readjusted to the requirements of the leaders' interest and the former's perception and evaluation of the contemporary situation. The ideology that was the foundation for the Assam movement launched by the All Assam Students' Union and the Assam Gana Parishad remained no longer the ideology once the Assam Gana Parishad came to power even though the goal legitimized by the ideology had no longer been fulfilled. Similar is the case with the Gorkhaland movement and the constant change in the policies, programmes and postures of the Gorkha National Liberation Front, and of the leadership in particular.

NOTES & REFERENCES

1. Brass, Paul R.: *The Politics of India Since Independence*, New Delhi: Foundation Books, 1995, p. 15.
2. *Ibid.*, p. 152.
3. *Ibid.*, p. 153.
4. *Ibid.*, p. 153.

5. *Ibid.*, p. 155.

6. Verma, S.P.: "The Crisis in South Asia: An Overview", in Phadnis, Urmila; Muni, S.D. and Bahadur, Kalim (eds.): *Domestic Conflicts South Asia*, Vol. I, New Delhi: South Asian Publishers, 1986, pp. 9-10.

7. Brass, Paul R.: *op. cit.*, p. 155. Also Mukherjee, I.N.: "Economic Growth and Social Justice in South Asia: Growing Potential for Domestic Conflict", in Phadnis, Urmila; Muni, S.D. and Bahadur, Kalim (eds.): *op. cit.*, pp. 1-25.

8. Brass, Paul R.: *op. cit.*, p. 155.

9. For a systematic classification of social movements:

   Aberle, D.F.: *The Peyote Religion Among the Navaho*, Viking Publications in Anthropology, No. 42, New York: Wenner-Gren Foundation, 1966, p. 366;

   Smelser, Neil: *Theory of Collective Behaviour*, London: Routledge and Kegan Paul, 1962.

   Wallacs, A.F.C.: "Revitalization Movements", in *American Anthropology*, Vol. 58, April 1956, pp. 264-281.

10. Rao, M.S.A.: *Social Movements and Social Transformation: A Study of Two Backward Classes Movements in India*, Madras: Macmillan, 1979, p. 13.

11. Oommen, T.K.: *Protest and Change: Studies in Social Movements*, New Delhi: Sage Publications, 1990, p. 57.

12. Mukherjee, Partha N.: 'Social Movements and Social Change: Towards a Conceptual Clarification and Theoretical Framework", in *Sociological Bulletin*, Vol. XXVI, No. 1, pp. 38-59. Also, "Naxalbari Movement and the Peasant Revolt in North Bengal", in Rao, M.S.A. (ed.): *Social Movements in India*, Vol. 1, Delhi: Manohar, 1978, pp. 17-90

13. Oommen, T.K.: *Charisma, Stability and Change: An Analysis of Bhoodan Gramdan Movement in India*, Delhi: Thompson Press, 1972.

14. Damle, Y.B.: "Protest, Dissent and Social Reform: A Conceptual Note", in Malik, S.C. (ed.): *Dissent, Protest and Reform in Indian Civilization*, Simla: Indian Institute of Advanced Study, 1977, pp 28-33.

15. Oommen, T.K.: "Sociological Issues in the Analysis of Social Movements in Independent India", in *Sociological Bulletin*, Vol. XXVII, No. 1, 1977, p. 37.

16. Chandra, Bipan: "Peasantry and National Integration in Contemporary India", in Chandra, B. (ed.): *Nationalism and Colonialism in Modern India,* New Delhi: Orient Longman, 1979, pp. 328-367.

17. Parvarthamma, C.: "Veerasaivism: A Saivite Sectarian Movement of Protest in Karnataka", in Malik, S.C. (ed.): *op. cit.*, pp. 188-198. Also,

    Saraswati, Baidyanath: "Notes on Kabir: A Non-literate Intellectual", in Malik, S.C. (ed.): *op. cit.*, pp. 167-187.

18. Gaugh, Kathleen: "Indian Peasant Uprising", in *Economic and Political Weekly*, Vol. XI, Nos. 32-34 (special number), 1974, pp. 1391-1412.

19. Oommen, T.K.: *Protest and Change: Studies in Social Movements, op. cit.*, p. 55.

20. Farquhar, J.N.: *Modern Religious Movements in India,* New York: Macmillan, 1967.

21. Heimsath, C.: *Indian Nationalism and Hindu Social Reform,* Princeton: Princeton University Press, 1964.

22. Oommen, T.K.: *Protest and Change: Studies in Social Movements, op. cit., p.* 59.

23. Shah, Ghanshyam: *Social Movements in India: A Review of Literature*, New Delhi: Sage Publication, 1990, pp. 27-28.

24. Kumar, Kapil: *Peasants Revolt: Tenants, Landless, Congress and the Raj in Oudh*, Delhi: Manohar, 1984, p. 221.

25. Banerjee, Sumanta: *In the Wake of Naxalbari,* Calcutta: Subarnarekha, 1980.

26. Chatterjee, Partha: "The Colonial State and Peasant Resistance in Bengal 1920-47", in *Past and Present*, 110, February 1986, pp. 203-204.

27. Mitter, Swati: *Peasant Movements in West Bengal,* Cambridge: University of Cambridge, 1977.

28. Mukherji, Partha: "Naxalite Movement and the Peasant Revolt in North Bengal", in Rao, M.S.A. (ed.): *Social Movements in India,* Vol. 1, *op. cit.,* pp. 75-76.

29. Singh, K.S.: *Dust Storm and Changing Mist: Story of Birsa Munda and His Movements in Chhotonagpur,* Calcutta: Firma KLM, 1966.

30. Fuchs, Stephen: "Messianic Movement in Tribal India", in *The*

Journal of the Asiatic Society of Bombay, Vol. XX, Nos. 1-2, 1967, p. 229.

31. Singh, K.S.: *Tribal Society in India: An Anthropo-Historical Perspective*, Delhi: Manohar, 1985, p. 151.

32. Weiner, Myron: *Sons of the Soil*, Delhi: Oxford University Press, 1978, p. 137. Also,

    Shah, Ghanshaym: *Economic Differentiations and Tribal Identity*, Delhi: Ajanta Publishers, 1984.

33. Mies, Maria: "Peasant Movement in Maharastra: Its Development and its Perspective", in *The Journal of Peasant Studies*, Vol. III, No. 3, July 1976. Also,

    Parulekar, S.V.: "The Liberation Movement Among Varlis", in Desai, A.R. (ed.): *Peasant Struggle in India*, Delhi: Oxford University Press, 1979;

    De Silva, G.V.S.; Mehta, V. and others: "Bhumi Sena: From the Village to the Global Order", in *National Labour Institute Bulletin*, Vol. V, Nos. 1-2, 1979;

    Banerjee, S.: *In the Wake of Naxalbari*, *op. cit.*

    Banerjee, Tarun Kumar: "Girijan Movement in Srikakulam – 1967-70" in *Society and Change*, Vol. 1, No. 4, October-December, 1980.

34. De Silva, G.V.S.; Mehta, V. *et al.*: *op. cit.* Also

    Kulkarni, S.D.: "The Bhill Movement in the Dhulia District ", in Singh, K.S. (ed.): *Tribal Movements in India*, Vol. 1, Delhi: Manohar Publications, 1983.

35. Zelliot, Eleanor: "Gandhi and Ambedkar: A Study of Leadrship", in Mahar, Michael (ed.): *The Untouchables in Contemporary India*, Tucson: The University of Arizona Press, 1972, p. 77.

36. Juergensmeyer, Mack: *Region as Social Vision: The Movement Against Untouchability in 20th Century Punjab*, Berkeley: University of California Press, 1982, p. 44.

37. O'Hanlon, Rosalind: *Caste, Conflict and Ideology: Mahatma Jotirao Phule and Low Caste Protest in Ninteenth Century Western India*, Bombay: Orient Longman, 1985, p. 11.

38. Omvedt, Gail: *Cultural Revolt in a Colonial Society: The Non-Brahmin Movement in Western India 1873-1930*, Bombay: Scientific Socialist Education, 1976, p. 23.

39. Ram, Mohan: "Ramaswami Naikar and the Dravidian Movement", in *Economic and Political Weekly*, Vol. XI, Nos. 6-8 (Annual Number), 1974.

40. Ross, Aileen, D.: *Student Unrest in India*, London: McGil-Queen's University Press, 1969.

41. Marx, Karl: *A Contribution to the Critique of Political Economy*, Chicago: Charles H. Kerr, 1904.

42. Mannheim, Karl: *Ideology and Utopia*, London: Routledge and Keagan Paul, 1960.

43. Geertz, Clifford: "Idiology as a Cultural System", in Aptrer, David E. (ed.): *Ideology and Discontent*, New York: Free Press, pp. 47-76.

44. Rao, M.S.A.: *Social Movements and Social Transformation*, *op. cit.*, p. 247.

45. Rao, M.S.A.: *Social Movements and Social Transformation*, *op. cit.*, p. 211.

46. *Ibid.*, p. 248.

Chapter – 5

Protests, Movements and Politics in India: Politics of Inclusion and Exclusion – An Assessment

The preceding chapters of the present study have shown the various dimensions of protest movements in India since independence – major theories of movements and protests and their relevance to the understanding of protest movements in India; social, economic, political-ethnic, cultural, religious contradictions of the Indian society that act as the breeding grounds for the eruption of different types of protests and agitations; historical and analytical aspects of different types, nature, ideology, leadership and issues of protest movements in India. But any study on protest movements remains incomplete unless it is followed by the analyses of the impact of those movements on the various segments of political life of the society. This is one of the basic objectives of the present study and the present chapter addresses to this aspect of the study of protest movements in India.

Any movement originates to bring about change or resist change. By that logic, a movement may either be progressive, status-quo-oriented or conservative. Whatever may be the nature of the direction of the movement it leaves some impact on various segments of socio-political life. The impact may be positive, contributing to the social cohesion, economic growth and political maturity and development, or negative, pulling the overall societal progress backward. The impact is also dependent on the perceptions of those who view movements and protests from different perspectives. Thus, a movement may be of positive impact and hence, progressive to the adherents of the movement while it may be of negative impact and hence, reactionary to those against whom the movement is directed. Under the circumstances, an objective assessment of the impact of a protest movement becomes difficult. Given this, it becomes pertinent to make a brief analysis of the concept of 'impact' itself.

There has been growing volume of writings on 'impact'. Social impact assessment is understood as a broad range of impacts or effects or consequences that are likely to be experienced by an equally broad range of social groups as a result of some course of action.[1] Therefore, it implies that impact studies are 'prospective' unlike evaluation studies which are 'retrospective'. Such studies began in the early 70s after the National Environmental Policy Act of 1969 was passed in the United States. Initially, social impact assessment studies were essentially environmental impact statements.[2] It came to social sciences in 1973 after the Council of the American Sociological Association formed a Committee "to develop guidelines for sociological contribution to environmental impact assessments".[3] The Chairman of the Committee, C.P. Wolf, is credited to be the founder of this sub-discipline. His work in collaboration with Kurt Finsterbusch is an influential text on impact assessment in the United States.[4]

Most of the empirical studies in the United States and Canada on social impact studies have dealt with one or the other of the following things: forests, recreations, policy considerations, specific construction projects, urban renewal and urban highway construction, and large-scale energy development. But the accuracy of such studies has been strongly challenged.[5] However, by now, the practioners of the impact assessments have largely agreed to the following propositions.[6]

(a) Socio-cultural variables need to be examined as well as economic or demographic ones;

(b) Impact assessment should not be limited to whatever

may appear to be available;

(c) Impact assessments should not be limited to variables that are easily quantified and or politically salient;

(d) Quality of life is a key dependent variable to be looked into; and

(e) Impact assessment should focus more on the tendency of projects to redistribute resources at all levels.

In fine, it appears from the above discussion that a distinction is made between "impact" and "evaluation". While impact denotes prospective effects or consequences, evaluation aims at retrospective effects or consequences. In this sense, evaluation should have been the appropriate term for the purpose of the present study as it seeks to measure the effects of the protest movements in India which have already taken place – a retrospective study by definition. This is the convention that is followed in the West.[7] However, there are a number of limitations of the prospective studies and for those limitations prospective impact studies on protest movements have not been carried on a massive scale. Given this, the present study uses the terms 'evaluation' and 'impact' interchangeably substituting 'impact' for 'evaluation' of the convention of the West.

In Chapter II of the present study it has been found that due to the social, cultural, ethnic, religious, economic and political contradictions that are found deep rooted in the Indian system, protests of different forms and scales emanate. These protests sometimes recede within absorbable time without much challenge to the unity, integrity and existence of the system. But some protests, in course of time, assume much higher scale and operational area posing substantial threat to the existence and functioning of the political system. Similarly, some protest movements are found to lead the system to a better direction thus contributing to the inculcation of positive change in the system while others turn to be disruptive force questioning the very legitimacy of the political system. Thus, protest movements in India are viewed from two distinct perspectives. First, protest movements are viewed as instruments for bringing about desired change in the system. It is assumed that protests reflect the unfulfilled aspirations of the protesting groups and thus act as pressure groups to direct action on the part of the government. Second, protest movements are thought to be negative means to pressurize the politico-social system. These emanate from irrational primordial considerations and also are made to crop up by the vested interests on those irrational considerations for irrational parochial interests. Thus, protest movements are assumed to be disruptive threat to the existence and persistence of the political system. Given this background, the present section ventures to identify the impacts of protest movements on the political process of India.

In the pre-independence period in India there was a wide range of protests, extending from courteous application to the authorities on the one hand to violent insurrection or non-violent civil disobedience on the other. And although the political parameters changed substantially after 1947, protests in one form or the other remained essentially the same. The fact is that the gaining of independence has marked very little change in the use of the more direct and agitational modes of public suasion.[8] The movements of public protests not merely continue even after the establishment of a Parliamentary democracy in India but as some observers like Bayley, Kothari, Harrison, Weiner, Oommen, Rao, Mukherjee, Shah and others have indicated, these movements have been increasing in number and have been gathering momentum, threatening even the very existence of the Parliamentary federal form of Government and the pluralist socio-cultural structure.

India is the largest democracy in the world. Its record in the defence of political freedom and in the translation of democratic theory into practical reality is remarkable not only among the developing countries but among the countries of the Western world as well. Public protest and even violence in the politics of a nation do indicate that all is not well with the nature of that system. Great Britain and the United States have both been the scenes of violence and protest in recent years. Just as it would be wrong in these instances to argue from protest and violence of extinction of democratic attributes, so too in the Indian case a discussion of public protest should not be read as implicit denial of the vitality of its democratic process.[9] But it should be added here that the Indian government is faced with a pervasive and continued threat to the maintenance of law and order the and law and order are jeopardized to an extent known only infrequently in either the United States or Great Britain and then never for prolonged periods of time.[10]

Under the circumstances, the questions that crop up are as to what interests and concerns are affected by the manifestations of these protests and why a government concerned with the strengthening of democracy, should feel impelled to undertake constraining action toward public protests of this magnitude. At least six closely connected reasons may be given for governmental anxiety and action.[11]

First, public protests impose an economic burden upon the nation. This cost is a consequence of the physical destruction visited upon public and private property, the loss of life and health to individuals, the diversion of resources, time and energy from constructive economic programmes to the essentially neutral task of maintaining law and order. In an economy already straining to the utmost for rapid economic development the cost may be unacceptable, spelling the difference between plan success and plan failure. Protests in any form, but more particularly in its illegal forms, cause some reallocation of resources that established industrial countries may be able to afford it, India perhaps cannot.

Second, one of the fundamental duties of any government is the preservation of minimal conditions of law and order. No government, whatever its political form, can outlive a successful challenge to its ability to meet this end. If the government is unable to contain violent public protest and enforce its rules and regulations, it may lose its justification for existence, its claim to legitimacy.

Third, coercive public protest which succeeds in its object of affecting the decisions of government represents a derogation from majority rule. It is possible, of course, that demonstrators sometimes present a truer picture of majority sentiments than elected representatives sample. Rather special circumstances must exist to support this proposition, circumstances which in the Indian case are most uncommon. Usually, coercive public protest has been the tool of an aggrieved minority. As such, it strikes the basic premise of democratic government, namely, that the will of the majority as expressed in free elections and through elected representatives is sovereign. If coercive public protest is seen to succeed, the representative integrity and efficacy of the erstwhile democratic government will be lost.

Fourth, coercive public protest represents not only the introduction of a supplementary means for the suasion of government, but a fundamental threat to the rule of law. If laws can be disregarded, sloughed aside arbitrarily, the prospect of equality and impartiality before the law is destroyed, and the efficacy of constituted means of representation and adjudication is impaired.

Fifth, as a result of the destruction of the rule of law and of the rule of the majority, a sort of Gresham's law begins to affect the nature of political responses. Direct action and social violence – either threatened or actual – begin to drive out the orderly, constitutional responses demanded in a democratic state. Every success for direct action sets of precedent for its utilization by other groups and individuals. Coercive protest movements, if allowed to go unrestrained, will be more widely imitated and become an ever greater rival to the processes of peaceful change through democratic government.

Sixth, democracy demands a considerable measure of social discipline in order to work successfully. Coercive protest movements involving forms which are illegal or violent represents a breakdown of discipline. It is based upon the destructive principle that certain ends justify recourse to undemocratic means of resolution. If government fails to apply its sanctions, it allows new linkages to become established between ends and means. Due to the default of government, people are permitted to protest in the belief that certain deeply felt needs, desires, or interests are beyond compromise and that extreme solutions are appropriate to satisfy them. Social accommodation based on compromise tends to give way to a series of internecine wars. The failure of government to restrain coercive protest movements represents a failure to secure acceptance of legitimate rules established to govern the relation between articulated wants and the procedure for their fulfillment.

As has already been discussed, protest movements in India assume many forms. For example, there are legal and illegal forms of protest. The illegal forms come in two varieties: violent and non-violent. Satyagraha or non-violent civil disobedience, is a non-violent but often illegal form of protest. Violent illegal protests refer primarily to riots, although it may include assassinations, coups d'etat, rebellions, insurrections, terrorism, etc.

In India, people compel official attention and constrain decision-making by deliberately engaging in activities that threaten public order. Violence or the threat of violence has become important instruments in Indian politics. Group violence, like the wider category of protest, comes in many varieties. It is possible, however, to distinguish three general kinds, one of which has an explicitly political motivation and purpose. These three forms of violence may be termed the "Violence of Remonstrance", the "Violence of Confrontation", and the "Violence of Frustration".[12] These three forms are differentiated according to the target of the violence, the precipitating or catalyzing agency, the amount of prior organization, the length of time required for the generation of violence, the visibility of the growth process, the nature of the participants, and the locations of the event.

Violence of Remonstrance refers to riots and public clashes growing out of agitational activities which have as their target governmental authority in some form. Violence here is a product of interaction between protestors and the representatives of the authority or public order in general – most commonly, the police. Violence of Remonstrance may not be organized but the activities preceding it certainly are. The process by which the violence is generated is visible and usually prolonged. The participants in the violence of Remonstrance are, by and large, members of modern social groups, such as labor unions, universities, political parties and professional societies. Violence of Remonstrance is more common in urban than in rural areas. Examples of this kind of violence are the anti-Hindu agitations in Madras in 1965 and 1966, the martyr's memorial agitation in Ahmedabad, 1958, students' riots against higher fees and food price campaigns in 1958, and again in 1966, Nava Nirman Andolan in Gujarat in 1974, movement for total Revolution in Bihar in 1974-75, and the anti-reservation agitation following the acceptance of the Mandal Commission Report by the V.P. Singh government.[13]

Violence of confrontation refers to riots that grow out of the antagonism of private groups. In this kind of violence, public agencies are not directly involved; they are not the immediate target of violence. The prime examples of confrontation are communal, ethnic riots and faction fights. In the violence of confrontation there is very little organization either in conduct or in the activities leading up to it. It is generated by a process which is invisible, involving feelings and attitudes that have matured over the years, sometimes over generations. The violence of confrontation does not generally escalate through clearly defined stages as does the violence of remonstrance. Participants in this kind of violence tend to be members of traditional grops.[14]

Violence of frustration encompasses commuter riots in large cities when trains are delayed, or attacks by mobs upon food shops that refuse to open, or when unemployed persons beseige an employment office. The violence of frustration does not have a definable target – unless it be the society as a whole. It is not an attack upon government or upon specific private group. It is frenzied lasting out at a state of affairs, galling largely because of its impersonality. The pretext for this kind of violence is impersonal too. There is no specific organization to the violence of frustration; it is abrupt and spontaneous. Participants in this kind of violence may be anyone, not modern or traditional people particularly. It is more common in urban areas.[15]

The point to be noted here is that the common variety of social violence in modern India has an explicitly political motivation, and it stems from a desire to shape government policy. It also follows that political protest and the deliberate use of violence are a tactic of people in the modern sector of Indian life; traditional people do not utilize these means as a matter of course but only to further particular issues about which they feel very deeply – they use protests in proportion to their attachment to particular issues. For example, whenever students resort to protests there is always the danger that violence may ensue. Peasants, on the other hand, grow violent more selectively. However, as the traditional people become more politicized and more conscious of their rights, they learn to use the systems of agitational modes as well as its formal and institutional ones. It suggests, therefore, that Panchayati Raj, to the extent that it is a successful instrument for political socialization, may unleash, as it does particularly in West Bengal, forces that cannot be contained in its institutional framework.

There is no evidence that patterns of participation in protests have changed over the years, nor do the issues serving as pretexts for protests today differ much from those in the past. On the question of the amount of prevalence of public protest which, by threatening law and order, coerces governmental decision-making, it has been observed that the growth of violence in the country has taken a turn for the worse since the death of Lal Bahadur Shastri.[17] The evidence indicates that the amount of public protest as well as of the violence has increased during the last four decades. The expectations of Indian political life, which have been stable for so long, have been upset. Where once there was acceptance of Congress predominance which bred apathy and cynicism, there is now ferment. In the past, the government could absorb a considerable amount of disruption and the political system seemed immune from the effects of violence. Now the possibilities to be achieved through protests have been enhanced because a decline in the capacity of the system to govern properly appears to have taken place.[18] This being so, recourse to public protest appears much more tempting as well as more significant.

It is a fundamental premise that the ruling elite in all societies grab resources, power and status to themselves and leaves large sections of the society unsatisfied. This obviously creates conditions of conflict in all political settings. During the liberation struggle, the Congress Party as an umbrella organization had politicized the masses to gain their support for ending the colonial rule which has held responsible for poverty, misery, hunger and exploitation of the people of India. After the attainment of independence, those laud promises and lofty ideals were overlooked and the ruling Congress party came to be controlled by a new elite class which started manipulating politics of India to their own interests. The capitalist path of development enabled the elite class comprising the upper castes and big industrial bourgeoisie to corner fruits of economic development to themselves. Not much was done for ameliorating the economic conditions of the rural landless poor, the depressed section of the society including the tribals, the adivasis, and the dalits. This path of modernization and development, as Myron Weiner[19] and Rajni Kothari[20] observe, has given birth to the phenomenon of two Indias – one very modern on the path of progress having access to resources, information and technology and the other very much left behind, in fact, bearing the brunt of exploitations, depressions and oppressions. The spectacle of the poor becoming poorer and the rich becoming richer – an ever widening gap between the rich few and poor many alienates them from the system, unleashes in them a lava of desperate energy.[21] Hence, it becomes easier to turn them into a mob, sometimes riotous. Again, when men live close to economic margins it is easy to capitalize on them for political ends. Thus, economic frustration is an important catalyst agent of protest movement in India including direct action.

Under the circumstances, regional imbalances become more visible. Numerous ethnic identities based on race, language, religion, culture and region feel alienated from the political system as they have failed to get equitable share in fruits of economic development and proper share in the decision-making process of the country. Nehru's accommodative model was bypassed by Mrs. Gandhi and evolved her own system of authoritarianism which was built up through a systematic approach of populistic politics.[22] During her regime, all these identities were designated as fissiparous and secessionist posing threat to integrity and unity of India. The ethnic identities naturally reacted sharply to it. Some of the ethnic identities launched movements for demanding more autonomy to the states and also demanded the creation of some new states. One may mention in this connection that the whole of the North-East India had to be linguistically reorganized to pacify these identities. It, therefore, suggests that ethnic aspirations coupled with economic, social and political factors are responsible for giving birth to many protest movements in India.

Now the question that needs to be addressed is whether protest movements are compatible with democratic form of government like that of India. The place of protest movements in Indian political context has been discussed by a galaxy of scholars, notable among them are Y.B. Chavan, David Bailey and Rajni Kothari.

Chavan distinguishes "Public Protests" into two categories: "Peaceful demonstrations or any peaceful movement for ventilating certain grievances" and "Direct Action which is organized defiance of law on a large or mass scale. According to him, large-scale demonstration of grievances and expression of feelings in a peaceful way is permissible in a parliamentary democracy, but direct action, that is, "organized defiance of law on a mass scale has no place in parliamentary democracy because it means the end of it".[23]

To him, there are four types of Direct Action taking place in India: (1) Wherein a group of persons take law into their hands and administer direct punishment to the supposed wrong-doer without going through the due processes of law; (2) wherein a particular group of people (particular religious, economic or caste group) feels wronged and takes vengeance against the other group by methods not permitted by law; (3) when a group of persons feeling aggrieved on occasions by the policy of the government or party in power launches organized defiance of law as a technique of solving problems; (4) actions launched by groups which are impatient to realize those "natural agro-cultural urges which make (them) aspire for better form of economic society for better social ideologies and political ideologies (they) are impatient to have it earlier in their own way in accordance with their time table".[24] Organized defiance of law of the above mentioned categories according to Chavan, is not permissible in parliamentary democracy.

However, he permits Direct Action in three exceptional circumstances: (1) Organized defiance of law by individuals who, like Mahatma Gandhi, though having fundamental respect for law, "by reason of conscience are faced with situations where Satyagraha is necessary" and like Mahatma Gandhi "are fit to undertake such individual action". (2) "...even in the functioning of democratic government, there is one very important exception in resort to direct action. Any government that is itself out to destroy the values of parliamentary democracy". (3) Direct Action carried out by men with moral stature and who, though few, are individuals representing a large section of humanity in a particular situation where humanity's future hangs in danger, for example, the use of nuclear power.[25]

Chavan's argument that Direct Action, except under three exceptional circumstances, is incompatible with parliamentary democracy, is founded on his perception of the principles underlying parliamentary democracy. To him, parliamentary democracy is a rule of law and a type of democracy in which there are periodical election based on adult franchise. Again, there are fundamental liberties of freedom of expression and freedom of association and the most vital thing is the existence of an independent judiciary to enforce these fundamental rights. In this type a government is not irremovable and after a specific period, the government itself offers to be replaced.[26]

But it should be noted that Chavan discusses the main tenets of parliamentary democracy at a 19th century liberal democratic level of logic. He does not take into consideration even the observations of eminent students of parliamentary democracy from Mosca to Mills, from Bryce, Finer, Laski to a large number of social democrats, or the philosophical basis, institutional weaknesses, nor the limitations seen in the actual experiences of the functioning of parliamentary forms of governments during the 19th and 20th centuries. He does not even refer to the crucial fact, observed by almost all sensitive observers of parliamentary form of governments, viz., the growing concentration of power in the hands of a few, and the reduction of mass of people to insignificance and their transformation into voting hands manipulated by powerful groups possessing economic power and monopolizing instruments of mass communication. He also eschews reference to the fact that why the parliamentary democratic governments, in the name of democracy, rule of law, and the preservation of law and order or bringing about national integration, are inaugurating increasing authoritarian, undemocratic curbs on even the limited rights given to citizens, within the frame of a capitalist democratic constitution.[27]

Again, as far as the functioning of parliamentary democracy in India is concerned, Chavan did not take into consideration the crucial feature pointed out by the All India Civil Liberties Council that India is "the only democratic country in the world whose fundamental law sanctions detention without trial in time of peace and in a situation which is not in the nature of an emergency".[28] Nor does he examine the potential antidemocratic limitations which have been attached to every clause of fundamental rights. Nor has he examined how far fundamental rights remain fundamental if they are subordinated to law and order requirements of the government. It, therefore, suggests that for Chavan, struggle against unemployment, against the economic measures which increasingly lower the conditions of living of the masses, the struggle to eradicate a social order which is founded on exploitation of man by man and buttressed, protected and defended by the coercive apparatus of the state should not take the form of Direct Action.[29]

Chavan's discussion of Direct Action and the need to suppress it by the democratic government, leaves out of account the analysis of the fundamental causes that lead to Direct Action. It also completely leaves out of account the possibility of transforming the anti-democratic measures adopted by the governments to preserve law and order and suppress public protests. Nor does Chavan examine how far the so-called philosophical, institutional premises underlying the specific form of government have stood the test of experience and life. David Bayley takes up the problems of the first type and Rajni Kothari the second aspects of the problems left undiscussed by Chavan.

Bayley attempts to examine the problem of relation of Direct Action and parliamentary form of government form a totally different angle. He wants to consider whether the parliamentary form of government in the process of suppressing Direct Action as well as in the anxiety to preserve law and order, or speed up economic advance in the country, will itself not violate some of the basic canons of democracy and thereby endanger the very democratic foundations of its existence. He presumes that in the context of Indian historical development "coercive public protests" have become characteristic of the political life in India and these protests have increased in number and intensity. He is, therefore, more anxious to find out not merely the limits which should be put on public protests but also a certain amount of permissibility to such actions by the democratic government if it wants to strengthen the democratic government democratically. Bayley believes that the Government of India is aware of the need to curb the coercive public protests in India, but less attention...has been given to the...other problem namely, to an examination of the possible consequences of successfully restraining coercive public protest" on the democratic government itself.[30]

Bayley assumes that the Indian government is faced with a pervasive and continued threat to the maintenance of law and order and law and order are jeopardized to an extent known extremely infrequently in the United States or United Kingdom. He also takes into account the possible arguments which may be put forth by the Government to control 'coercive public protests' namely, that such protests impose an economic burden upon the nation; will prevent the government from performing its most fundamental duties, namely the preservation of minimal conditions of law and order; will destroy the basis of majority rule; not merely introduce a supplementary means for suasion of government, but a fundamental threat to the rule of law; will encourage replacing orderly, constitutional responses demanded in a democratic state; become an even greater rival of the process of peaceful change through democratic government; and destroy the assumption of natural harmony, and social accommodation based on compromise by all groups and generate a belief that certain deeply felt needs, desires or interests are beyond compromise and that extreme solutions are appropriate to satisfy them.[31]

All these arguments, according to Bayley, attain great efficacy in an underdeveloped country like India where the democratic spirit does not prevail in the society. However, the Indian government while being aware of these consequences of permitting direct action, does not take into account the effect of measures adopted by the government to suppress 'coercive public protest' on its own self. He points out a number of dangers which may arise if the government adopts a stringent policy of suppression of all forms of public protests including illegal and violent forms. These may be: (1) the stopping of a socially useful or functional response; (2) the weakening of the consensus between rulers and the ruled; (3) the intensification of the Gandhian Martyrdom Syndrome;(4) the creation of situations tactically advantageous for the non-democratic political opposition; (5) the alienation of people from the police and court system; (6) danger of suppression of all unwanted opinion by the government in the process of disciplining the popular opinion as expressed through 'coercive public protests'; (7) the danger of the task of regulating coercive public protest degenerating into authoritarian suppression of all protests. This danger is more real because of the fact that in India an elite group composed of officials and policymakers is already separated from the masses by a chasm of education, training and experience, and are likely to easily extend a policy of tutelage in the rules of democratic interaction; (8) in the absence of institutional countervailing forces operating in Indian society, the after-effect of controlling tightly the various forms of political protests so popular in contemporary India may be that the agents of governmental authority may acquire a habit of using more and more power for solving problems and thus slowly slide down to an authoritarian regime.[32] Bayley thus points out how the process of curbing public protests in the Indian setting has grave consequences for the very democratic parliamentary form itself.

Bayley's analysis of coercive public protests and parliamentary government, while an interesting as well as thought provoking piece of formal analysis, neither examine the socio-economic causes which generate mounting coercive protests, nor provides any clue to find out whether the parliamentary form of government will be able to eradicate the underlying socio-economic causes generating coercive public protests and threatening the very fabric of the rule of law created under parliamentary democracy. He does not even pose the problem of alienation of individuals which has taken place in capitalist profit oriented competitive industrial societies, nor does he examine why people develop fear of freedom or want to escape from freedom. The findings of thinkers like Tonnies, Weber, Reisman, Tawney, Laski, Erich From, Michels and a host of sociologists, psychologists, political thinkers and others show that the phrase "freedom of individual" has become a cliché in the new mass-societies emerging in the capitalist world, with its large-sized bureaucratic organizations, wherein the individual is transformed into commodity, into a robot manipulated by the powerful monopolists controlling economic resources and state power and manipulating gigantic mass communication media, for conditioning his views and preparing him to work as a guinea pig to be exploited in the drive for profits of the monopolies or to be slaughtered in the gigantic wars, launched by them in their drive for markets.[33] Thus, Bayley offers only a verbal fetish of freedom plus a dose of advice to the leaders of the government to be pragmatic in their approach, and suggests a policy of an opportunistic handling of the situation. He has nothing to offer to the majority of the population, as to how they should develop movements which would help them destroy restraints imposed by parliamentary government, on their concrete economic, political, social and cultural democratic rights.

Rajni Kothari takes up the problem of protest and direct action and parliamentary democracy at a deeper level. He observes how the parliamentary form of democracy has failed to embody the idea of democracy as understood in its essential sense and this failure principally stems from the fact that under it there is little scope for popular participation in political processes. This lack of participation leads to a sense of insignificance in the people, especially in those sections which are more politically conscious. Faced with a situation in which power is concentrated they grow under a sense of powerlessness, a feeling which is in sharp contradiction to the ideology of democracy.[34] What we find in reality is that power tends to get concentrated under parliamentary government.

The participation of the people in the process of government is kept to a minimum. Effectively, parliamentary democracy becomes a rule of minority. Decisions taken at the seat of the power and enforced by its agents come as a fait accompli to the people. Thus, grievances accumulate. The normal channels provided for removing the accumulated grievances prove to be impotent. The stage is set for direct action.[35]

Kothari thus comes to the conclusion that direct action is inevitable under parliamentary democracy. He points out, "it is easy to dismiss direct action as impermissible under parliamentary democracy; it is difficult to obtain conditions under which the need for direct action is wholly removed".[36] After establishing the inevitability of protest movements in parliamentary democracy he tried to dispose of the formal arguments which are usually put forth to oppose protest movements, namely, (1) it would result in anarchy and chaos, (2) that it could be justified against foreign government but highly inappropriate under a government which is "our own government", (3) that the electorate ought to give a fair chance to the government in power, because the electorate is free to change it in the next election, (4) that it would make a mockery of the sovereignty of parliament.

According to Kothari, fear of anarchy and chaos in the body politic is itself a symptom of a deep-seated malady prevailing in society, which reveals that some drastic steps are required to settle the issue. The argument of the irrelevance of protest movements in self-government is founded on a hollow reasoning. Because parliamentary democracy, by permitting only the single act of choosing a representative, and denying every other mode of participating in political action never permits the people to feel even the representative government as 'self-government'. The argument that the elected government should be given a fair chance by the electorate is also very feeble according to Kothari because elections in parliamentary democracy, are no more than a rubber stamp on one party's manifesto or another's which may be drawn up deceptively leaving out measures which are likely to be unpalatable to the public. Finally, Kothari refutes the fourth argument against protest and direct action, namely, that it will make a mockery of the sovereignty of the parliament by pointing out that the parliamentary sovereignty in effect turns out to be the sovereignty of an organized minority, with majority having the little participation in the political powers, and he argues that the curious fact indeed is that the only real participation possible for a majority of people under such a form of government is the participation in direct action.[37]

Kothari's discussion of parliamentary democracy and protest movements, though stimulating, carries on the discussion at a formal level, and thus offers no basic clues to the understanding of the problem. After a brilliant exposure of the limitations of parliamentary democracy as a fetter on conscious, purposive and free participation of people in the political processes, he does not deepen his discussion. While recognizing that parliamentary government has failed, and therefore compels people to take to direct action, Kothari still glorifies freedom of speech, freedom of assembly, and freedom of press, which he feels are its essential features. He does not point out the truth that these freedoms in the context of a capitalist framework are accessible only to a small group of capitalists, landlords, exploiters and profiteers. He does not examine why the parliamentary democratic constitution in India has categorically laid down restrictions on fundamental rights, and has declared certain categories of rights as fundamental. He further remains completely silent over the fact that the Preventive Detention Act, and a number of other undemocratic clauses, to mention the POTA in particular, have armed the government with such powers that it can rule by suppressing all democratic liberties cherished by him. In fact, in the end Kothari ends curiously as a defender of the status quo – permitting only those direct actions which would only fertilize parliamentary form of government and he is opposed to other direct actions.[38]

In fine, it may thus be noted that parliamentary democracy as we experience in India is not completely satisfactory and hence inadequate to meet the grievances. Thus, protest in any form is inevitable. The protests and movements will continue till adequate institutional forms and mechanisms for the rationalization and exercise of concrete democratic rights and social and economic environment conducive to the expression of the best selves of the individual is found and attained,

On the impact of the protest movements in India, T.K. Oommen[39] views it from a different angle. He first classifies the protest movements on their type of collectivity, nature of the goal, type of movements and their macro and micro consequences. These different types of protest movements thus vary in terms of their consequences for the system. To Oomen, collectivities may broadly be classified into three: biological, primordial and civil. These three different types of collectivities pursue goals that are symbolic, instrumental and both symbolic and instrumental simultaneously. Each category of the collectivities may thus take three different but overlapping forms, namely, biological-symbolic, biological-instrumental, and biological-symbolic and instrumental. Similar to these categories are also found in the case of primordial and civil collectivities. When a protest movement takes place for increasing and/or decreasing the age at marriage or for the right of admission to public places by women/black/ untouchables, this is an example of biological symbolic movement. A movement by women for equal wages or a youth movement for lowering the age of franchise or for reservation/ dereservation falls in the category of biological-instrumental protest movement. A movement of a racial category for establishing a new nation-state comes under the category of biological with both symbolic and instrumental goals. So far as the primordial collectivities are concerned, caste mobility movements, conversion or reform movements of religious collectivities; linguistic collectivities fighting for cultural autonomy fall in the category of primordial-symbolic movements. When the movement of religious, linguistic, caste or tribal group is organized for political purposes like political representation or for economic opportunities it comes under primordial instrumental category. Secessionist movements by religious, linguistic or tribal collectivities are regarded as primordial movements with symbolic and instrumental goal. Finally, civil collectivities may resort to movements such as workers' movements to get May Day declared as a holiday, students' mobilization to abolish the compulsory attendance system and these movements are civil-symbolic movements. Students' movement for participation in University decisional processes, farmers' mobilization for agricultural subsidies, worker's demand for sharing of profits with owners fall in the category of civil-instrumental type. Finally, most of the movements by the civil collectivities combine both symbolic and instrumental goals but when the instrumental goal provides the thrust these movements are of civil with symbolic and instrumental type.

Movements which pursue exclusively symbolic goals rarely question the basic values and principles involved in the prevalent distribution of goods and services; they only strive towards a change in the system. Similarly, movements which pursue exclusively instrumental goals are capable of bringing about change within the system alone. But some of these movements may cause structural transformation, that is, change of the system, through an accretive process. For example, lowering of age of franchise has brought about substantial change in the distribution of political power in favor of the youth as they constitute a substantial proportion of the population. Similarly, workers' movements for sharing of profits, if successful, can gradually undermine capitalism as a system. The case of movements which combine both symbolic and instrumental goals is quite different. As for civil collectivities, such protests exist in large number but are rarely a threat to the nation-state. The possibility of emergence of movements threatening the nation-state is the greatest when the collective actors are constituted by primordial collectivities such as religious, linguistic or tribal groups. In so far as these collectivities pursue both symbolic and instrumental goals simultaneously, secessionism is almost the inescapable demand.[40]

Given the different collectivities with their different goals and consequences on the nation and the state, we get a variety of protest movements in India all of which pose a threat, albeit in varying degrees, to the nation-state. The threat emanates from two sources; the nature of responses from the deprived, and that of the collectivity. On the one hand of the continuum is the eagerness on the part of the dominant collectivity to absorb all other collectivities into its fold, leading to the crystallization of assimilationist movements. If secessionism cannot be supported from the nationalist point of view, assimilationism cannot be defended from the humanist perspective. In between these polar opposites, separatist, insulationist and welfarist movements may be identified with their corresponding impact on the system as a whole and the parts of the system.[41]

The bases of secessionist movements in independent India are basically three: language, e.g., the Dravidian movement at the initial stage; tribe, e.g., Naga National Movement, Mizo National Front, Gorkha National Liberation Front; and religion, e.g., the movement for independent Kashmir, the movement for a Sikh state, Khalistan. Whatever may be the bases of group formation, to the extent that the tendency towards extra-territorial loyalty persists or the 'aspiration' for disengagement from the nation-state continues, it is an indicator of inadequate welding of the constituents into the nation-state. Secessionist movements, if successful, will lead to the disintegration of the state and thus redrawing of boundaries. This, in turn, brings about independence, autonomy to the collectivities pursuing secessionist protests. Religion provides the most salient basis of secessionism in India. All secessionist movements in independent India have had a religious content. Dravidian Tamil nationalism was not only against Hindi but also against Aryan Hinduism. The majority of Mizos and Nagas look upon themselves not only as tribes but also as Christians. But the persistent secessionist movements of independent Kashmir and Khalistan – are clearly based on religious ideologies, those of Islam and Sikhism.

The tendency towards proliferation of states within the nation-state is a manifestation of separatist movements. Once language has been accepted as the basis of state formation it is inevitable that endemic demands for separate states based on language should crystallize in a country like India with a multiplicity of languages. Accepting language as the sole or even the dominant criterion of state formation foments recurrent demands. Further, once language is accepted as the basis of state formation, those cases where language and other factors coexist pose severe problems. The identification, though perhaps wrongly, of the Punjabi language with Sikhism and Urdu with Islam are cases in point. Again, if the people speaking a language are not concentrated in a definite territory, in all probability, the development of their language and culture, for want of political patronage and administrative nurture, would be adversely affected. The case of Sindhi and to a certain extent, that of Urdu are examples. This would provide for the grounds for the emergence of separatist movements.

Once language is accepted as the dominant basis of state formation, other primordial bases would be used for mobilization – region, dialect and tribe. The persisting demand for a separate Jharkhand state – bringing together the tribal groups belonging to the border districts of Bihar, Orissa and West Bengal is simultaneously a demand to recognize Jharkhand as a specific cultural region and for tribal autonomy. The tendency in such contexts would often be to rediscover traditional identities which frozen or even to invent new myths of identity. Finally, the total neglect of administrative viability, ecological variations and developmental imbalances and the sole reliance on language for state reorganization gave birth to a series of regional movements such as the Telangana separatist movement between 1969-71, and the resurrection of the erstwhile Vidharbha movement. In fine, the separatist movements cause erosion of state authority at the center and the emergence of federal polity. For the constituent units, separatist movements lead to limited autonomy within the framework of nation-state.

The logical extension of establishing states based on language is the emergence of animosity towards outsiders, that is, towards those linguistic groups outside the region, giving birth to insulationsit movements. The widespread tendency to emphasize the rights of sons of the soil and the proliferation of 'senas' are too well-known. This type of movement usually emerges either in advanced urban industrial towns or in backward rural areas. While the arch-type of this variety of movements is the Shiv Sena of Mumbai, the emergence of 'Lachit Sena', Kannada Chaluvaligars only indicate the widespread tendency in this direction. An extension of this tendency may also be discerned in the emergence of regional political parties such as the Bangla Congress, Kerala Congress and Dravidian parties. Similarly, the proverbial hatred and suspicion that the tribals have towards the outsiders or "dikus" is well-known. Generally, the contentions in this context anchor around employment, admission to educational institutions, licenses for new economic ventures, etc. The mobilizations in Assam against Bengalis labelling them as 'foreigners', adds a new dimension to the already vexing problem.[42] The consequences of insulationist movement thus becomes weakening of the concept of unitary citizenship and hence of the overarching nature of the nation-state. As far as the micro structures of the nation-state is concerned, insulationist movements result in confrontations between two or more local structures and hence, hostility among constituent units within the nation-state.[43]

While a culturally plural situation gives birth to the crystallization of identities and movements based on language, region and religion, a socially plural situation is likely to facilitate the emergence of identities based on social rank and prestige, giving birth to welfarist movements. These movements are geared to the welfare of their clientele in the broadest sense of the term. Given the fact that inequality was institutionalized in traditional Indian society through the caste system and the values and norms that were associated with it, it is not surprising that a large number of movements led by those who experienced deprivation under the rigidity of the caste system rebelled, particularly when the new democratic framework assured them equality, fraternity and freedom. Under the welfarist movement there is the possibility of traditional vested interests getting disenchanted and hence fomenting unrest. Thus, welfarist movement causes social development of the traditionally underprivileged primordial collectivities and hence there is the likelihood of animosity from entrenched collectivities. The virulent anti-Brahmin movement in Tamil Nadu[44], the Chamar movement in part of Uttar Pradesh[45], are some of the well-known movements of this variety.

Finally, the 'assimilationist' movement has been a part of the Indian ethos for centuries. Thus, though the Hindu mode of absorption[48], the tribal people, particularly in South-Central India, had been gradually assimilated into the Hindu fold. Similarly, through the process of 'Sanskritization'[49], the lower castes have been attempting to move up in the caste hierarchy. Under the assimilationist movement, the nation-state is consolidated but at a very high social cost because it leads to the eclipse of local identities and what Oommen calls 'culturocide'.[50] Among the religions of Indian origin, the Jains follow, by and large, a policy of socio-cultural assimilation with the dominant religious collectivity, the Hindus. As for the neo-Buddhists, the recent converts from Dalits, who constitute the bulk of Indian Buddhists today, the tendency is to assert their status in caste rather than in religious terms. Among the religions of alien origin the tendency to undergo a process of enculturation or Indianization of their life style is clearly discernible.[51] In the context of language too, the twin process of assertion and assimilation are at work.[52] Most Hindus and some Muslims prefer the amalgamation of Hindi and Urdu and the resultant Hindustani.

Given these general patterns of protest movements and their tacit and manifest impacts on the nation-state of India and its constituent units, exploration and identification of concrete and perceived impacts of the protest movements on the Indian political process may be ventured. These may not be all inclusive and exhaustive but will indicate the major pattern that is being shaped along which more comprehensive and pinpointed investigation could be made.

Since the late sixties, many things have changed – stability of leadership, party, government and the system as a whole. These changes have been, to a great extent, due to mobilization and protests on the part of various groups and collectivities. Two themes have marked India's political history most in these later years – political awakening and political decay.[53]

Political awakening is a process by which individuals and social groups develop a fuller understanding of the workings and implications of open representative politics, and become more active in seeking to participate in it. They increasingly understand that elected politicians are supposed to represent and respond to felt needs, that problems are often shared by many other in their caste, class, occupational group, region, locality, etc. and this fact places their social group in conflict with others. These groups have grown more assertive, so that conflicts quicken, as do the political rivalries that naturally follow from this. This awakening has been taking place among all sections of Indian society. It started earlier and has gone further among more prosperous and literate groups becoming conscious of their identity, status and position and the rights due to them. It has occurred among the poor and illiterate many as well. As these disadvantaged groups crystallize into active elements in the political process through their mobilization, they become less willing to tolerate. This awakening is reflected in all areas of life which concern them – from the immediate cause of deprivation to ecological subject – and people assert by mobilization and protest. In other words, people are no longer passive receiver as they had been. The awakening has thus made India more genuine democracy as well as more difficult country to govern – a characteristic that is designated as political decay.

Political decay may be described as a decline in the capacity of political institutions to respond creatively or even adequately to discontent and the aspirations of social groups. Since the late sixties, both the formal institutions of the state in India such as legislature, the Judiciary, and the bureaucracy, and informal institutions especially political parties have undergone decay. Broadly speaking, this has occurred for the loss, or decline of legitimacy of these institutions in the face of protest movements in India. Thus, the simultaneous occurrence of both awakening and decay resulting mostly from mobilization and protest has led to serious disorder and something close to political crisis.

This phenomenon has resulted in a divergence of the state and society giving birth to two trends – 'statism' among those near the apex of the political system that followed from the increasing isolation of the state from the society, and 'anti-politics' that follows from the increasing isolation of the society from the state.[54] Statists seek a strong state, some wanting a state whose strength resides mainly in its capacity for brisk, assertive leadership while others stress the importance of the state's coercive powers. These views are arrived at as a consequence of recent political decay and of the loss of confidence in the state as an agency for creative change in society. Since the state cannot play much of a mediating role in this increasingly conflictual society, it must either provide clear, compelling leadership or must arm itself to meet social turbulence with force, or both.

The growth of statism at the apex of the system is paralleled by a reaction at and near the base of the system. At times, it is merely anti-statist, seeking a decent realization of power within the political system, but it also contains more uncompromising elements voicing sentiments that are fully anti-political – that is, they oppose involvement of any kind with the state. Instead, faith is placed in voluntary self-help associations, initiatives, protests and movements at the grassroots all across India. Thus, it is to be noted that the protests and movements in India flow from the different contradictions of the society including the dysfunctional role of the state that have their impact in the state making the latter centralized, authoritarian and interventionist.

India, like most of the developing countries, emerged as an independent state but it is yet to mature as a nation. Maturity to a nation implies an emotional-affective attachment of an average citizen to one's own country, transcending those based on his primordial attachments of religion, language, caste, race, etc.[55] This passage from a "nation-in-the-becoming" to a "nation-in-the-being" is the period of "nation-building". The coming into being of the nation-state implied a national consensus on the institutions and mechanisms of the state, through which social conflicts keep getting articulated and resolved. But before such a consensus is reached, more often than not, this period is likely to be characterized by internal strifes and conflicts over clashing values and interests, over issues of exploitation, discrimination, and oppression. Hence, conflicts of scale taking place within a state need not be interpreted necessarily as destabilizing, anti-national forces bent upon destroying the country. On the contrary, these should be considered as constituting very stuff out of which a nation-state will get galvanized.[56]

Viewed thus, protest movements in India do not pose threat to the nation-state of India. Rather these movements contribute to the process of nation-building by helping to reach the consensus on which the 'nation-in-the-being' will be founded. However, this may be one side of the coin. Protest movements do indeed contribute but the negative aspect of the impact of these movements should not be lost sight of. Movements based on irrational grounds[57] of parochial vested interests with a veil of a broad rational goal only pull the state to fragmentations thus destroying the process of building the nation. The emergence of a number of protests and movements in India such as those of the Gorkhaland movement, Assam movement, Bodoland movement, movements for Khalistan and Kashmir has more negative impacts on the nation than their positive impacts. In other words, it may be said that some of the protests and movements in India have virtually weakened the nation of India thus weakening also the state.

Under the circumstances, in the face of numerous protest movements the government began to lose its command over the country. There was found the erosion in the legitimacy of the regime. This crisis of legitimacy and hence governability led the government, particularly during Indira Gandhi's tenure, to be more authoritarian and interventionist to counter those movements by the coercive power of the state. This was a clear departure from the earlier regimes, where the accommodative norm was followed to meet the agitations and protests. But the interventionist and authoritarian policies and actions could not meet the grievances of the agitating and protesting groups. On the other hand, authoritarianism only fuelled to the fire of the grievances.

Given the volatile situation, we witness a new era in Indian political process – an era of political accords. In order to pacify the protesting groups in the name of protecting India's sovereignty and integrity a number of accords has been signed by the government with the protesting groups. Mention may be made of the Punjab Accord 1985, Assam Accord 1985, Bodo Accord 1993, Accord on Darjeeling 1988, Mizo Accord 1986, Shillong Accord 1975, and Peace Accords in Tripura. Besides these, there have been some agreements with the protesting groups and concessions in the form of autonomy have been conceded. Various autonomous councils within the boundary of provinces are the examples of this sort.

In line with the Anandpur Sahib Resolution of 1977 the Memorandum of Settlement was signed by Prime Minister Rajiv Gandhi and Sant Harchand Singh Longowal, President, Shirmoli Akali Dal on July 24, 1985 which is commonly known as Rajiv Longowal Accord. The Accord comprises eleven clauses with a number of sub-clauses. It intended to settle some long standing problems of Punjab along with settling some immediate problems that came with the assassination of Indira Gandhi and the subsequent riots and revolts. In the Accord, a number of concessions were granted including the territorial claims that Punjab had been having for long-the transfer of Chandigarh and other areas of Punjabi speaking people to Punjab.[58]

The memorandum of settlement signed by the Union Government and the Government of Assam with All Assam

Students' Union (AASU) and All Assam Gana Sangram Parishad (AAGSP) which had spearheaded movement on the issue of foreign nationals in Assam, brought to an end the prolonged agitation. The settlement sought to resolve the foreigners issue by fixing a base year (1966), assured constitutional, legislative and administrative safeguards for the protection, preservation and promotion of cultural, social, linguistic identity and heritage of the Assamese people.[59] The Bodo Accord was signed on February 20, 1993 after a long dialogue between the Government of India, the All Bodo Students' Union (ABSU) and the Bodo Peoples' Action Committee (BPAC), and the State Government of Assam. As a result a scheme was finalized under which it was considered necessary to provide maximum autonomy within the framework of the Constitution of India to the Bodos for social, economic, educational, ethnic and cultural advancement. The scheme provided detailed provisions for the autonomy, powers and functions of the designated Bodo Autonomous Council.[60]

The demands of the agitating Gorkha National Liberation Front (GNLF) having been considered by the Government of India and the Government of West Bengal and consequent upon the tripartite meeting between Buta Singh, Union Home Minister, Jyoti Basu, Chielf Minister of West Bengal and Subhas Ghising, President, GNLF at New Delhi on August 25, 1988, the agreement for the establishment of Darjeeling Gorkha Hill Council was signed. The GNLF dropped the demand for a separate state of Gorkhaland and for the social, economic, educational and cultural advancement of the people residing in the hill areas of Darjeeling district came the autonomous hill council, the Darjeeling Gorkha Hill Council by an Act of the Government of West Bengal. The council was allotted as many as nineteen subjects of basic nature to be dealt with.[61]

In order to satisfy the protesting and agitating people of Mizoram the process of negotiation and settlement started in 1971 with the 27th Constitutional Amendment Act and reached its climax with the 53rd Amendment Act, 1986 via the Mizo Accord of 1986. with a view to satisfying the desires and aspirations of all sections of the people of Miozoram, the Government of India, in the memorandum of Settlement, 1986, considered it necessary to grant statehood to Mizoram and also conceded some special rights to be enjoyed by the people of Mizoram. All these were, however, conditional to the cooperation of the Mizo National Front to be acceded in the form of giving up arms and entering into the mainstream within the constitutional framework of India.

The process of negotiation with the agitating Nagas started as early as in 1947 with the Naga-Akbar Hydari Accord. Under the Accord, the right of the Nagas to develop themselves according to their freely expressed wishes was recognized. This was followed by the Sixteen Point Agreement of 1960 which sought to extend another set of concessions to the Nagas including the status of a full-fledged statehood. The 13th Amendment Act of the Constitution of India, 1962 inserted a special provision of Article 371A in the constitution guaranteeing some special privileges to the Nagas. Finally came the Shillong Accord of 1975 and the Supplementary Agreement to the Shillong Accord of January 1976 under which the underground Nagas agreed to accept the Constitution of India and in turn, their proper rehabilitation was assured.[63]

The 49th Amendment Act, 1984 and the 50th Amendment Act, 1984 in the Constitution of India were adopted to satisfy the aspirations of the agitating people in Tripura. These Acts were followed by the ultimate Memorandum of Settlement, 1988. the Accord was the outcome of a changed position adopted by the Tripura National Volunteers (TNV) under the leadership of Bijay Kumar Hranugkhawl to abjure violence, give up secessionist demand and to hold negotiations for a peaceful solution of all the problems of Tripura within the Constitution of India. In exchange, the Government of India and the Government of Tripura declared some special privileges and concessions to the TNV including provisions for resettlement and rehabilitation of the TNV undergrounds.[64]

Besides these peace accords some other agreements were also signed to pacify the agitating groups and concessions in the form of autonomy were extended. The Jharkhand Autonomous Area Council (JAAC) is the example of this type of concessions and that ultimately resulted in creation of the Jharkhand state.

However, an analysis of these accords and agreements show that most of these accords had been signed under the initiative of Prime Minister Rajiv Gandhi who lacked the quality of his mother Indira Gandhi to resort to authoritarian moves. Instead, he started the process of appeasement to the protesting groups. Thus, a review of these Accords show that these were more for gaining political mileage than to solve the problems of these areas. Again, it also shows that the Accords could not redress the deprivation and powerlessness of the agitating people. This implies that the agitations and protests did not cover the genuine deprivation and the resultant powerlessness of the common men for whom those agitations and protests were said to have launched. Similarly, these organized protests and the resultant accords have exposed the governability crisis of the system having its bearing on the entire political process thereby reflecting the message of a weak regime scared of its legitimacy thus resorting to the politics of appeasement.

It is also argued from some quarters that the constitutional schemes of federalism in India is one of the breeding grounds of deprivation of the regions thus leading to protests and movements for redressing the perceived deprivation. Viewed thus, the protest movements in India work as a contributory force to redefine the federal framework of India. But, in practice, one witnesses in India a number of movements that have been launched on sheer parochial ground to satisfy some narrow vested interests. These movements, though under the shadow of perceived deprivation by the centre of the region or group, are in no way contributory to the Indian federal system and the process. The demand for a separate state of Kamtapur within the West Bengal on the grounds of separate culture, language and identity is a case in point. The fragmentation of the existing states to create new states as the protests intensify will open the flood gate and new protests for new states will get articulated, organized and intensified thereby posing question to the very federal identity of India. Thus, the regime requires to convey the message that the grievances of the protesting region or group may be redressed without creating new states. The present BJP-led government could have avoided the decision to create new states of 'Bananchal', 'Uttaranchal' and 'Chattisgarh' for the sake of the future of the Indian federal structure. The decision seems to be more politically motivated than pragmatically need-based.

Under the circumstances, however, the broad Indian political context is characterized by weakening political institutions and increasing power struggles. This results in the simultaneous tendencies in India towards increase in centralization and in powerlessness. Decision-making under successive governments continue to be highly centralized but that did little to enhance the government's ability to define and pursue clear policy goals. Personalization of power is closely connected with the issues of institutional weakness, which in turn necessitates a populist orientation in order to earn legitimacy and sustain popular support. Thus, the institutional weakness and the power struggles threaten the prospect for establishing legitimate and coherent authority.[65]

Given all these, the following concluding observations may be drawn keeping in mind the broad research questions formulated for the purpose of exploration of the problem of the overall impact of the protest movements on the political process in India. In general, protest movements originate from the perceived deprivation, injustice, conditions of powerlessness or loss of identity of a section of people. The broad general theory of Relative Deprivation concerning the social movements and also the Strain theory revolve around this assumption. If a protest movement is articulated and organized on these lines the movement becomes rational and justified. A protest movement of this type is certainly capable of expressing the legitimized conditions of powerlessness, injustice, deprivation of the different sections of the people and hence, essentially remedial in nature. But often it is found that protest movements originate on relative deprivation, not of the section of the people, but of the leadership who, for some reasons or the other has been out of the helms of power and wants to be around the power center. Protest movements of this type are not capable of expressing the aspiration of the people in whose name the movements are launched. Rather, the movements under the garb of peoples' movement seek to redress the deprivation of the leadership – deprivation of his share in the power center. In India, too, not all the protest movements are of the first category. The protest movements launched by the Assam Gana Parishad and the All Assam Students' Union, the Gorkhaland movement launched by the Gorkha National Liberation Front and the Kamtapur movement launched by the Kamtapur Peoples' Party are more of leader-oriented in the objectives than people-oriented. In all these movements even though the cause of people's powerlessness, injustice and deprivation was highlighted, the real motive behind the movements have been the desire of the leaders to enjoy power who could not enjoy it through the accepted legitimate means. This becomes evident when one notices the compromise made by the Assam Chief Minister, Prafulla Kumar Mohanto, one of the important leaders of the Assam movement on issues of foreigners over which the entire Assam movement was founded. Logically, it follows that he wants to be around power and for power he can compromise the cause of the people that was showed to be the root cause of the movement. Similarly, whenever the legitimacy of the rule of GNLF chief, Subhas Ghising, appears to be eroding thus posing question to his existence and identity he renews the movement in the hill areas of the State of West Bengal. Finally, the limited section of the Rajbangshis of the northern part of West Bengal who have been educated, have earned social position, want to share the power but cannot, through the legitimate means. In this situation, they exploit the primordial sentiments of the passive Rajbangshis of this region in the name of deprivation and exploitation to raise to power through protests and movements.

To the protest movements in India the reaction of the Indian state has been a mix of both positive, assimilating, adaptive, accommodative as well as negative, harsh and oppressive responses. During the Nehru era, the state response to the various protests and movements has been one of accommodation. But after Nehru, the state has, in most of the cases, been negative and intolerant in its approach to the protest movements. Even though effects were made to redress the grievances of the protesting sections by signing accords during Indira Gandhi and Rajiv Gandhi's tenure, these accords were more politically motivated than to redress the grievances. In fine, the overall state response to the protest movements in India has been one of interventionism, intolerance and suppression because these protest movements were perceived to be threat to the rule of the regime. In fact, there has been game of politics played by different regimes to suit their narrow political interests. The politics of inclusion and the politics of exclusion played by successive regimes have virtually worsened the situation resulting in deprivation and alienation. In fact, the politics of, and with, protest movements has led to the inclusion for some while exclusion, deprivation and marginalization for others. And this has resulted in the growing and intensifying regionalization of Indian politics taking recourse to primordial loyalties and identities – religious, ethnic, linguistic and regional. As a result, the plural society of India has been sharply polarized and many Indias with diverse value systems coexist on a sharp edge of mistrust and distrust. This has inevitably caused an erosion in nationalistic values in spirit and action. Above all, the process of globalization has further opened the avenues for harvesting benefits from the system thus causing more divide among the included and disgruntled elites. Needless to say, this enhances the possibility of more protests on primordial counts in the main causing further stress on the already weakening state and compelling the latter for more and more compromise and concessions leaving the sharply polarized society into a situation worse confounded.

However, the protest movements in India, whatever might be its scale, intensity and magnitude of operations, have not been able to impair the basic structure of the Indian political system and the process. It is the elasticity of the Indian political system that has helped it to absorb the shock of different types of protest movements thereby helping the system from being disrupted or being broken into pieces in the face of the protest movements of different type and magnitude. This happens to be a unique quality of the Indian political system. Thus, even though there has been governability crisis, legitimacy has been questioned in the face of the protest movements and as such, sudden jerks have been felt in the system but the system has proved to be capable enough to absorb those jerks and remain intact with all its basic characteristics. The protest movements have not been able to pull the Indian political system to fragmentation.

NOTES & REFERENCES

1. Freudenberg, William R.: "Social Impact Assessment", in *Annual Review of Sociology*, Vol. 12, 1986, pp. 451-78.
2. *Ibid.*, p. 453.
3. Dunlap, R.E. and W.R. Catton: "Environmental Sociology", in *Annual Review of Sociology*, Vol. 5, 1979, p. 246.
4. Wolf, C.P. and Kurt Finsterbusch,: *Methodology of Social Impact Assessment*, New York: American Sociological Association, 1977.
5. Murdock, S.M.; Leistritz, F.L.; Hamm, R.R. and Hwang, S.S.: "An Assessment of the Accuracy and Utility of Socio-economic impact Assessments" in Mekell, C.M. *et al.* (eds.): *Paradoxes of Western Energy Development*, Colorado: Westview Press, 1984, p. 292.
6. Freudenberg, William R.: *op. cit.*, pp. 463-71.
7. Subba, T.B.: *Ethnicity, State and Development: A Case Study of the Gorkhaland Movement in Darjeeling*, New Delhi: Har-Anand Publications, 1992.
8. Bayley, David: "The Pedology of Democracy: Coercive Public Protests in India", in *The American Political Science Review*, Vol. LVI, September 1962, p. 663.
9. Bayley, David: "Public Protest and the Political Process in India"; in *Pacific Affairs*, Vol. XLII, No. 1 (Spring), 1969, p. 5.
10. Bayley, David: "Violent Agitation and Democratic Process in

India", *Ph.D. Dissertation*, Princeton University, 1961, cited in "The Pedology of Democracy: Coercive Public Protest in India", *op. cit.*, p. 664.

11. Bayley, David: "The Pedology of Democracy: Coercive Public Protest in India", *op. cit.* pp. 664-665.
12. Bayley, David: "Public Protest and Political Process in India", *op. cit.*, pp. 5-6.
13. Bayley, David: *Ibid.*, p. 6.
14. Bayley, David: *Ibid.*, p. 6.
15. Bayley, David: *Ibid.*, pp. 6-7.
16. Bayley, David: *Ibid.* pp. 7-8.
17. Aiyar, S.P. (ed.): *The Politics of Mass Violence in India*, Bombay: Manaktalas, 1967, p. 15.
18. Mitra, Subrata K.: "Crowds and Power: Democracy and the Crisis of 'Governability' in India", in Baxi, Upendra and Parekh, Bhikhu (eds.): *Crisis and Change in Contemporary India*, New Delhi: Sage Publication, 1995, pp. 216-245.

    Also, Kohli, Atul: *Democracy and Discontent: India's Growing Crisis of Governability*, Cambridge: Cambridge University Press, 1990.

    And, Brass, Paul R.: *The Politics of India since Independence*, New Delhi: Foundation Books, 1995.
19. Weiner, Myron: "The Political Consequences of Preferential Policies: A Comparative Perspective", *Comparative Politics*, Vol. XVI, No. 1, October, 1983, pp. 35-52.

    Also, Weiner, Myron: "The Political Economy of Industrial Growth in India", *World Politics*, Vol. XXXVIII, No. 4, July 1986, pp. 596-610.

    And, Weiner, Myron: *The Indian Paradoxes: Essays in Indian Politics*, Delhi: Sage Publications, 1989.
20. Kothari, Rajni: *Politics and the People: In Search of a Humane India*, Delhi: Ajanta Publications, 1989.
21. Mahendru, K.C.: "Public Protests and Civil Liberties in India", *Political Science Review*, Vol. XIII, No. 1-4, 1974, p. 206.
22. Singh, Dalip: "Protest Movements in India", *Indian Journal of Political Science*, Vol. 52, No. 4, October-December, 1991, pp. 453-454.
23. Chavan, Y.B.: "Direct Action and Parliamentary Democracy",

Mavalankar Memorial Lecture, 1961, Harold Laski Institute of Political Science, Ahmedabad, 1961, p. 6.

24. *Ibid.*, p. 8.

25. *Ibid.*, pp. 11-12.

26. *Ibid.*, p. 5.

27. Desai, A.R.: "Public Protest and Parliamentary Democracy", in Aiyar, S.P. and Srinivasan, R. (eds.): *Studies in Indian Democracy*, Bombay: Allied Publishers, 1965, pp. 303-304.

28. All India Civil Liberties Council quoted in *The Indian Civil Liberties Bulletin*, August, 1957, p. 310.

29. Desai, A.R.: *op. cit.*, pp. 304-05.

30. Bayley, David: "The Pedogogy of Democracy: Coercive Public Protest in India", *op. cit.*, p. 665.

31. *Ibid.*, pp. 663-664.

32. *Ibid.*, pp. 664-65.

33. Desai, A.R.: *op. cit.*, p. 309.

34. Kothari, Rajni: "Direct Action – A Pattern of Political Behaviour", in *Quest*, January-March, 1960, p. 25.

35. *Ibid.*, p. 26.

36. *Ibid.*, p. 26.

37. *Ibid.*, pp. 25-27.

38. Desai, A.R.: *op. cit.*, pp. 317-19.

39. Oommen, T.K.: *Protest and Change: Studies in Social Movements*, New Delhi: Sage Publications, 1990, pp. 164-169.

40. *Ibid.*, pp. 167-168.

41. *Ibid.*, pp. 169-182.

42. Oommen T.K.: "Insiders and Outsiders in India: Primordial Collectivism and Cultural Pluralism in Nation-Building" in *International Sociology*, Vol. 1, No. 1, March, 1986, pp. 41-64.

43. Oommen, T.K.: Protest and Change, *op.cit.*, pp. 175-76.

44. Hardgrave, R.L.: *The Dravidian Movement*, Bombay: Popular Prakashan, 1965.

45. Omvedt, Gail: *Cultural Revolt in a Colonial Society: The Non-Brahmin Movement in Western India 1873-1930*, Bombay: Scientific

Socialist Education Trust, 1976.

46. Rao, M.S.A.: *Social Movement and Social Transformation in India: A Study of Two Backward Classes Movements*, New Delhi, Macmillan, 1978.

47. Lynch, Owen: *The Politics of Untouchability: Social Mobolity and Social Change in a City of India*, Columbia: Columbia University Press, 1969.

48. Bose, N.K.: *Culture and Society in India*, Bombay: Asia Publishing House, 1967.

49. Srinivas, M.N.: *Caste in Modern India and Other Essays*, London: Asia Publishing House, 1962.

50. 'By culturocide' Oommen means a systematic annihilation of cultures. Oommen, T.K.: "Insiders and Outsiders in India: Primordial Collectivism and Cultural Pluralism in Nation-Building", *op. cit.*, pp. 53-74.

51. Ahmed, Imtiaz: *Ritual and Religion among Muslims in India*, New Delhi: Monohar Publications, 1981.

52. Khubchandani, Lachman M.: *Plural Language, Plural Cultures: Communication, Identity and Socio-Political Change in Contemporary India*, Honolulu: University of Hawai Press, 1983.

53. Manor, James: "The State of Governance", in Roy, Subroto and James William E. (eds.): *Foundations of Indian Political Economy Towards an Agenda for the 1990s*, New Delhi, Sage Publications, 1992, pp. 37-59.

54. *Ibid.*, pp. 50-53.

55. Mukherjee, Partha N.: "Social Conflicts in India: Nation Building or Nation Destroying? An Agenda for Urgent Research", *Man and Development*, Vol. XIV, No. 4, December 1992, pp. 21-32.

56. *Ibid.*, pp. 27-28.

57. A number of movements and protests in India are organized by the frustrated leaders who want to be around power centers but fail to. Thus they exploit the primordial considerations to incite the otherwise passive common masses for a movement but effectively for their own narrow interests. This has been suggested by the present authors as a separate theoretical framework in this study, vide Chapter-1 of the present study.

58. Memorandum of Settlement (Rajiv-Longowal Pact) 1985, quoted in Dutta, P.S.: *Ethnic Peace Accords in India*, New Delhi: Vikas

Publishing House, 1995, pp. 190-93.

59. Quoted in Dutta, P.S.: *Ibid.*, pp. 34-39.
60. Quoted in Dutta, P.S.: *Ibid.*, pp. 41-78.
61. Quoted in Dutta, P.S.: *Ibid.*, pp. 79-141.
62. Quoted in Dutta, P.S.: *Ibid.*, pp. 142-152.
63. Quoted in Dutta, P.S.: *Ibid.*, pp. 153-168.
64. Quoted in Dutta, P.S.: *Ibid.*, pp. 223-231.
65. Kohli, Atul: *op. cit.* p. 304.

Select Bibliography

Abbi, B.L. (ed.): *North East Region: Problems and Prospects of Development*, Chandigarh: Centre for Research and Industrial Development, 1984.

Aberle, D.F.: *The Peyote Religion among the Novaho*, Viking Fund Publication in Anthropology, No. 42, New York: Wenner, Green Foundation, 1966.

Ahluwalia, Isher J.: *Industrial Growth in India: Stagnation Since Mid Sixties*, Delhi: Oxford University Press, 1985.

Ahmed, Imtiaz: *Ritual and Religion Among Muslims in India*, New Delhi: Manohar Publications, 1981.

Ahmed, Imtiaz: "Secularism and Communalism", *Economic and Political Weekly*, Vol. 4, Nos. 28-29 and 30 (Special Number), 1969.

Ahmed, Bashiruddin: "Emerging Indian Political System", *The Administrator*, Vol. 31, No. 1, 1986.

Ahmed, Bashiruddin and Eldersveld, Sommuel J.: *Citizen and Politics: Mass Political Behaviour in India*, Chicago: University of Chicago Press, 1978.

Aiyar, S.P. (ed.): *The Politics of Mass Violence in India*, Bombay: Manaktalas, 1966.

Akhter, Majeed (ed.): *Regionalism: Developmental Tensions in India*, Delhi: Cosmo Publications, 1984.

Alavi, Hamja: "Peasants and Revolutions", Millband, R. and

Saville, J. (eds.): *Socialist Register*, New York: Monthly Review Press, 1965.

Alam, Zaved: "Peasantry, Politics and Historiography: Critique of New Trend in Relations to Marxism", *Social Scientist*, Vol. II, No. 2, 1983.

Anand, V.K.: *Conflict in Nagaland*, Delhi: Chanakya Publications, 1980.

Anderson, W.K. and Damle, Sridhar D.: *The Brotherhood in Saffron: The Rashtriya Sawamsevak Sangh and Hindu Revivalism*, New Delhi: Vistaar Publications, 1987.

Anderson, Robert and Walter, Huber: *The Hour of the Fox: Tropical Forests, the World Bank and Indigenous People in Central India*, Seattle: University of Washington Press, 1988.

Ansari, M.M.: "Financing of the State Plans: Perspectives for Regional Development", *Economic and Political Weekly*, Vol. 18, No. 49, 1983.

Aslam, Mohammad: "State Communalism and the Reassertion of Muslim Identity", in Hasan, Zoya; Jha, S.N. and Khan, Rasheeduddin (eds.): *The State, Political Process and Identity: Reflections in Modern India*, New Delhi: Sage Publications, 1989.

Azeem, Anwar: "Urdu – A Victim of Cultural Genocide?", Imam, Zafar (ed.): *Muslims in India*, New Delhi: Orient Longman, 1975.

Badrinath, C.: "Dissent, Protest and Social Reform: The Hinstorical Context", Malik, S.C. (ed.): *Dissent, Protest and Reform in Indian Civilization*, Simla: Indian Institute of Advanced Study, 1977.

Bahuguna, Sunderlal: "Womens Non-Violent Power in the Chipko Movement", Kishwar, Madhu and Ruth, Vanitha (eds.): *In Search of Answers*, London: Zed Books, 1984.

Bailey, F.G.: *Politics and Social Change: Orissa in 1959*, Berkeley: University of California Press, 1963.

Balagopal, K.: "An Ideology for the Provincial Propertied Class", *Economic and Political Weekly*, Vol. 22, No. 50, 1987.

Balagopal, R.: "Congress(I) vs. Telegu Desam Party: At Last a Lawful means for Overthrowing a Lawfully Constituted Government", *Economic and Political Weekly*, Vol. 22, No. 4, 1987.

Balasubramanyam, V.N.: *The Economy of India*, London: Weidenfeld and Nicolson, 1984.

Banerjee, Ashis: "The Ideology and Politics of India's National Identity", Hasan, Zoya; Jha, S.N. and Khan, Rasheeduddin (eds.): *The State, Political Process and Identity*, New Delhi: Sage Publications, 1989.

Banerjee, Sumanta: *In the Wake of Naxalbari*, Calcutta: Subarnarekha, 1980.

Banerjee, Tarun Kumar: "Girijan Movement in Srikakulam 1967-70", *Society and Change*, Vol. 1, No. 4, 1980.

Banton, M.: "Ethnic Groups and the Theory of Rational Choice", *Sociological Theories: Race and Colonialism*, Paris: UNESCO, 1980.

Banton, M.: *Agrarian Radicalism in South India*, Princeton N.J.: Princeton University Press, 1985.

Bardhan, Pranab: *The Political Economy of Development in India*, Oxford: Basil Blackwell, 1984.

Bardhan, Pranab: "On Class Relations in Indian Agriculture: A Comment", *Economic and Political Weekly*, Vol. 14, No. 19, 1979.

Bardhan, Pranab: "Dominant Proprietory Class and India's Democracy", Kohli, Atul (ed.): *India's Democracy: An Analysis of Changing State-Society Relations*, Princeton N.J.: Princeton University Press, 1988.

Barnett, M. Ross: *The Politics of Cultural Nationalism in South India*, Princeton N.J.: Princeton University Press, 1976.

Barua, Sanjib: "Immigration, Ethnic Conflict and Political

Turmoil – Assam, 1979-1985", *Asian Survey*, Vol. 26, No. 11, 1986.

Basu, Sajal: *Politics of Violence: A Case Study of West Bengal*, Calcutta: Minerva Associates, 1982.

Basu, Sajal: *West Bengal: The Violent Years*, Calcutta: Prachi Publications, 1979.

Bawa, Noorjahan: "Environmental Movements for Sustainable Development", in Chaube, S.K. and Chakraborty, B. (eds.): *Social Movements in Contemporary India*, Calcutta: K.P. Bagchi, 1991.

Baxi, Upendra and Parekh, Bhikhu (eds.): *Crisis and Change in Contemporary India*, New Delhi: Sage Publications, 1995.

Bayley, David H.: "The Pedagogy of Democracy: Coercive Public Protest in India", *American Political Science Review*, Vol. 56, No. 3, 1962.

Bayley, David H.: "Public Protest and Political Process in India", *Pacific Affairs*, Vol. 62, No. 1, 1969.

Bayley, David H.: "Violent Agitation and Democratic Process in India", *Ph.D. Dissertation*, Princeton University, 1961.

Bayley, David H.: *The Police and Political Development in India*, Princeton N.J.: Princeton University Press, 1969.

Beteille, Andre: *Studies in Agrarian Social Structure*, Delhi: Oxfod University Press, 1974.

Bhambri, C.P.: "Indian Political System: Nature of Contradictions", Phadnis, Urmila, Muni, S.D. and Bahadur, Kalim (eds.): *Domestic Conflicts in South Asia*, Vol. I, New Delhi: South Asian Publishers, 1986.

Bhambri, C.P.: *Politics in India 1947-87*, New Delhi: Vikas Publishing House, 1988.

Bhatt, Anil: "Caste and Political Mobilization in a Gujarat District", Kothari, Rajani (ed.): *Caste in Indian Politics*, New Delhi: Orient Longman, 1973.

Bhattacharjee, Chandana: *Ethnicity and Autonomy Movement:*

Case of Bodo-Kacharis of Assam, New Delhi: Vikas Publishing House, 1996.

Bhattacharya, S.: *Genesis of Tribal Extremism in Tripura*, New Delhi: Gian Publishing House, 1991.

Bhowmick, Sarit K.: "Development Perspectives for Tribals", *Economic and Political Weekly*, Vol. 23, No. 20, 1988.

Blair, Marry W.: *Voting, Caste, Community and Society*, New Delhi: Young Asia Publications, 1979.

Bombwall, K.R. (ed.): *National Power and State Autonomy*, Meerut: Meenakshi Publications, 1978.

Bose, N.K.: *Culture and Society in India*, Bombay: Asia Publishing House, 1967.

Brass, Paul R.: "Language, Religion and Politics", Roy, Subroto and James, William J.(eds.): *Foundations of India's Political Economy: Towards an Agenda for the 1990s*, New Delhi: Sage Publications, 1992.

Brass, Paul R.: *Language, Religion and Politics in North India*, Cambridge: Cambridge University Press, 1974.

Brass, Paul R.: *The Politics of India since Independence*, New Delhi: Foundation Books, 1994.

Brass, Paul R.: *Ethnicity and Nationalism: Theory and Comparison*, New Delhi: Sage Publications, 1991.

Brass, Paul R.: "Class, Ethnic Group and Party in Indian Politics", *World Politics*, Vol. 32, No. 3, 1981.

Brass, Paul R.: "Pluralism, Regionalism and Decentralizing Tendencies in Contemporary Indian Politics", Wilson, A.J. and Dalton, Dennis (Eds.): *The States of South Asia: Problems of National Integration*, London: C. Hurst, 1982.

Brass Paul R.: "The Punjab Crisis and the Unity of India", Kohli, Atul (ed.): *India's Democracy: An Analysis of Changing State-society Relations*, Princeton N.J.: Princeton University Press, 1988.

Brass Paul R. and Franda, M.: *Radical Politics in South Asia,* Cambridge MA: MIT Press, 1973.

Broomfield, John: *Elite Conflict in a Plural Society,* Berkeley: University of California Press, 1968.

Calman, Leslie J.: *Protest in Democratic India—Authority's Response to Challenge,* Boulder Co.: Westview, 1985.

Chakravarty, Renu: *Communists in India's Women's Movement,* Delhi: People's Publishing House, 1980.

Chandra, Bipan: *Communalism in Modern India,* New Delhi: Vikas Publishing House, 1993.

Chandra, Bipan: "Peasantry and National Integration in Contemporary India", Chandra, Bipan (ed.): *Nationalism and Colonialism in Modern India,* New Delhi: Orient Longman, 1979.

Chandra, Bipan (ed.): *Nationalism and Colonialism in Modern India,* New Delhi: Orient Longman, 1979.

Chandra, Pratap: "Study of Ideological Discord in Ancient India: Search for a Suitable Model", Malik, S.C. (ed.): *Dessent, Protest and Reform in Indian Civilization,* Simla: Indian Institute of Advanced Study, 1977.

Chopra, Suneet: "Missing Correct Perspective", *Social Scientist,* Vol. 10, No. 8, 1982.

Chatterjee, P.: "Peasants, Politics and Historiography: A Response", *Social Scientist,* Vol. II, No. 5, 1983.

Chatterjee, P.: "Models of Power: Some Classifications", *Socialist Scientist,* Vol. 13, No. 2, 1985.

Chatterjee, P.: "The Colonial State and Peasant Resistance in Bengal 1920-47", *Past and Present,* No. 110, 1986.

Chatterjee, Rakhahari: "Democracy and Opposition in India", *Economic and Political Weekly,* Vol. 33, No. 17, 1988.

Chattopadhyay, D.K.: *History of Assam Movement since 1947,* Calcutta: Minerva Associates, 1990.

Chaube, S.K. and Chanraborty, B. (eds.): *Social Movements in Contemporary India*, Calcutta: K.P. Bagchi, 1999.

Chaudhury, B.B.: "Peasant Movements in Bengal 1850-1900", *Nineteenth Century Studies*, No. 3, 1973.

Choudhury, Sukhbir: *Moplah Uprising (1921-23)*, Delhi: Agan Prakashan, 1979.

Chavan, Y.B.: "Direct Action and Parliamentary Democracy", *Mavalankar Memorial Lecture 1961*, Ahmedabad: Harold Laski Institute of Political Science, 1961.

Custers, Peter: *Women in the Tebhaga Uprising*, Calcutta: Naya Prakash, 1987.

Custers, Peter: "Women's Role in Tebhaga Movement", *Economic and Political Weekly*, Vol. 21, No. 43, 1986.

Das, Arvind N. (ed.): *Agrarian Movements in India*, London: Frank Cass, 1982.

Das, Arvind N. (ed.): *Agrarian Unrest and Socio-Economic Change in Bihar 1900-1980*, Delhi: Manohar Publishers, 1983.

Das, Victor: *Jharkhand: Castle Over the Grave*, New Delhi: Inter-India Publications, 1978.

Dale, Stephen: "The Moppila Outbreak: Ideology and Social Conflict in 19th Century Kerala", *Journal of Asian Studies*, Vol. 33, No. 1, 1975.

Damle, Y.B.: "Protest, Dissent and Social Reform: A Conceptual Note", Malik, S.C. (ed.): *Dissent, Protest and Reform in Indian Civilization*, Simla: Indian Institute of Advanced Study, 1977.

Dandavate, Madhu: "Social Roots of Gender Injustice", *Mainstream*, December 23, 2000.

Dandekar, V.M.: "Unitary Elements in a Federal Constitution", *Economic and Political Weekly*, Vol. 22, No. 44, 1987.

Dandekar, V.M.: "Indian Economy Since Independence", *Economic and Political Weekly*, Vol. 23, Nos. 1&2, 1988.

Dandekar, V.M. and Rath, N.: "Poverty in India: Dimensions and Trends", *Economic and Political Weekly*, Vol. 6, No. 1, 1971.

Dasgupta, Biplab: *The Naxalite Movement*, Bombay: Allied Publishers, 1974.

Dasgupta, Jyotirindra: "The Janata Phase: Reorganisation and Redirection in Indian Politics", *Asian Survey*, Vol. 19, No. 4, 1979.

Dasgupta, Sugata; Bhattacharjee, Ronen and Singh, Surendra: *The Great Gherao of 1969: A Case Study of Campus Violence and Protest Methods*, Bombay: Orient Longman, 1974.

Deka, K.N.: "Assam: The Challenge of Political Integration and Congress Leadership", Narain, Iqbal (ed.): *State Politics in India*, Meerut: Meenakshi Publications, 1976.

Desai, A.R.: *Social Background of Indian Nationalism*, Bombay: Popular Book Depot, 1954.

Desai, A.R. (ed.).: *Peasant Struggles in India*, Delhi: Oxford University Press, 1979.

Desai, A.R.: "Public Protest and Parliamentary Democracy", Aiyar, S.P. and Srinivasan, R. (eds.): *Studies in Indian Democracy*, Bombay: Allied Publishers, 1965.

Desai, A.R. (ed.): *Violation of Democratic Rights in India*, Bombay: Popular Prakashan, 1986.

Desai, A.R.: *Repression and Resistance in India*, Bombay: Popular Prakashan, 1990.

Desai, I.P.: "Anti-reservation Agitation and Structure of Gujarat Society", *Economic and Political Weekly*, Vol. 16, No. 12, 1979.

De Silva, G.V.S.; Mehta, V. *et al.*: "Bhumi Sena: From the Village to the Global Order", *National Labour Institute Bulletin*, Vol. 5, Nos. 1-2, 1979.

Dev, Acharya Narendra: *Presidential Address*, All India Kiṣan Conference, Gaya, 1939.

Dhami, M.S.: "Political Parties and State—Autonomy Issues:

A Case Study of Akali Party", Bombwall, K.R. (ed.): *National Power and State Autonomy*, Meerut: Meenakshi Publications, 1978.

Dhanagare, D.: *Peasant Movements in India 1920-50*, Delhi: Oxford University Press, 1983.

Dhanagare, D.: "Peasant Protest and Politics – The Tebhaga Movement in Bengal (India) 1946-47", *The Journal of Peasant Studies*, Vol. 8, No. 3, 1976.

Dhanagare, D.: "Social Origins of the Peasant Insurrection in Telengana, 1946-51", *Contributions to Indian Sociology*, New Series, No. 8, 1974.

Diamond, Larry; Link, Juan J. and Lipset, S.M. (eds.): *Democracy in Asia*, New Delhi: Vistaar Publications, 1989.

Dogra, Bharat: *Forests and People: Rishikesh*, Himalayan Darshan Prakashan Society, 1980.

Dumont, Louis: "Nationalism and Communalism", *Religion, Politics and History in India: Collected Papers in Indian Sociology*, Paris: Mouton Publishers, 1970.

Dunlop, R.E. and Catton, W.R.: "Environmental Sociology", *Annual Review of Sociology*, Vol. 5, 1979.

Dutta, Prabhat K.: "Secessionist Movements in North East India", *Indian Journal of Political Science*, Vol. 53, No. 4, 1992.

Dutta, P.S.: *Autonomy Movements in Assam: Documents*, New Delhi: Omsons, 1993.

Dutta, P.S.: *Ethnic Peace Accords in India*, New Delhi: Vikas Publishing House, 1995.

Eckstein, Harry: *Division and Cohesion in Democracy: A Study of Norway*, Princeton: Princeton University Press, 1966.

Elliot, C.M.: "Decline of a Patrimonial Regime: The Telangana Rebellion in India 1946-51", *The Journal of Asian Studies*, Vol. 32, No. 1, 1974.

Engineer, Ashgar Ali: " A Theory of Communal Riots", *Seminar*, 291, 1983.

Engineer, Ashgar Ali: "Socio-Economic Basis of Communalism", Grover, Verinder (ed.): *Sociological Aspects of Indian Political System*, New Delhi: Deep and Deep Publications, 1990.

Engineer, Ashgar Ali: "From Caste to Communal Violence", *Economic and Political Weekly*, Vol. 20, No. 15, 1985.

Engineer, Ashgar Ali (ed.): *Communal Riot in Post-Independence India*, Hyderabad: Sangam Books, 1984.

Enloe, C.H.: *Ethnic Conflict and Political Development*, Boston: Little Brown and Company, 1973.

Everett, Jona Matson: *Women and Social Change in India*, Delhi: Heritage Publications, 1979.

Everyman's, July 20, 1974.

Everyman's, November 9, 1974.

Fairchild, H.P. (ed.): *Dictionary of Sociology*, New York: Philosophical Library (No Date).

Farquhar, J.N.: *Modern Religious Movements in India*, New York: Macmillan, 1967.

Franda, Marcus: *Radical Politics in West Bengal*, Cambridge, Mass: MIT Press, 1972.

Franda, Marcus: *West Bengal and Federalizing Process in India*, Princeton N.J.: Princeton University Press, 1968.

Franda, Marcus: *Small is Politics: Organizational Alternatives in India's Rural Development*, New Delhi: Willey Eastern, 1979.

Frank, Andre Gunder and Fuentes, Marta: "Nine Theses on Social Movements", *Economic and Political Weekly*, Vol. 32, No. 35, 1987.

Frankel, Francis: *India's Political Economy, 1947-1977; The Gradual Revolution*, Princeton N.J.: Princeton University Press, 1971.

Frankel, Francis and Rao, M.S.A. (eds.): *Dominance and State Power in Modern India: Decline of a Social Order*, Vols. I&II, New Delhi: Oxford University Press, 1989 and 1990.

Freudenberg, William R.: "Social Impact Assessment", *Annual Review of Sociology*, Vol. 12, 1986.

Friedman, Yohanan: "The Attitude of the YAMIYYAT-ULAMA-HIND to the Indian National Movement and the Establishment of Pakistan", *Asian and African Studies*, No. 7, 1971.

Frykenberg, Robert Eric: "The Emergence of Modern 'Hinduism' as a Concept and as a Constitution: A Reappraisal with Special Reference to South India", Gunter, S. and Herman, Kulke (eds.): *Hinduism Reconsidered*, Heidelberg: South Asia Institute, 1988.

Fuchs, Stephen: "Messianic Movements in Tribal India", *Journal of the Asiatic Society of Bombay*, Vol. 20, Nos. 1-2, 1967.

Geertz, Clifford: "Ideology as a Cultural System", Apter, David (ed.): *Ideology and Discontent*, New York: Free Press, 1971.

Ghose, Anjan: "Caste Idiom from Clas Conflict: Cases of Khanjawala", *Economic and Political Weekly*, Vol. 14, Nos. 5&6, 1979.

Ghose, Sankar: *The Disinherited State: A Study of West Bengal, 1967-70*, Bombay: Orient Longman, 1971.

Gill, Sucha Singh and Singhal, K.C.: "The Punjab Problem: In Historical Roots", *Economic and Political Weekly*, Vol. 19, No. 14, 1984.

Gopalan, N.C.: *The Moplah Rebellion*, Calcutta: The Author, 1921.

Goswami, Atul and Gogoi, Jayanta K.: "Migration and Transformation of Assam", Abbi, B.L. (ed.): *North East Region: Problems and Prospects of Development*, Chandigarh: Centre for Research in Rural and Industrial Development, 1984.

Goswami, B.B.: *The Mizo Unrest*, Jaipur: Alekh Publications, 1979.

Gough, Kathleen: "Indian Peasant Uprising", *Economic and Political Weekly*, Vol. 9, Nos. 31-34 (Special Number), 1974.

Gough, Kathleen and Sharma, H.P. (eds.): *Imperialism and Revolution in South Asia*, New York: Monthly Review Press, 1973.

Government of India: *The First Five Year Plan*, Delhi: Planning Commission, 1951.

Government of India: *The Second Five Year Plan*, Delhi: Planning Commission, 1956.

Grierson, G.A. (ed.): *Linguistic Survey of India*, Delhi: Motilal Banarasidas, 1967-68.

Guha, Ranjit: *Elementary Aspects of Peasant Insurgency in Colonial India*, Delhi: Oxford University Press, 1983.

Guha, Ranjit: "The Prose of Counter Insurgency", Guha, Ranjit (ed.): *Subaltern Studies*, Vol. II, Delhi: Oxford University Press, 1983.

Guha, Ranjit (ed.): *Subaltern Studies*, Vols. I, II, III, IV, V, Delhi: Oxford University Press, 1983.

Gupta, Dipankar: "On Altering the Ego in History: Paradoxes of the Ethnic Opinion", *Peasant Studies*, Vol. 13, No. 2, 1985.

Gupta, Dipankar: "The State and Ethnicity in India", *Asian Studies*, No. 10, 1992.

Gupta, Dipankar: "The Communalizing of Punjab, 1980-85", *Economic and Political Weekly*, Vol. 20, No. 28, 1985.

Gurr, T.R.: *Why Men Rebel*, Princeton N.J.: Princeton University Press, 1970.

Habib, Irfan: "The Peasant in Indian History", *Social Scientist*, Vol. II, No. 3, 1983.

Hall, R.L.: *Ethnic Autonomy – Comparative Analysis: The Americas, Europe and the Developing World*, Vol. II, New York: Macmillan, 1933.

Hamja, Alavi: "Peasants and Revolutions", Gough, Kathleen and Sharma, H.P. (eds.): *Imperialism and Revolution in South Asia*, New York: Monthly Review Press, 1973.

Hardgrave, Robert L.: *India Under Pressure: Prospects for Political*

Stability, Boulder Colo: Westview Press, 1984.

Hardgrave, Robert L.: *The Dravidian Movement*, Bombay: Popular Prakashan, 1965.

Hardgrave, Robert L.: "The Mopilla Rebellion 1921: Peasant Revolt in Malabar", *Modern Asian Studies*, Vol. 2, No. 1, 1977.

Hardgrave, Robert L. and Kochanek, Staneley A.: *India: Government and Politics of Developig Nation*, San Diego: H.B., Jovanovich, 1986.

Hardiman, David: *The Coming of the Devi: Adivasi Assertion in Western India*, Delhi: Oxford University Press, 1987.

Harrison, Selig: *India: The Most Dangerous Decades*, Princeton: Princeton University Press, 1960.

Hart, Henri C.: "The Indian Constitution: Political Development and Decay", *Asian Survey*, Vol. 20, No. 4, 1980.

Hasan, Zoya; Jha, S.N. and Khan, Rasheeduddin (eds.): *The State, Political Process and Identity: Reflection on Modern India*, New Delhi: Sage Publications, 1989.

Heberle, Rudolf: *Social Movements: An Introduction to Political Sociology*, New York : Appleton-Century-Crafts Inc., 1951.

Heberle, Rudolf: "Types and Functions of Social Movements", *International Encyclopaedia of Social Science*, New York: Collien Macmillan, 1968.

Heimsath, C.: *Indian Nationalism and Hindu Social Reform*, Princeton: Princeton University Press, 1964.

Henningham, Stephen: *Peasant Movements in Colonial India, North Bihar 1917-42*, Canberra: Australian National Universoty, 1982.

Hitchock, R.H.: *Peasant Revolt in Malabar: A History of Malabar Rebellion, 1921*, Delhi: Usha Publications, 1983.

Huntington, S.P.: *Political Order in Changing Societies*, New Haven: Yale University Press, 1968.

Hussain, Monirul: *The Assam Movement; Class, Ideology, Identity*,

Delhi: Har-Anand, 1993.

Hussain, Monirul: "Tribal Movement for Autonomous State in Assam", *Economic and Political Weekly*, Vol. 22, No. 32, 1987.

Imam, Zafar: *Muslims in India,* New Delhi: Orient Longman, 1975.

Innaih, N.: *Saffron Star Over Andhra Pradesh,* Hyderabad: Book Links Corporation, 1984.

Irani, C.R.: *Bengal: The Communist Challenge,* Bombay: Lalvani Publishing House, 1968.

Jain, Devaki: "Gandhian Contributions towards a Theory of Feminist Ethic", Jain, Devaki and Diana Eck (eds.): *Speaking of Faith: Cross Cultural Perspectives in Women, Religious and Social Change,* Delhi: Kali for Women, 1986.

Jain, Shobhita: "Women and Peoples Ecological Movement: A Case Study of Women's Rule in the Chipko Movements in Uttar Pradesh", *Economic and Political Weekly,* Vol. 19, No. 41, 1984.

Januzzi, T.F.: *Agrarian Crisis in India: The Case of Bihar,* Austin: University of Texas Press, 1973.

Jeffery, Robin: *What's Happeinging to India? Punjab, Ethnic Conflicts, Mrs. Gandhi's Death and the Test for Federalism,* Basingstoke: Macmillan, 1986.

Jha, Hetukar: "Tradition, Violence and Modernization: Understanding the Legitimation Crisis of Indian Political Order", *The Eastern Anthropologist,* Vol. 47, No. 4, 1994.

Jha, Prem Shankar: *India: A Political Economy of Stagnation,* Bombay: Oxford University Press, 1980.

Johnson, Chalmers: *Revolutionary Change,* Boston: Little Brown, 1966.

Jones, Kenneth W.: "Communalism in the Punjab: The Arya Samaj Contribution", *Journal of Asian Studies,* Vol. 28, No. 1, 1968.

Joshi, P.C.: "Economic Background of Communalism in India:

A Model of Analysis", Nanda, B.R. (ed.): *Essays in Modern Indian History*, Delhi: Oxford University Press, 1980.

Juergensmeyer, Mark: *Region as Social Vision: The Movement Against Untouchability in Twentieth Century Punjab*, Berkeley: University of California Press, 1982.

Kakati, S.C.: "From Phizo to ULFA in NORTH EAST", *The Statesman*, Calcutta: February 14, 1991.

Kamble, J.R.: *Rise and Awakening of Depressed Classes in India*, Delhi: National Publishing House, 1979.

Kannan, K.P.: *Of Rural Proletarian Struggle: Mobilization and Organization of Rural Workers in South West India*, Delhi: Oxford University Press, 1988.

Kapoor, Rajiv: *Sikh Separatism: The Politics of Faith*, London: Allen and Unwin, 1986.

Katzenstein, Marry F.: *Ethnicity and Equality: The Shiv Sena Party and Preferrential Policies in Bombay*, Ithaca, New York: Cornell University Press, 1979.

Kaushik, Susheela: "Women Movements in India", in Chaube, S.K. and Chakraborty, B. (eds.): *Social Movements in Contemporary India*, Calcutta: K.P. Bagchi, 1999.

Kaviraj, Narahari: *A Peasant Uprising in Bengal*, New Delhi: People's Publishing House, 1972.

Kadourie, E.: *Nationalism*, London: Hutchinson, 1960.

Kadourie, E. (ed.): *Nationalism in Asia and Africa*, London: Weidenfeld and Nicolson, 1971.

Kelkar, Govind: "Women's Movement Studies: A Critique of the Historiography", *Samya Sakti – A Journal of Women Studies*, Vol. I, No. 2, 1984.

Khan, Rasheeduddin: "The Total State and the Indian Political System", Hasan, Zoya; Jha, S.N. and Khan, Rasheeduddin (eds.): *The State, Political Process and Identity: Reflections on Modern India*, New Delhi: Sage Publications, 1989.

Khubchandani, Lachman M.: *Plural Language, Plural Cultures:*

Communication, Identity and Socio-Political Change in Contemporary India, Honolulu: University of Hawaii Press, 1983.

Kishwar, Madhu: "Gandhi on Women", *Economic and Political Weekly*, Vol. 20, No. 40, 1985.

Kishwar, Madhu and Ruth, Vanitha (eds.): *In Search of Answers*, London: Zed Books, 1985.

Kling, B.B.: *The Blue Mutiny: The Indigo Distrubances in Bengal, 1859-1862*, Calcutta: Firma KLM, 1977.

Kochanek, Stanley A.: *Business and Politics in India*, Berkeley: University of California Press, 1979.

Kohli, Atul: *The State and Poverty in India: The Politics of Reform*, Cambridge: Cambridge University Press, 1987.

Kohli, Atul: "Democracy, Economic Growth and Inequality in India's Development", *World Politics*, Vol. 32, No. 4, 1980.

Kohli, Atul: *The State and Development in the Third World*, Princeton N.J.: Princeton University Press, 1986.

Kohli, Atul: *Democracy and Discontent: India's Growing Crisis of Governability*, New Delhi: Cambridge University Press, 1991.

Kohli, Atul (ed.): *India's Democracy: An Analysis of Changing State-Society Relations*, Princeton N.J.: Princeton University Press, 1988.

Kornhouser, W.: "Mass Society", Shills, David (ed.): *International Encyclopaedia of Social Sciences*, Vol. 9, New York: Macmillan, 1968.

Kothari, Rajni: "The Crisis of Moderate State and the Decline of Democracy", Lyon, P. and Manor, J. (eds.): *Transfer and Transformation: Political Institutions in the New Commonwealth*, Leicester UK: Leicester University Press, 1983.

Kothari, Rajni: "Masses, Classes and the State", *Economic and Political Weekly*, Vol. 21, No. 5, 1986.

Kothari, Rajni: "Direct Action: A Pattern of Political Behaviour", *Quest*, No. 24, January-March, 1990.

Kothari, Rajni: "The Non-Party Political Process", *Economic and Political Weekly*, Vol. 19, No. 5, 1984.

Kothari, Rajni: *State Against Democracy: In Search of a Humane Governance*, Delhi: Ajanta Publications, 1988.

Kothari, Rajni: *Transformation and Survival: In Search of a Humane World Order*, Delhi: Ajanta Publications, 1988.

Kothari, Rajni: *Rethinking Development: In Search of Humane Alternatives*, Delhi: Ajanta Publications, 1989.

Kothari, Rajni: *Politics and the People: In Search of the Humane India*, Delhi: Ajanta Publications, 1989.

Kothari, Rajni (ed.): *Caste in Indian Politics*, Delhi: Orient Longman, 1971.

Kulkarni, S.D.: "The Bhil Movement in the Dhulia District", Singh, K.S. (ed.): *Tribal Movement in India*, Vol. I, Delhi: Manohar Publications, 1983.

Kumar, Kapil: *Peasants Revolt: Tenants, Landless, Congress and the Raj in Oudh*, Delhi: Manohar Publications, 1984.

Lama, M.P.: "Unquiet Hills", *The Statesman*, April 19 & 21, 1988.

Landsberger, Henri A.: "Peasant Unrest: Themes and Variations", Landsberger, Henri A. (ed.): *Rural Protest: Peasant Movements and Social Change*, London: Macmillan, 1974.

Lele, Jayant: *Elite Pluralism and Class Rule: Political Development in Maharashtra*, Bombay: Popular Prakashan, 1982.

Liddle, Joanna and Joshi, Rama: *Daughters of Independence: Gandhi, Caste and Class in India*, New Delhi: Kali of Women, 1986.

Lijphart, Arendt: *Democracy in Plural Societies: A Comparative Exploration*, Bombay: Popular Prakashan, 1989.

Linj, Juna: *The Breakdown of Democratic Regimes*, Baltimore: John

Hopkins University Press, 1978.

Linch, Woen: *The Politics of Untouchability*, New York: Columbia University Press, 1968.

Lyon, P. and Manor, J. (eds.): *Transfer and Transformation: Political Institutions in the New Commonwealth*, Leicester UK: Leicester University Press, 1983.

Mackenzie, W.J.M.: *Politics and Social Science*, Harmondsworth: Middlesex, 1967.

Madan, T.N.: "Secularism in its Place", *Journal of Asian Studies*, Vol. 66, No. 4, 1987.

Maheshwari, S.R.: "Anomic Situations and Political Legitimacy in India", *Political Science Review*, Vol. 13, Nos. 1-4, 1974.

Mahendru, K.C.: "Public Protests and Civil Liberties in India", *Political Science Review*, Vol. 13, Nos. 1-4, 1974.

Majumdar, Vina: "The Social Reform Movement in India: From Ranade to Nehru", in Nanda, B.R. (ed.): *Indian Women from Purdah to Modernity*, Delhi: Vikas Publishing House, 1976.

Malik, S.C. (ed.): *Dissent, Protest and Reform in Indian Civilization*, Simla: Indian Institute of Advanced Study, 1977.

Manor, James: "The State of Governance", Roy Subroto and James, William E. (eds.): *Foundations of Indian Political Economy: Towards an Agenda for the 1990s*, New Delhi: Sage Publications, 1992.

Manimala: "Zanen Kenkar? And Jote Onkar? The Story of Women's Participation in Bodhgaya Struggle", *Manushi*, Vol. 3, No. 2, 1983.

Marx, Karl: *A Contribution to the Critique of Political Economy*, Chicago: Charles H. Kerr, 1904.

Marx, Karl and Engels, Fredrick: *Selected Works*, (Three Volumes), Moscow: Progress Publishers, 1973.

Mathew, G. (ed.): *Shift in Indian Politics*, New Delhi, Concept Publishing Co., 1984.

Mathur, L.P.: *Resistance Movement of Tribals of India*, Udaipur: Himangshu Publications, 1988.

Merton, R.K. and Rosset, Alice Kitt: "Contribution to the Theory of Reference Group Behaviour", Merton, R.K. and Lazarsfeld, P.F. (eds.): *Continuities and Social Research*, New York: The Free Press, 1966.

Mannheim, Karl: *Ideology and Utopia*, London: Routledge and Kegan Paul, 1960.

Mies, Maria: "Peasant Movement in Maharashtra: Its Development and its Perspectives", *Journal of Peasant Studies*, Vol. 3, No. 3, 1976.

Migdal, Joel: *Strong Societies and Weak States: State Society Relations and State Capabilities in the Third World*, Princeton N.J.: Princeton University Press, 1989.

Minogue, K.: *Nationalism*, London: Batsford, 1967.

Minault, Gail: "Some Reflections on Islamic Revivalism vs. Assimilation among Muslims in India", *Contributions to Indian Sociology*, Vol. 18, No. 2, 1984.

Mitra, Manoshi: "Tribal Women and Tribal Movements", *Samya-Shakti – A Journal of Women Studies*, Vol. 1, No. 2, 1984.

Mitra, Subrata K.: "Crowds and Power: Democracy and the Crisis of Governability in India", in Baxi, Upendra and Parekh, Bhikhu (eds.): *Crisis and Change in Contemporary India*, New Delhi: Sage Publications, 1995.

Mitra, Subrata K.: "The Perils of Promoting Equality: The Latent Significance of the Anti-Reservation Movement in India", *Journal of Commonwealth and Comparative Politics*, Vol. 25, No. 3, 1987.

Mitra, S.K.: *Peasant Uprising and Mahatma Gandhi in North Bihar*, Meerut: Anu Prakashan, 1978.

Mitter, Swasti: *Peasant Movements in West Bengal*, Cambridge: University of Cambridge, 1977.

Mohan, Purnima: *Encyclopaedia of Women*, Delhi: Indian

Publishers Distributors, 2000.

Moore, Barrington Jr.: *Social Origins of Dictatorship and Democracy*, London: Allen Lane, 1967.

Morris-Jones, W.H.: *The Government and Politics of India*, London: Hutchinson University Library, 1963.

Morris-Jones, W.H.: *Politics Mainly India*, Madras: Orient Longman, 1978.

Morris-Jones, W.H.: "India: The Trial of Leadership", *Asian Survey*, Vol. 6, No. 2, 1966.

Mukherjee, I.N.: "Economic Growth and Social Justice in South Asia: Growing Potential for Domestic Conflict", in Phadnis, Urmila; Muni, S.D. and Bahadur, Kalim (eds.): *Domestic Conflicts in South Asia*, Vol. 1, New Delhi: South Asian Publishers, 1986.

Mukherjee, Partha N.: "Social Movements and Social Change: Towards a Conceptual Clarification and Theoretical Framework", *Sociological Bulletin*, Vol. 26, No. 1, 1977.

Mukherjee, Partha N.: "The Gorkhaland Movement: Some Theoretical Formulations and Propositions", *Social Action*, Vol. 46, No. 2, 1985.

Mukherjee, Partha N.: "Naxalbari Movement and the Peasant Revolt in North Bengal, in Rao, M.S.A. (ed.): *Social Movements in India*, Delhi: Manohar Publications, 1978.

Mukherjee, Partha N.: "Social Conflicts in India: Nation Building or Nation Destroying? An Agenda for Urgent Research", *Man and Development*, Vol. 14, No. 4, 1992.

Munshi, Saldana Indra: "Tribal Women in the Warli Revolt 1945-47: Class and Gender in the Left Perspective", *Economic and Political Weekly*, Vol. 2, No. 17, 1986.

Murdock, S.M.; Leistritz, F.L.; Hamm, R.R. and Hwarg, S.S.: "An Assessment of the Accuracy and Utility of Socio-Economic Impact Assessments", Meckel, C.M. *et al.* (eds.): *Paradoxes of Western Energy Development*, Colorado: Westview Press, 1984.

Murti, V.K. Ramana: "Nationalism and Sub-Nationalism in Contemporary India", *Quest* (Bombay), No. 56, 1968.

Naidu, Ratna: *Communal Edge to Plural Societies: India and Malayasia*, Delhi: Vikas Publishing House, 1980.

Namboodiripad, E.M.S.: *Crisis into Chaos*, New Delhi: Sangam Books, 1981.

Namboodiripad, E.M.S.: *A Short History of the Peasant Movement in Kerala*, Peoples Publishing House, 1943.

Nandy, Ashis: "The Politics of Secularism and the Recovery of Religious Tolerance", *Alternatives*, No. 3, 1988.

Narain, Iqbal (ed.): *State Politics in India*, Meerut: Meenakshi Publications, 1968.

Narain, Iqbal and Mathur, P.C.: *Politics in Changing India*, Jaipur: Rawat Publications, 1994.

Narain, Iqbal: "A Conceptual Analysis in Indian Context", Akhtar, Majeed (ed.): *Regionalism: Developmental Tensions in India*, Delhi: Cosmo Publications, 1984.

Narang, A.S.: *Storm Over the Sutlej: Akali Politics*, New Delhi: Gitanjali Publishing House, 1983.

Natarajan, L.: "Indigo Cultivators Strike 1860", Desai, A.R. (ed.): *Peasant Struggle in India*, Delhi: Oxford University Press, 1979.

Nayar, Baldev Raj: *Violence and Crime in India: A Quantitative Study*, Delhi: Macmillan, 1975.

Nibedan, N.: *The North East India: The Ethnic Explosion*, New Delhi: Lancers, 1981.

Nisbet, R.: *The Quest for Community*, New York: Oxford University Press, 1953.

O'Hanton, Rosalind: *Caste, Conflict and Ideology: Mahatma Jotirao Phule and Low Caste Protest in Nineteenth Century Western India*, Bombay: Orient Longman, 1985.

O'Malley, L.S.S. (ed.): *Modern India and the West: A Study of the*

Interaction of their Civilization, London: Oxford University Press, 1941.

Oommen, T.K.: *Protest and Change: Studies in Social Movements*, New Delhi: Sage Publications, 1990.

Oommen, T.K.: *State and Society in India: Studies in Nation-Building*, New Delhi: Sage Publications, 1990.

Oommen, T.K.: *From Mobilization to Institutionalization: The Dynamics of Agrarian Movement in 20th Century Kerala*, Bombay: Popular Prakashan, 1985.

Oommen, T.K.: "Sociological Issues in the Analysis of Social Movements in Independent India", *Sociological Bulletin*, Vol. 26, No. 1, 1977.

Oommen, T.K.: "Insiders and Outsiders in India: Primordial Collectivism and Cultural Pluralism in Nation-Building", *International Sociology*, Vol. 1, No. 1, 1986.

Oommen, T.K.: *Charisma, Stability and Change: An Analysis of Bhoodan Gramdan Movement in India*, Delhi: Thompson Press, 1972.

Omvedt, Gail: *Cultural Revolt in a Colonial Society: The Non-Brahmin Movement in Western India 1873-1930*, Bombay: Scientific Socialist Education Trust, 1976.

Omvedt, Gail: "Women and Rural Revolt in India", *Journal of Peasant Studies*, Vol. 5, No. 3, 1978.

Palanithurai, G.: "Ethnic Identity and National Loyalty of an Ethnic Group in India", *Indian Journal of Political Science*, Vol. 51, No. 1, 1990.

Pant, K.C.: "Violence in a Period of Social Change", *Mainstream*, Vol. 3, Nos. 29-30, 1970.

Parvathamma, C.: "Veerasaivism: A Saivite Sectarian Movement of Protest in Karnataka:, Mallik, S.C. (ed.): *Dissent, Protest and Reform in Indian Civilization*, Simla: Indian Institute of Advanced Study, 1977.

Patel, Sujata: "Construction and Reconstruction of Women in

Gandhi", *Economic and Political Weekly,* Vol. 20, No. 33, 1985.

Patel, Sujata: "Legitimacy, Crisis and Growing Anthoritarianism", *Economic and Political Weekly,* Vol. 23, No. 19, 1988.

Patel, Sujata: "Debacle of Populist Politics", *Economic and Political Weekly,* Vol. 20, No. 16, 1985.

Pavier, B.: *The Telengana Movement 1944-51,* Delhi: Vikas Publishing House, 1981.

Perulekar, S.V.: "The Liberation Movement among Varlis", Desai, A.R. (ed.): *Peasant Struggle in India,* Delhi: Oxford University Press, 1979.

Plettigrew Joyce: "Take Not Arms against Thy Sovereign", *South Asian Research,* Vol. 9, No. 2, 1984.

Phadke, U.D.: "The Historical Background of Mass Violence in India", Aiyar, S.P. (ed.): *The Politics of Mass Violence in India,* Bombay: Manaktalas, 1966.

Phadnis, Urmila, Muni, S.D. and Bahadur, Kalim (eds.): *Domestic Conflicts in South Asia,* Vols. I and II, New Delhi: South Asian Publishers, 1984.

Pimpley, Prakash and Sharma, Satis (eds.): *Struggle for Status,* Delhi: B.R. Publishing Corporation, 1985.

Puranik, S.N.: "The Problem of Communal Harmony in India", Grover, Verinder (ed.): *Sociological Aspects of the Indian Political System,* New Delhi: Deep and Deep Publications, 1990.

Puri, Harish K.: "The Akali Agitation: An Analysis of Socio-Economic Bases of Protest", *Economic and Political Weekly,* Vol. 23, No. 3, 1988.

Rai, S.M.: "Gandhi and Communal Politics in India", *Indian Political Science Review,* Vol. 4, No. 1, 1969-70.

Raj, A.L.: "Ideology and Hegemony in Jharkhand Movement", *Economic and Political Weekly,* Vol. XXVII, No. 5, 1992.

Rajendran, G.: *The Izhava Community and Kerala Politics*, Trivandrum: The Kerala Academy of Political Science, 1974.

Ram, Mohan: "Ramaswami Naikar and the Dravidian Movement", *Economic and Political Weekly*, Vol. 9, Nos. 6-8 (Annual Number), 1974.

Ram, Mohan: "The Telengana Peasant Armed Srtuggle 1946-51", *Economic and Political Weekly*, Vol. 8, No. 23, 1973.

Ranga, N.G. and Saraswati, Swami Sahajananda: *History of the Kisan Movement*, Madras: All India Kisan Publications, 1939.

Ranga, N.G.: *Revolutionary Peasants*, New Delhi: Armi Book Company, 1949.

Rao, M.S.A.: *Social Movements in India*, Vol. I and II, New Delhi: Manohar Publications, 1979.

Rao, C.R.M.: "The Levels of Indian Politics: A Problem of Authoritarian Tradition and Democratic Modernity", Aiyar, S.P. and Srinivasan, R. (eds.): *Studies in Indian Democracy*, New Delhi: Allied Publishers, 1965.

Rao, R.: *The Historical Telengana Struggle*, New Delhi: Communist Party of India, 1972.

Reddi, K. Madhusudhan: "Indian Polity : From Consensus to Fragmentation", *Indian Journal of Political Science*, Vol. 54, Nos. 3-4, 1993.

Robinson, Francis: "Nation-Formation: The Brass Thesis and Muslim Separatism", *Journal of Commonwealth and Comparative Politics*, Vol. 15, No. 3, 1977.

Rosenthal, Donald B.: *The Expansive Elite: District Politics and State Policy Making in India*, Berkeley: University of California Press, 1977.

Ross, Aileen D.: *Student Unrest in India*, London: McGill-Queens University Press, 1969.

Rothschild, Joseph: *Ethno-Politics: A Conceptual Analysis*, New York: Columbia University Press, 1981.

Roy, Ajit: "Darjeeling: Hopeful Turn and Remaining Obstacles",

Economic and Political Weekly, Vol. 23, No. 30, 1988.

Rubin, Barnett R.: "The Civil Liberties Movement in India: New Approaches to the State and Social Change", *Asian Survey*, Vol. 27, No.3, 1987.

Rudolph, Lloyd I. and Rudolph, Susanne H.: *In Pursuit of Laxmi: The Political Economy of the Indian State*, New Delhi: Orient Longman, 1987.

Rudolph, Lloyd I. and Rudolph, Susanne H.: "Determinants and Varieties of Agrarian Mobilizations" Desai, Meghnad *et al* (eds.): *Agrarian Power and Agricultural Productivity in South Asia*, Delhi: Oxford Univeristy Press, 1984.

Runciman, W.C.: *Relative Deprivation and Social Justice*, London: Routledge and Kegan Paul, 1966.

Saberwal, Satish: "Elements of Communalism" I and II, *Mainstream*, Nos. 29 and 30, March 21 and 28, 1981.

Sahni, Ruchi Ram: *Struggles for Reform in Sikh Shrines*, Amritsar: S.G.P.C. (Undated).

Saraswati, Baidyanath: "Notes on Kabir: A Non-Literate Intellectual", Mallik, S.C. (ed.): *Dissent, Protest and Reform in Indian Civilization*, Simla: Indian Institute of Advanced Study, 1977.

Sareen, H.K.: *Insurgency in North-East India: A Study of Sino-American Role*, New Delhi: Sterling Publishers, 1980.

Sarkar, Ajeya: "Regionalism, State and the Emerging Political Pattern in India", *Indian Journal of Political Science*, Vol. 51, No. 4, 1990.

Sarkar, K.K.: "Kakdwip Tebhaga Movement", Desai, A.R. (ed.): *Peasant Struggles in India*, Delhi: Oxford University Press, 1979.

Sathyamurthy, T.V.: "Contemporary European Scholarship on Political and Social Change in South Asia: An Essay in the Sociology of Knowledge", *Economic and Political Weekly*, Vol. 22, No. 11, 1987.

Sathyamurthy, T.V. (ed.): *Class Fromation and Political Transformation in Post-Colonial India*, Vol. 4, New Delhi: Oxford University Press, 1996.

Sen, Sunil: *Agrarian Struggles in Bengal 1946-47*, New Delhi: Peoples' Publishing House, 1972.

Sen, Sunil: *Peasant Movements in India – Mid Nineteenth and Twentieth Centuries*, Calcutta: K.P. Bagchi, 1982.

Sengupta, Nirmal: "The Social and Economic Basis of Current Tribal Movements", *Social Action*, October-December, 1990.

Sengupta, Nirmal: "Background of the Jharkhand Question", Sengupta, Nirmal (ed.): *Fourth World Dynamics: Jharkhand*, Delhi: Shankar Printing Service, 1982.

Sengupta, Nirmal (ed.): *Fourth World Dynamics: Jharkhand*, Delhi: Shankar Printing Service, 1982.

Sengupta, Pradip K.: *India: Constitutional Dynamics of Changed Polity*, Allahabad: Chugh Publications, 1991.

Sengupta, Pramod: *Naxalbari and Indian Revolution*, Calcutta: Research India Publications, 1983.

Sethi, J.D.: "Jayaprakash Narayan and His Revolution", *Gandhi Marg*, January, 1975.

Shah, Ghanshyam: *Politics of Scheduled Castes and Scheduled Tribes*, Bimbay: Vora Publications, 1975.

Shah, Ghanshyam: *Caste Association and Political Process in Gujarat: A Study of the Kshatriya Sabha*, Bombay: Popular Prakashan, 1975.

Shah, Ghanshyam: *Economic Differentiation and Tribal Identity*, Delhi: Ajanta Publications, 1984.

Shah, Ghanshyam: *Protest Movements in Two Indian States*, Delhi: Ajanta Publications, 1977.

Shah, Ghanshyam: *Social Movements in India: A Review of Literature*, New Delhi: Sage Publications, 1990.

Shah, Ghanshyam: "Direct Action in India: A Study of Gujarat and Bihar Agitations", *Contributions to Asian Studies*, No. 14, 1979.

Shah, Kalpana: *Womens' Liberation and Voluntary Action*, Delhi: Ajanta Publishers, 1984.

Shakir, Moin: "Class Character of the Indian State", Grover, V. (ed.): *Sociological Aspects of Indian Political System*, New Delhi: Deep and Deep Publications, 1990.

Sharma, K.L.: "Jharkhand Movement in Bihar", *Economic and Political Weekly*, Vol. XI, No. 2, 1976.

Sheth, Parveen: *Patterns of Political Behaviour in Gujarat*, Ahmedabad: Sahitya Mudranalaya, 1976.

Shills, Edward: "The Political Class in the Age of Mass Society: Collective Liberalism and Social Democracy", Chudnowski, M. (ed.): *Does Who Govern Matter? Elite Circulation of Contemporary Societies*, De Kalib: Northern Illinois University Press, 1982.

Shyamlal: *Caste and Political Mobilization*, Jaipur: Panchsheel Prakashan, 1981.

Singh, A. (ed.): *Punjab in Indian Politics*, Delhi: Ajanta Publications, 1985.

Singh, B.P.: "North-East India: Demography, Culture and Identity Crisis", *Modern Asian Studies*, Vol. XXI, No. 2, 1987.

Singh, Iqbal: *Punjab Under Seige: A Critical Analysis*, New York: Allen, Macmillan and Enderson, 1986.

Singh, Dalip: "Protest Movements in India", *Indian Journal of Political Science*, Vol. 52, No. 4, 1991

Singh, K.S. (ed.): *Tribal Movements in India*, Vols. 1&2, Delhi: Manohar Publications, 1982 and 1983.

Singh, K.S.: *Tribal Society in India: An Anthropo-Historical Perspective*, Delhi: Manohar Publications, 1985.

Singh, K.S.: *Dust Storm and Changing Mist: Story of Birsa Munda and His Movement in Chhotonagpur*, Calcutta: Firma KLM, 1966.

Singh, Mohinder: *The Akali Movement*, Delhi: Macmillan, 1978.

Singh, Rajendra: "Agrarian Social Structure and Peasant Unrest: A Study of Land Grab Movement in District Basti, East U.P.", *Sociological Bulletin*, No. 1, 1974.

Singh, Sangeeta; Menon, Meenakshi *et al.*: "Subaltern Studies II: A Review Article", *Social Scientist*, Vol. 12, No. 10, 1984.

Singh, Yogendra: "Contemporary Social 'Crisis' in India and its Dimensions", *Man and Development*, Vol. XIV, No. 4, 1992.

Singh, Yogendra: *Modernization of Indian Tradition*, New Delhi: Thomson Press (India) Ltd., 1973.

Sinha, Arun: "Recurrent Patterns of Jharkhand Politics", *Economic and Political Weekly*, Vol. XXII, No. 45, 1987.

Skocpol, Theda: *States and Social Revolutions*, Cambridge: Cambridge University Press, 1979.

Smelser, Neil: *Theory of Collective Behaviour*, London: Routledge and Kegan Paul, 1962.

Smith, A.D.: *Theories of Nationalism*, London: Duckworth, 1971.

Smith, Donald E.: *India as a Secular State*, Princeton N.J.: Princeton University Press, 1963.

Smith, W.C.: Modern Islam in India, cited in Engineer, Ashgar Ali: "Socio-Economic Basis of Communalism", Grover, Verinder (ed.): *Sociological Aspects of Indian Political System*, New Delhi: Deep and Deep Publications, 1990.

Srinivas, M.N.: *Social Change in Modern India*, Los Angels: California University Press, 1966.

Srinivas, M.N.: *Caste in Modern India and other Essays*, London: Asia Publishing House, 1962.

Srinivas, M.N.: "The Indian Road to Equality", *Economic and Political Weekly*, Vol. 12, June (Special Number), 1960.

Srinivas, R.: "Democracy and the Revolt of the Masses", Aiyar, S.P. (ed.): *The Politics of Mass Violence in India*, Bombay: Manaktalas, 1966.

Stokes, Eric: *The Peasants and the Raj: Studies in Agrarian Society and Peasant rebellion in Colonial India*, Delhi: Vikas Publishing House, 1978.

Stouffer, Samuel A. *et al.* (eds.): *The American Soldier: Adjustment During Army Life*, Vol. 1, Princeton: Princeton University Press, 1949.

Subba, T.B.: *Ethnicity, State and Development: A Case Study of the Gorkhaland Movement in Darjeeling*, New Delhi: Har-Anand Publications, 1992.

Sunday, Calcutta: February 20, 1986.

Swaminathan, M.S.: "Foreword" to Ismail Seragaldin: Promoting Sustainable Development: Towards a New Paradigm, *Rajiv Gandhi Institute of Contemporary Studies*, Paper-12, 1994.

Syangden, Bipin and Moktan, Ashok: *Gorkhas Speak*, Darjeeling: B.B. Tamang Publishers, 1986.

Taylor, David and Yapp, Malcolm (eds.): *Political Identity in South Asia*, London: Curzon Press, 1979.

Thappar, Romila: "Ethics, Religion and Social Protest in the First Millennium BC in Northern India", Malik, S.C. (ed.): *Dissent, Protest and Reform in Indian Civilization*, Simla: Indian Institute of Advanced Study, 1977.

The Indian Nation, March 16, 1974.

Thimmaiah, G. and Aziz, Abdul: "The Political Economy of Land Reforms in Karnataka, a South India State", *Asian Survey*, Vol. 23, No. 7, 1983.

Thompson, D.L. and Roness, D. (eds.): *Ethnicity, Politics and Development*, Colorado: Lynn Riesner Publishers, 1986.

Thorner, Daniel: *The Shaping of Modern India*, Bombay: Allied Publishers, 1980.

Tilly, Charles: *From Mobilization to Revolution*, Mass: Addision Westely, 1979.

Upreti, P.N.: *Religion and Politics in Punjab in 1920s*, Delhi:

Sterling Publishers, 1982.

Velayudhan, Meera: "Women Workers and Struggle in Alleppey", *Samya-Shakti – A Journal of Women Studies*, Vol. 1, No. 2.

Verba, S.; Ahmed, B. and Bhatt, A.: *Race, Caste and Politics*, New York: Sage Publications, 1972.

Verma, S.P.: "The Crisis in South Asia: An Overview", in Phadnis, Urmila; Munshi, S.D. and Bahadur, Kalim (eds.): *Domestic Conflicts in South Asia*, Vol. 1, New Delhi: South Asian Publishers, 1986.

Wallace, A.F.C.: "Revitalization Movements", *American Anthropologist*, 58, 1964.

Weiner, Myron: "The Political Economy of Industrial Growth in India", *World Politics*, Vol. 38, No. 4, 1986.

Weiner, Myron: *The Indian Paradoxes: Essays in Indian Politics*, Delhi: Sage Publications, 1989.

Weiner, Myron: *The Politics of Scarcity*, Bombay: Asia Publishing House, 1963.

Weiner, Myron: *Sons of the Soil*, Delhi: Oxford University Press, 1978.

Weiner, Myron: "India's Two Political Cultures", Weiner, Myron (ed.): *Political Change in South Asia*, Calcutta: Firma KLM, 1963.

Weiner, Myron (ed.): *Political Change in South Asia*, Calcutta: Firma KLM, 1963.

Weiner, Myron and Eisenstadt, S.N. *et al.*: *Orthodoxy, Heterodoxy and Dissent in India*, Berlin: Mouton, 1984.

Weiner, Myron and Katzenstein, Marry F.: *India's Preferrential Politics: Migrants, the Middle Class and Ethnic Equality*, Chicago: University of Chicago Press, 1981.

Weldon, T.D.: *The Vocabulary of Politics*, London: Harmondsworth, 1955.

Wilkinson, Paul: *Social Movement*, London: Macmillan, 1971.

Wilson, T.H.: *Introduction to Social Movements*, New York: Basic Books.

Wolf, C.P. and Finterbusch, Kurt: *Methodology of Social Impact Assessment*, New York: American Sociological Association, 1977.

Wolf, Eric R.: *Peasants*, Engelwood Cliffs N.J.: Princeton Hall, 1966.

Wolf, Wric R.: *Peasant Wars in the Twentieth Century*, New York: Harper and Row, 1970.

Wolf, Eric R.: "Types of Latin American Peasantry: A Preliminary Discussion", *American Anthropologist*, Vol. 57, No. 3, 1955.

Wood, John, R. (ed.): *State Politics in Contemporary India: Crisis or Continuity?*, Boulder Co.: Westview Press, 1984.

Wood, John R.: "Extra-parliamentary Opposition in India: An Analysis of Populist Agitations in Gujarat and Bihar", *Pacific Affairs*, Vol. 68, No. 3, 1975.

Zakaria, R.: *Rise of Muslims in Indian Politics*, Bombay: Samaiya Publications, 1970.

Zelliot, Eleanor: "Gandhi and Ambedkar: A Study of Leadership", Mahar, Michael (ed.): *The Untouchables in Contemporary India*, Tucson: The University of Arizona Press, 1972.

Appendix – I

Peace Accords in Assam

Problem of Foreigners in Assam
Memorandum of Settlement

Chief Minister, Assam
August 16, 1985.

The issue of foreign nationals in Assam, which had agitated the popular mind, has been resolved to the satisfaction of all sections of the people of the State. The Memorandum of Settlement, signed by the Union Government and the Government of Assam with the AASU and AAGSP which had spearheaded a movement on the issue, brought to an end the prolonged agitations and has opened up new possibilities of social and economic development in the State. The Memorandum, which accommodates all shades of opinion and satisfies all concerned sectrions apart from taking into full consideration the national commitments and international and humanitarian obligations, will go down in the country's history as a shining example of popular wisdom so brilliantly symbolized by the country's Prime Minister.

We present in the following pages the full text of the historic Memorandum of Settlement with the hope that the people in general will fully comprehend the spirit of the historic settlement and will entend full cooperation to the Government in implementing it.

Janata Bhavan, HITESHWAR SAIKIA

Memorandum of Settlement

Sd/- (Biraj Sharma)

1. Government have all along been most anxious to find a satiafactory solution to the problem of foreigners in Assam. The All Assam Students Union (AASU) and the All Assam Gana Sangram Parishad (AAGSP) have also expressed their keenness to find such a solution.

Sd/- (P.K. Mahanta)

2. The AASU through their Memorandum dated 2nd February, 1980, presented to the late Prime Minister Smt. Indira Gandhi, conveyed their profound sense of apprehensions regarding the continuing influx of foreign nationals into Assam and the fear about adverse effects upon the political, social, cultural and economic life of the State.

Sd/- (B.K. Phukan)

3. Being fully alive to the genuine apprehensions of the people of Assam, the then Prime Minister initiated the dialogue with the AASU/AAGSP. Subsequently, talks were held at the Prime Minister and Home Minister's levels during the period 1980-83. Several rounds of informal talks were held during 1984. Formal discussions were resumed in March 1985.

Foreigners Issue

5.1 For purpose of detection and deletion of foreigners, 1.1.1966 shall be the base date and year.

5.2. All persons who came to Assam prior to 1.1.1966, including those amongst whose names appeared on the electoral rolls used in 1967 elections, shall be regularized.

5.3 Foreigners who came to Assam after 1.1.1966 (inclusive) and upto 24th March, 1971 shall be detected in accordance with the provisions of the Foreigners Act, 1946 and the Foreigners (Tribunals) Order 1964.

Sd/- (Biraj Sharma)

5.4 Name of the foreigners so detected will be deleted from the electoral roll in force. Such persons will be required to register themselves before the Registration Officers of the respective districts in accordance with the provisions of the Registration of Foreigners Act, 1939 and the Registration of Foreigners Rule, 1939.

Sd/- (P.K. Mahanta)

5.5 For the purpose, Government of India will undertake suitable strengthening of the governmental machinery.

5.6 On the expiry of a period of ten years following the date of detection, the names of all such persons which have been deleted from the electoral rolls shall be restored.

5.7 All persons who were expelled earlier, but have since re-entered illegally into Assam, shall be expelled.

5.8 Foreigners who came to Assam on or after March 25, 1971 shall continue to be detected, and expelled in accordance with law. Immediate and practical steps shall be taken to expel such foreigners.

5.9. The government will give due consideration to certain difficulties expressed by the AASU/AAGSP regarding the implementation of the Illegal migrants (Determination by Tribunals) Act, 1983.

Safeguards and Economic Developments

6. Constitutional. Legislative and administrative safeguards, as may be appropriate shall be provided to protect, preserve

and promote the cultural, social, linguistic identity and heritage of the Assamese people.

7. The Government take this opportunity to renew their commitment for the speedy all round economic development of Assam, so as to improve the standard of living of the people. Special emphasis will be placed on education and science & technology through establishment of national institutions.

Other Issues

8.1 The Government will arrange for the issue of citizenship certificates in future only by the authorities of the Central Government.

Sd/- (P.K. Mahanta)

8.2 Specific complaints that may be made by the AASU/ AAGSP about irregular issuance of Indian Citizenship Certificate (ICC) will be looked into.

Sd/- (Bijan Sharma)

9. The international border shall be made sucure against future infiltration by erection of physical barriers like walls, barbed wire fencing and other obstacles at appropriate places. Patrolling by security forces on land and reverine routes all along the international border shall be adequately intensified. In order to further strengthen the security arrangements, to prevent effectively future infiltration, an adequate number of check posts shall be set up.

9.2 Besides the arrangements mentioned above and keeping in view security consideration, a road all along the international border shall be constructed so as to facilitate patrolling by security forces. Land between border and the road would be kept free on human habitation, wherever possible. Riverine patrolling along the international border would be intensified. An effective measures would be adopted to prevent infiltrators crossing or attempting to cross the international border.

10. It will be ensured that relevant laws for prevention of encroachment of government lands and lands in tribal belts and blocks are strictly enforced and unauthorized encroachers evicted as laid down under such laws.

11. It will be ensured that the relevant law restricting acquisition of immovable property by foreigners in Assam is strictly enforced.

12. It will be ensured that Birth and Death Registers are duly maintained.

Restorarion of Normalcy

Sd/- (P.K. Mahanta)

13. The All Assam Students Union (AASU) and the All Assam Gana Sangram Parishad (AAGSP) call off the agitation, assure all cooperation and dedicate themselves towards the development of the country.

Sd/- (Biraj Sharma)

14. The Central and the State Government have agreed to:

    (a) review with sympathy and withdraw cases of disciplinary action taken against employees in the context of the agitation and to ensure that there is no victimization;

    (b) frame a scheme for ex-gratia payment to next to kin of those who were killed in the course of the agitation;

    (c) give sympathetic consideration to proposal for relaxation of upper age limit for employment in public services in Assam, having regard to exceptional situation that prevailed in holding of academic and competitive examinations, etc. in the context of agitation in Assam;

    (d) undertake review of detention cases, if any, as well as cases against persons charged with criminal offences in connection with the agitation, except those charged with commission of heinous offences;

(e) consider withdrawal of the prohibitory orders/ notification in force, if any.

15. The Ministry of Home Affairs will be the nodal Ministry for the implementation of the above.

Sd/-
(P.K. Mahanta)
President
All Assam Students Union

Sd/-
(R.D. Pradhan)
Home Secretary
Government of India

Sd/-
(B.K. Phukan)
General Secretary
All Assam Students Union

Sd/-
(Biraj Sharma)
Convenor
All Assam Gana
Sangram Parishad

Sd/-
(Smt. P.P. Trivedi)
Chief Secretary
Govt. of Assam

In the presence of

Sd/-
(Rajiv Gandhi)
Prime Minister of India

Date: 15th August, 1985
Place: New Delhi

1. Election Coimmission will be requested to ensure preparation of fair electoral rolls.
2. Time for submission of claims and objections will be extended by 30 days, subject to this being consistent with the Election Rules.
3. The Election Commission will be requested to send Central Observers.

Sd/-
Home Secretary

1. Oil refinery will be established in Assam.
2. Central Government will render full assistance to the State Government in their efforts to reopen:
   (i) Ashok Paper Mills
   (ii) Jute Mills
3. I.I.T. will be set up in Assam.

Memorandum of Settlement (Bodo Accord)

February 20, 1993, Guwahati

1. Preamble

(i) Both the Government of India and the Government of Assam have been making efforts to bring about an amicable solution to the problems of the Bodos and Other Plains Tribals living in the north bank of rive Brahmaputra within Assam.

(ii) Towards this end, the Government of India held a series of meeting with the State Government as well as with the leaders of All Bodo Students Union (ABSU) and Bodo People's Action Committee (BPAC). The State Government has also separately held discussion with the Bodo leaders. As a result, it has been considered necessary to set-up an administrative authority within the State of Assam under a scheme, the details of which are outlined in the succeeding paragraphs:

2. Objective

The objective of this scheme is to provide maximum autonomy wihin the framework of the Constitution to the Bodos for social, economic, educational, ethnic and cultural advancement.

3. (a) Name: Bodoland Autonomous Council (BAC)

There shall be formed, by an Act of Assam Legislative Assembly, a Bodoland Autonomous Council (BAC) within the State of Assam comprising continuos geographical areas between river Sankos and Mazat river Pasnoi. The land records authority of the State will scrutinize the list of villages furnished by ABSU/BPAC having 50% and more of tribal population which shall be included in the BAC. For the purpose of providing contiguous areas, even the villages having less than 50% tribal population shall be included. BAC will also include Researve Forests as per the guidelines laid by Ministry of Defence and Miistry of Environment and Forests, Govt. of India, not otherwise required by the Government for manning the international border and tea gardens located completely within the BAC contiguous area.

(b) Powers

The BAC will comprise of a General Council comprising 40 members, 35 elected on the basis of adult suffrage and having a life of five years. The Government will have powers to nominate 5 members of the Council, particularly from groups which could not otherwise be represented. This Council will have powers to make bye-laws, rules and orders for application within the BAC area on the subjects enumeratred in Schedule 'A'.

(c) The Executive Authority of the BAC would be exercised by its Executive Body to be known as Bodoland Executive Council (BEC). The BEC will be responsible for implementation within the BAC area of the laws of subjects enumerated in Schedule 'A'.

(d) The General Council and the BEC will hold office during the pleasure of the Governor of Assam. Consultation with the State Law Department of Government of Assam would be necessary if the Governor proposes to dissolve either the General Council or the BEC before the expiry of its term in accoedance with the provisions of law. The executive authority of the BEC will be exercised by the party enjoying a simple majority in the General Council. On completion of elections, the Governor would invie the leader of the majority party to constitute the BEC.

4. Finances

(i) (a) The finances for the BAC will be earmarked under a separate subhead within the State budget, in keeping with the guidelines laid down by the Government of India from time to time. The government of Assam would have no powers to divert this earmarked allocation to other heads/ areas except in exigencies when there is unavoidable overall Budget cut.

(b) The provisions made in 4(i) (a) regarding allocation of funds should be in the line with the spirit of the Constitution (Seventy Second) and (Seventy Third) amendment.

(ii) The BAC would also receive grant-in-aid from time to time within the principles and policies enunciated by the Government of India.

(iii) The General Council will have powers to raise financies from levies/fees/taxes etc. on subjects mentioned in Schedule 'A' subject to Constitutional amendment mentioned above.

(iv) The finances for the BAC will be managed exclusively by its General Council and the statement of its annual audited accounts will be laid on the table of the State Assembly.

5. Powers of Appointment

The Bodoland Executive Committee would have powers to appoint Class III and Class IV Staff within its jurisdiction for implementation of schemes connected with the subjects enumerated in Schedule 'A'.

6. Reservation of Seats

The Election Commission of India will be requested by the BAC to consider seat reservation and delimitation of constituencies, both Lok Sabha and State Assembly, within the BAC area, to the extent permitted by the Constitution and the law.

7. Special Provisions for the BAC Area

The Genral Council shall be consulted and its views shall be given due regard before any law made on the following subjects is implemented in the BAC area.

(i) the religious or social practice of the Bodos;

(ii) the Bodo customary laws and procedures; and

(iii) the ownership and transfer of land within the BAC area.

8. Special Status for the Bodoland and Autonomous Council

The BAC shall, within the laws of the land, take steps to protect the demographic complexion of the areas falling within its jurisdictioin.

9. Special Courts

Action will be taken in consultation with the Guwahati High Court to set up within BAC Special Courts as specified below to try suits and cases between parties all of whom belong to Scheduled Tribe or Tribes in accordance with the tribal customary law and procedure, if any:

(a) Village Courts; (b) subordinate District Customary Law Courts within a civil Sub-Divisional Territory, and (c) District Customary Law Court.

10. Appointment in the Central Bodies

The claims of the Bodos shall be considered for appointment to the North-Eastern Council.

11. Official Language

The general Council can lay down policy with regard to use of Bodo languages as medium of official correspondence within the BAC area. However, while corresponding with offices outside the BAC area, correspondence will have to be in bilingual form in accordance with the Article 345 of the Constitution and the provision of law in this behalf.

12. Changes in Geographical Boundary

The geographical areas of the Bodoland Autonomous Council as agreed upon can be changed with the mutual consent of the BAC and the Government of Assam.

13. Revision of List of Scheduled Caste and Scheduled Tribes

The scheduling and de-scheduling of Scheduled Caste and Scheduled Tribes residing within the Bodo areas will be done as per the Commission appointed by the Government of India under the Constitution.

14. Trade and Commerce

The General Council will have powers to regulate trade and commerce within its jurisdiction in accordance with the existing law. For this purpose, it can issue permits and licences to individuals within the BAC areas. The Government of Assam and the Union Government while considering allotment of permits to people residing within the BAC areas will give preference to the Bodos.

15. Employment Opportunities

The BAC will have power to reserve jobs for Scheduled

Tribes within its jurisdiction. However, exercise of such powers shall be in accordance with the existing constitutional and legal provisions.

16. Civil and Police Services

(i) The Government of Assam may from time to time post officers of the rank of Class II and above to posts within the BAC in accordance with the exigencies. While making these postings due regard will be given the views of BAC about officers being so posted.

(ii) The Officers posted to the BAC areas will be accountable to the BAC for the performance and the assessment of their work recorded by the BEC authorities, will be incorporated to their ACRs by the State Government.

(iii) The Central Government while making recruitment from the State of Assam to the Army, para-military forces and police units, will hold special recruitment drives within the BAC area.

17. Appointment of Interim Bodoland Executive Council

The Government of Assam will take steps for the formation of an Interim Bodoland Executive Council for the BAC from amongst the leaders of the present Bodoland movement who are signatories to this settlement, during the transition period, i.e., prior to the holding of elections. Such Interim council would be formed before a prescribed date mutually agreed between the Central and State Governments.

18. Relief and Rehabilitation

(i) ABSU-BPAC leaders will take immediate steps to bring overgound and deposit with the District authorities all arems, ammunition and explosives in the possession of their own supporters and will cooperate with the administration in bringing overground all

Bodo militants along with their arms and ammunition, etc. within one month of the formation of the Interim BEC. In order to ensure the smooth return to civil life of the cadre and to assist in the quick restoration of peace and normalcy, such surrenders made voluntarily, will not attract prosecution.

(ii) The Government of Assam will consider sympathetically the withdrawal of all cases against persons connected with the Bodoland Movements excluding those relating to heinous crimes.

(iii) The Government of India will initiate steps for review of action against the Bodo employees of Government of India and subordinate offices as well as in respect of Central Government Undertakings. Similar action would be taken by the Government of Assam.

(iv) The Government of Assam will initiate immediate steps for suitable rehabilitation of the Bodo militants coming overgroud as a result of this settlement. Similarly, the Government will organize ex-gratia payments as per rules to next of the kins killed during the Bodo agitation.

19. Share in Collection of Excise Duty on Tea

The Government of Assam will deposit in the BAC Fund revenue collected from the tea gardens falling within the BAC area.

20. Protection of Right of Non-Tribals

The Government of Assam and the BAC will jointly ensure that all rights and interests of the non-tribals as on date living in BAC area in matters pertaining to land as well as their language protected.

21. Ad-hoc Central Grant for Launching the BAC

After the signing of this settlement, an ad-hoc Budget on reasonable basis will be prepared by interim BEC and discussed with the State and Central Government for necessary financial support.

Sd/- S.K. Bwiswamutiary President, ABSU	Sd/- K.S. Rao Addl. Chief Secretary to the Government of Assam
Sd/- Rabi Ram Brahma General Secretary, ABSU	Sd/- Subhash Basumatari Chairman, BPAC

In the presence of

Sd/- Rajesh Pilot Minister of State (Internal Security) Ministry of Home Affairs Government of India	Sd/- Hiteswar Saikia Chief Minister of Assam State Govt. of Assam

Appendix–II

Peace Accord in the Sub-Himalaya Accord on Darjeeling

Text of the Accord on Darjeeling

The demands of the GNLF having been considered by the Government of India and the Government of West Bengal and consequent upon the tripartite meeting between Shri Buta Singh, Union Home Minister, Shri Jyoti Basu, Chief Minister of West Bengal and Shri Subhas Ghising, President GNLF at New Delhi o 25.7.88, it is hereby agreed between Government of India, Government of West Bengal and GNLF as below:

1. Separate State of Gorkhaland

In the overall national interest and in response to Prime Minister's call, the GNLF agree to drop the demand for a separate State of Gorkhaland. For the social, economic, education and cultural advancement of the people residing in the hill areas of Darjeeling district, it is agreed to have an autonomous hill council to be set up under a State Act. The salient features of the hill council would be as follows:

(i) The name of the Council will be Darjeeling Gorkha Hill Council.

(ii) The Council will cover the three hill sub-divisions of Darjeeling district namely, Darjeeling, Kalimpong and Kurseong, plus the Mouzas of Lohagarh T.G.,

Lohagarh Forest, Eangmohan, Barachenga, Panighata Chota Adalpur, Poharu, Sukna Forest, Sukna Part I, Pantapati Forest, Mahanadi forest and Salbari Chhat Part II within Siliguri subdivision.

(iii) The state government agrees to lease to the Council, after it formed, or acquire for it the use of such land as may be required and necessary for administrative and developmental purposes, anywhere in the State and in particular in or around 'Darjeeling More' in Siliguri subdivision.

(iv) The executive powers of the Council will cover the following subjects to the provision of the Central and State laws:

1. The allotment, occupation use or setting apart land other than any land which is reserved forest, for the purpose of agriculture or grazing or for residential or other than non-agricultural purposes or for any other purpose likely to promote the interest of the inhabitants of any village, locality or town;
2. The management of any forest, not being a reserved forest;
3. The use of any canal or water-course for the purpose of agriculture;
4. Agriculture;
5. Public health and sanitation, hospitals and dispensaries
6. Tourism;
7. Vocational training;
8. Public Works-Development
9. Construction and maintenance of all roads except national highways and state highways;

10. Transport and development of transport;
11. Management of burials and burial grounds, cremation and cremation grounds;
12. Preservation, protection and improvement of livestock and prevention of animal diseases, veterinary training and practice;
13. Pounds and the prevention of cattle trespass;
14. Water, that is to say water supplies, irrigation and canals, drainage and embankment, water storage;
15. Fisheries;
16. Management of markets and fairs not being already managed by municipal authorities, panchayat samiti or gram panchayats;
17. Education – primary, secondary and higher secondary;
18. Works, lands and buildings vested in or in the lawful possession of the council; and
19. Small scale and cottage industries.

(v) The Council shall exercise general powers of supervision over Panchayat Samitis, Gram Panchayats and Municipalities falling within the area of the Council's jurisdiction.

(vi) The general council will have a total of 42 members out of which 28 will be elected and the rest nominated by the State Government.

(vii) There will be an Executive Council and the Chairman and the Vice-Chairman of the General Council will be ex-officio members of the Executive Council with the Chairman, the general council functioning, as the Chief Executive Councillor. The Chief Executive Councillor will nominate five members to the executive council from out of the elected members of the council and the state government will nominate two members to the executive council from out of the non-official nominated members of the General Council.

(viii) The Chairman of the General Council cum Executive Councillor will have the ex-official status and privileges of a minister in the council of minister in the state.

(ix) The bill for setting up the hill council will be introduced and passed in a special session of the state legislature which has been summoned. The election to the hill council will be held by the 10 December, 1988.

2. Restoration of Normalcy

(i) *Review of Criminal Cases:* It is agreed that a review will be done by the State Government of all the cases registered under various laws against persons involved in the GNLF agitation. Action will be taken, in the light of the review, not to proceed with prosecution in all cases except those charged with murder. Release of persons in custody will follow the withdrawal of cases. This review will be completed within 15 days of signing of this agreement.

(ii) *Action against Government Servents:* The State Government agrees to withdraw all cases of disciplinary action taken against employees in the context of the agitation. There will be no victimization of government servants.

(iii) The GNLF agrees to issue a call to its cadre for the surrender of all unauthorized arms to the district administration. It will be made clear in the call that such surrenders made voluntarily within the prescribed date will not attract any prosecution.

(iv) The GNLF hereby agrees to withdraw all agitational activities and to extend full cooperation to the administration for the maintenance of peace and normalization of the political process in the hill areas of Darjeeling.

(Subhash Ghising)
President, GNLF

(R.N. Sengupta)
Chief Secretary on behalf of the Government of West Bengal

(C.G. Somiah)
Union Home Secretary on behalf of the Union Government

In the presence of Union Home Minister, Chief Minister, Govt. of West Bengal

Appendix – III

Peace Accords in Mizoram

MEMORANDUM OF SETTLEMENT, 1986
(THE MIZO ACCORD)

Preamble

1. Government of India have all along making earnest efforts to bring about an end to the disturbed conditions in Mizoram and to restore peace and harmony.
2. Towards this end, initiative was taken by the Prime Minister, Smt. Indira Gandhi, on the acceptance by Shri Laldenga on behalf of the Mizo national Front (MNF) of the two conditions namely cessation of violence by MNF and holding of talks within the framework of the Constitution of India, a series of discussions were held with Shri Laldenga. Settlement on various issues reached during the course of the talks is incorporated in the following paragraph.

Restoration of Normalcy

3.1 With a view to restoring peace and normalcy in Mizoram the MNF party, on their part, undertakes within the agreed timeframe, to take all necessary steps to end all under-ground personnel of the MNF with their arms, ammunition and equipment to ensure their return to civil life, to abjure violence and generally to help in the process of restoration of normalcy. The modalities of bringing out all underground personnel and the deposit of arms, ammunition and equipment will be worked out. The implementation of the foregoing will be under the supervision of the Central Government.

3.2 The MNF Party will take immediate steps to amend its Articles of Association so as to make them conform to the provision of law.

3.3 The Central Government will take steps for the resettlement and rehabilitation of underground MNF personnel coming overground after considering the schemes proposed in this regard by the Government of Mizoram.

3.4 The MNF undertakes not to extend any support to Tripura National Volunteers (TNV), Peoples' Liberation Army of Manipur (PLA) and any other such groups, by way of training, supply of arms or providing protection or in any other manner.

Legal Administrative and Other Steps

4.1 With a view to satisfying the desires and aspirations of all sections of the people of Mizoram, the Government will initiate measure to confer Statehood on the Union Territory of Mizoram, subject to other stipulations contained in this Memorandum of Settlement.

4.2 To give effect to the above, the necessary legislative and administrative measures will be undertaken, including those for the enactment of Bills for the amendment of the Constitution and other laws for the conferment of Statehood as aforesaid, to come into effect on a date to be notified by the Central Government.

4.3 The amendments aforesaid shall provide, among other things, for the following:

(i) The territory of Mizoram shall consist of the territory specified in Section 6 of the North Eastern Areas (Reorganisation) Act, 1971.

(ii) Notwithstanding anything contained in the Constitution, no Act of parliament in respect of:

(a) religious or social practices of the Mizos;

(b) Mizo customary law or procedure;

(c) Administration of Civil and Criminal justice involving decisions according to Mizo customary law; and

(d) Ownership and transfer of land;

Shall apply to the State of Mizoram unless the Legislative Assembly of Mizoram by a resolution so decides:

Provided that nothing in this clause shall apply to any Central Act in force in Mizoram immediately before that appointed day.

(iii) Article 170, Clause (1) shall, in relation to the Legislative Assembly of Mizoram, have effect as if for the word 'sixty', the word 'forty' has been substituted.

5. Soon after the Bill for conferment of Statehood becomes law, and when the President is satisfied that normalcy has returned and that conditions conducive to the holding of free and fair elections exist, the process of holding elections to the Legislative Assembly will be initiated.

6. (a) The Centre will transfer resources to the new Government keeping in view the change in status from Union Territory to a State and this will include resources to cover the revenue gap for the year.

(b) Central assistance for Plan will be fixed taking note of any residuary gap in resource so as to sustain the approved Plan outlay and the pattern of assistance will be in the case of special category States.

7. Border trade is locally produced or grown agricultural commodities could be allowed under the scheme to be formulated by the Central Government, subject to international agreements with neighbouring countries.

8. The Inner Line Regulations, as now in force in Mizoram, will not be amended or repealed without consulting the State Government.

Other Matters

9. The rights and privileges of the minorities in Mizoram as envisaged in the Constitution, shall continue to be preserved and protected and their social and economic advancement shall be ensured.

10. Steps will be taken by the Government of Mizoram at the earliest to review and codify the existing customs, practices, laws or other usages relating to the matters specified in clauses (a) to (d) of para 4.3 (II) of the Memorandum keeping in view that any individual Mizo may prefer to be governed by Act of parliament dealing with such matters and which are of general application.

11. The questions of the unification of Mizo inhabited areas of the States to form one administrative unit was raised by the MNF delegation. It was pointed out to them on behalf of the Government of India, that Article 3 of the Constitution of India prescribes the procedure in this regard but that the Government cannot make any commitment in this respect.

12. It was also pointed out on behalf of the Government that as soon as Mizoram becomes a State:

(i) the provisions of Part XVII of the Constitution will apply and the State will be at liberty to adopt any one or more of the languages in use in the State as the language to be used for all or any of the official purposes of the state;

(ii) It is open to the State to move for the establishment of a separate University in the State with the prescribed procedure; in the light of the Prime Minister's statement at the Joint Conferences of the Chief Justices, Chief Ministers and Law Ministers held at New Delhi on 31st August, 1985. Mizoram will be entitled to have a High Court of its own if so wishes:

(a) It was noted that there is already a scheme in force for payment of ex-gratia amount to heirs dependents of persons who were killed during diusturbances in 1966 and thereafter in the Union Territory of Mizoram. Arrangements will be made to expeditiously disburse payment to those eligible persons who had not been made over payment of the same.

(b) It was noted that consequent on verification done by a joint team of officers, the Government of India had already made arrangements for payment of compensation in respect of damge to crops; buildings destroyed/damaged during the action in Mizoram; and rental charges of buildings and lands occupied by the Security Forces. There may, however be some claims which were preferred and verified by the above team but have not yet been settled. These pending claims will be settled expeditiously. Arrangement will also be made for payment of pending claims of rental charges for lands/buildings occupied by the Security Forces.

LALDENGA	R.D. PRADHAN
On behalf of	Home Secretary
Mizo National Front	Govt. of India
Dated; 30th June, 1986	LALKHAMA
Place: New Delhi	Chief Secretary
	Govt. of Mizoram

Sequence of Events

The memorandum of Settlement contemplates the following sequence of event:

1. Coming overground of MNF personnel and depositing of atms, ammunition and equipment by them in accordance with the time bound programme as already agreed upon between the Ministry of Home Affairs and the MNF delegation.
2. The MNF Party should take immediate steps to amend its Articles of Association to make them conform to the provisions of law.
3. Government will initiate steps for rehabilitation of MNF personnel coming overground.
4. After completion of action under paragraphs (1) and (2) above, a Constitution Amendment Bill will be introduced in Parliament for the grant of Statehood and other consequential measures to be taken up.
5. After the Bill becomes law, preparations for delimitation of constituencies and holding election to the State Legislature will be taken on hand when the President is satisfied that normalcy has been restored.

LALDENGA	R.D. PRADHAN
On behalf of	Home Secretary
Mizo National Front	Govt. of India
Dated; 30th June, 1986	LALKHAMA
Place: New Delhi	Chief Secretary
	Govt. of Mizoram

5 Point Agreement between the Govt. of Mizoram and the HMAR People's Convention, 1993

1. To bring out an amicable solution to the problems arising out of the demands of the Hmar People's Convention.
2. To give adequate autonomy to the Council for social, economic, cultural and educational advancement of the people under the jurisdiction of the Council.
3. To initiate measures for use of Hmar language as a medium of instruction upto Primary level and recognition of the Hmar language as one of the major language of the State of Mizoram.
4. The name of Council shall be 'Sinlung Hills Development Council'.
5. To take immediate measures for inclusion of an area to be specified with the H.P.C. Demand Area of Mizoram and the other non-scheduled areas of Mizoram in the Scheduled (Tribal) Area of the Sixth Schedule to the Constitution of India so that the above mentioned area are safeguarded under the Sixth Schedule to the Constitution of India.

Final bilateral settlement shall be made after working out the details of the Council within the framework of the above agreed points.

Sd/-
Upa Thansung
Vice President

Sd/-
(Vaivenga)
Minister
Hmar People's Convention
Health and Family
Welfare etc.
Mizoram

September 29, 1993

Appendix – IV
Peace Accords in Nagaland

THE NAGA-AKBAR HYDARI ACCORD, 1947

Tribes Represented at Discussions on the 26th and 28th June, 1947, at Kohima

Western Angamis

Eastern Angamis

Kukis

Kacha Nagas (Mzemi)

Rengmas

Semas

Lothas

Aos

Sangtams

Changs

Heads of Proposed Understanding

That the right of the Nagas to develop themselves according to their freely espressed wishes is recognized.

1. *Judicial* : All cases whether civil or criminal arising between Nagas in the Naga Hills will be disposed of by duly constituted Naga Courts according to Naga

Customary law or such law as may be introduced with the consent of duly recognized Naga representative organizations; save that where a sentence of transportation or death has been passed there will be a right of appeal to the Governor.

In cases arising between Nagas and non-Nagas in (a) Kohima and Mokokchung town areas, and (b) in the neighbouring plains districts the judge if not a Naga will be assisted by a Naga assessor.

2. *Executive:* The general principle is accepted that what the Naga Council is prepared to pay for the Naga Council should control. This principle will apply equally to the work done as well as the staff employed.

While the District Officer will be appointed at the discretion of the Governor Subdivisions of the Naga Hills should be administered by a Subdivisional Council with a full time executive President paid by Naga Council who would be responsible to the District Officer for all matters falling within the latter's responsibility, and to the Naga Council for all matters falling within their responsibility.

In regard to: (a) Agriculture – the Naga Council will exercise all the powers now vested in the District Officer. (b) C.W.D. the Naga Council would take over full control. (c) Education and Forest Department – The Naga Council is prepared to pay for all the services and staff.

3. *Legislative:* That no law passed by the Provincial or Central Legislature which would materially affect the terms of this agreement or the religious practices of the Nagas shall have legal force in the Naga Hills without the consent of the Naga Council. In cases of dispute as to whether any law did so affect this agreement the matter would be referred by the Naga Council to the Governor who would then direct that the law in questin should not have legal force in the

Naga Hills pending the decision of the Central Government.

4. *Land:* That land with all its resources in the Naga Hills should not be alienated to a non-Naga without the consent of the Naga Council.

5. *Taxation:* That the Naga Council will be responsible for the imposition, collection, and executive of land revenue and house tax and of such other taxes as may be imposed by the Naga Council.

6. *Boundaries:* That present administrative divisions should be modified so as

   (i) to bring back into the Naga Hills Districts at the forests transferred to the Sibsagar and Nowgong Districts in the past, and

   (ii) to bring under one unified administrative unit as fas as possible all Nagas. All the areas so included would be within the scope of the present proposed agreement. No area should be transferred out of the Naga Hills without the consent of the Naga Council.

7. *Arms Act:* The Deputy Commissioner will act on the advice of the Naga Council in accordance with the provisions of the Arms Act.

8. *Regulations:* The Chin Hills Regulations and the Bengal Eastern Frontier Regulations will remain in force.

9. *Period of Agreement:* The Governor of Assam as the Agent of the Government of the Union will have a special responsibility for period of 10 years to ensure the due observance of this agreement; at the end of this period the Naga Council will be asked whether they require the above agreement to be extended for a further period or a new agreement regarding the future of Naga people arrived at.

The Sixteen Point Agreement, 1960

THE SIXTEEN POINT AGREEMENT ARRIVED AT BETWEEN THE NAGA PEOPLE'S CONVENTION AND THE GOVERNMENT OF INDIA IN JULY, 1960

The points placed by the delegates of the Naga People's Convention before the Prime Minister on 26 July, 1960, as finally recast by the Delegation in the light of discussions on 27th and 28th July 1960 with the Foreign Secretary.

1. The Name

The territories that were heretofore known as the Naga Hills – Tuensang Area under the Naga Hills-Tunesang Area Act 1957, shall form a State within the Indian Union and be hereafter known as Nagaland.

2. The Ministry Incharge

The Nagaland shall be under the Ministry of External Affairs of the Government of India.

3. The Governor of Nagaland

(1) The President of India shall appoint a Governor for Nagaland and he will be vested with the executive powers of the Government of Nagaland. He will have his headquarters in Nagaland.

(2) His administrative secretariat will be headed by a Chief Secretary stationed at the Headquarters with other

Secretariat Staff as necessary.

(3) The Governor shall have special responsibility with regard to law and order during the transitional period and for so long as the law and order situation continues to remain disturbed on account of hostile activities. In exercising this special responsibility, the Governor, shall, after consultation with the Ministry, act in his individual judgement. The special responsibility of the Governor will cease when normalcy returns.

4. Council of Ministers

(1) There shall be a Council of Ministers with a Chief Minister at the head to assist and advise the Governor in the exercise of his functions.

(2) The Council of Ministers shall be responsible to the Naga Legislative Assembly.

5. The Legislature

There shall be constituted a Legislative Assembly consisting of elected and nominated members as may be deemed necessary representing different tribes. (Further a duly constituted body of Experts may be formed to examine and determine the principles of representation on democratic basis).

6. Representation in Parliament

Two elected members shall represent Nagaland in the Union Parliament, that is to say one for the Lok Sabha and other for the Rajya Sabha.

7. Acts of Parliament

No act or law passed by the Union Parliament affecting the following provisions shall have legal force in the Nagaland unless specifically applied to it by a majority vote of the Nagaland Legislative Assembly.

(1) The Religious or Social Practices of the Nagas.

(2) Naga Customary Laws and Procedure.

(3) Civil and Criminal Justice so far as these concern decisions according to Naga Customary Law.

The existing laws relating to administration of civil and criminal justice as provided in the Rules for the Administration of Justice and Police in the Naga Hills District shall continue to be inforce.

(4) The ownership and transfer of land and its resources.

8. Local Self Government

Each tribe shall have the following units of rule-making and administrative local bodies with matters concerning the respective tribes and area:

(1) The Village Council

(2) The Range Council and

(3) The Tribal Council

These Councils will also deal with disputes and cases involving breaches of customary laws and usages.

9. Administration of Justice

(a) The existing system of administration of civil and criminal justice shall continue.

(b) Appellate Courts:

(1) The District Court-cum-Sessions Court (for each district), High Court and Supreme Court of India.

(2) The Naga Tribunal (for the whole of the Nagaland) in respect of cases decided according to Customary Law.

10. Administration of Tuensang District

(1) The Govrnor shall carry on the administration of the Tuensang District for a period of 10 (ten) years until

such time when the tribes in the Tuensang District are capable of shouldering more responsibility of the advanced system of administration. The commencement of the ten-year period of administration will start simultaneously with the enforcement of detailed workings of the constitution in other parts of the Nagaland.

(2) Provided further that regional Council shall be formed for Tuensang District by elected representatives from all the tribes in Tuensang District, and the Governor may nominate representatives to the Regional Council as well. The Deputy Commissioner will be the Ex-Officio Chairman of the Council. The Regional Council will elect members to the Naga Legislative Assembly to represent Tuensang District.

(3) Provided further that on the advice of the Regional Council, steps will be taken to start various Councils and Courts, in those areas where the people feel themselves capable of establishing such institutions.

(4) Provided further that no Act or Law passed by the Naga Legislative Assembly shall be applicable to Tuensang District unless specifically recommended by the Regional Council.

(5) Provided further that the Regional Council shall supervise and guide the working of the various Councils and Tribal Courts within Tuensang District and wherever necessary depute the local officers to act as Chairman thereof.

(6) Provided under the Councils of such areas inhabited by a mixed population or which have not as yet decided to which specific Tribal Council to be affiliated to shall be directly under the Regional Council for the time being. And at the end of ten years the situation will be reviewed and if the people so desire the period will be further extended.

11. Financial Assistance from the Government of India

To supplement the revenues of the Nagaland, there will be need for the Government of India to pay out of the Consolidated Fund of India.

(1) A lump sum each year for the development programme in the Nagaland and

(2) A grant-in-aid towards meeting the cost of administratiom.

Proposals for the above grants shall be prepared and submitted by the Government of Nagaland to the Government of India for their approval. The Governor will have general responsibility for ensuring that the funds made available by the Government of India are expended for purposes for which they have been approved.

12. Consolidation of Forest Areas

The delegation wished the following to be placed on record:

> The Naga delegation discussed the question of the inclusion of the Reserve Forests and of contiguous areas inhabited by the Nagas. They were referred to the provisions in Articles 3 and 4 of the Constitution, prescribing the procedure for the transfer of areas from one State to another.

13. Consolidation of Contiguous Naga Areas

The delegation wished the following to be placed on record:

> The Naga leaders expressed the wish for the contiguous areas to join the new State. It was pointed out to them on behalf of the Government of India that Articles 3 and 4 of the Constitution provided for increasing the area of any State, but that it was not possible for the Government of India to make any commitment in this regard at this stage.

14. Formation of Separate Naga Regiment

In order that the Naga people can fulfill their desire of playing a full role in the defence forces of India the question of raising a separate Naga Regiment should be duly examined for action.

15. Transitional Period

(a) On reaching the political settlement with the Government of India, the Government of India will prepare a Bill for such amendment of the Constitution, as may be necessary, in order to implement the decision. The Draft Bill, before presentation to Parliament, will be shown to the delegate of the NPC.

(b) There shall be constituted an Interim Body with the Governor in the administration of the Nagaland during the transitional period. The tenure of office of the Interim body will be 3 (three) years subject to reelection.

16. Inner Line Regulation

Rules embodied in the Bengal Eastern Frontier Regulation, 1873.

Shillong Accord, 1975

THE SHILLONG ACCORD OF 11 NOVEMBER 1975 BETWEEN THE GOVERNMENT OF INDIA AND THE UNDERGROUND NAGAS

1. The following representatives of the underground organizations met the Governor of Nagaland Shri L.P. Singh, representing the Government of India, at Shillong on 10 and 11 November 1975.

   1. **Shri I. Temjenba**
   2. **Shri S. Dahru**
   3. **Shri Z. Ramyo**
   4. **Shri M Assa**
   5. **Shri Kevi Yallay**

2. There was a series of four discussions. Some of the discussions were held with the Governor alone; at other, the Governor was assisted by the two Advisers for Nagaland, Shri Ramunny and Shri H. Zopianga and Shri M.L. Kampani, Joint Secretary in the Ministry of Home Affairs. All the five members of the Liasion Committee namely Rev. Longri Ao, Dr. M. Aram, Shri L. Lugaland, Shri Kemmeth Kerhuo and Shri Lungshim Shaiza, participated in the discussions.

3. The following were the outcome of the discussions:

(i) The representatives of the underground organisations conveyed their decision, of their own volition, to accept, without condition, the Constitution of India.

(ii) It was agreed that the arms, now underground, would be brought out and deposited at appointed places. Details for giving effect to this agreement will be worked out between them and representatives of the Government, the Security forces, and members of the Liasion Committee.

(iii) It was agreed that the representatives of the underground organisations should have reasonable time to formulate other issues for discussions for final settlement.

Dated, Shillong
11 November, 1975.

I. Temjenba; S. Dehru
Z. Ramyo; M. Assa; Kevi Yally
On behalf of the representatives of
Underground Organisations

L.P. Singh
On behalf of the
Government of India

SUPPLEMENTARY AGREEMENT TO THE SHILLONG ACCORD ON 5 JANUARY 1976

Implementation of Clause II of the Shillong Accord of 11 November 1975:

1. It was decided that the collection of arms initially at collection centres, would commence as early as possible, and will be completed by 25 January 1976. Initial places of collection to be decided through discussion between Commissioner, representatives of underground organizations and the members of the Liasion Committee.

2. Once all arms are collected, these will be handed over to Peace Council team at the respective places of collection.

3. Peace Council team will arrange to transport the arms

from collection centres to Chedema Peace Camp and arrange guards etc. for safe custody of arm.

4. Similar arrangement at agreed place/places will be made in Manipur with concurrence of the Manipur Government.

5. The underground may stay at peace camps to be established at suitable places, and their maintenance will be arranged only by the Peace Council. Any voluntary contribution from any source will be made to the Peace Council, who will utilize the fund according to necessity.

Biseto Medom Keyho; Pukrove Nakru; Z. Ramyo; I. Temjenba

L.P. Singh
Governor

Dated, Shillong
5 January, 1976

Appendix—V
Peace Accord in Punjab

MEMORANDUM OF SETTLEMENT
SIGNED BY
SHRI RAJIV GANDHI
PRIME MINISTER
&
SANT HARCHAND SINGH LONGOWAL
PRESIDENT, SHIROMANI AKALI DAL,
ON JULY 24, 1985

According to this historic document:

1. Compensation to Innocent Persons Killed

1.1. Along the exgratia payment to those innocent killed in agitation or any action after 1st August, 1982, compensation for property damaged will also be paid.

2. Army Recruitment

2.1 All citizens of the country have the right to enroll in the Army and merit will remain the criterion for selection.

3. Enquiry into November Incidents

3.1 The jurisdiction of Shri Justice Ranganath Mishra Commission enquiring into the November riots of

Delhi would be extended to cover the disturbances at Bokaro and Kanpur also.

4. Rehabilitation of those Discharged from the Army

4.1. For all those discharged, efforts will be made to rehabilitate and provide gainful employment.

5. All India Gurudwara Act

5.1 The Government of India agrees to consider the formulation of an All India Gurudwara Bill. Legilation will be brought forward for this purpose in consultation with Shirmani Akali Dal, others concerned and after fulfilling all relevant constitutional requirements.

6. Disposal of Pending Cases

6.1 The notifications applying the Armed Forces Special Powers Act to Punjab will be withdrawn. Existing Special Courts will try only cases relating to the following type of offences:

(a) Waging War

(b) Hijacking

6.2 All other cases will be transferred to ordinary courts and enabling legislation if needed will be brought forward in this session of Parliament.

7. Territorial Claims

7.1 The Capital Project Area of Chandigarh will go to Punjab. Some adjoining areas which were previously part of Hindi or the Punjabi regions were included in the Union Territory. With the capital region going to Punjab the areas which were added to the Union Territory from the Punjabi region of the erstwhile State of Punjab will be transferred to Punjab and those from Hindi regions to Haryana. The entire Sukhna lake will be kept as part of the Chandigarh and will thus go to

Punjab.

7.2 It had always been maintained by Smt. Indira Gahdhi that when Chandigarh is to go to Punjab, some Hindi speaking territories in Punjab will go to Haryana. A Commission will be constituted to determine the specific Hindi speaking areas of Punjab which should go to Haryana in lieu of Chandigarh.

The principle of contiguity and linguistic affinity with a village as a unit will be the basis of such determination. The Commission will be required to give its findings by 31st December. 1985 and these will be binding on both sides. The work of the Commission will be limited to this aspect and will be distinct from the boundary claims which the other Commission referred to in para 7.4 will handle.

7.3 The actual transfer of Chandigarh to Punjab and areas in lieu thereof to Haryana will take place simultaneously on 26th January, 1986.

7.4 There are other claims and counterclaims for readjustment of the existing Punjab-Haryana boundaries. The Government will appoint another Commission to consider these matters and give its findings. Such findings will be binding on the concerned States. The terms of reference will be based on a village as a unit, linguistic affinity and congruity.

8. Centre-State Relations

8.1 Shirmoni Akali Dal states that the Anandapur Sahib Resolution is entirely within the framework of the Indian Constitution: that it attempts to define the concept of Centre-State relations in a manner which may bring out the true federal characteristics of our unitary Constitution and that the purpose of the Resolution is to provide greater autonomy to the State with a view to strengthening the unity and integrity of the country, since unity in diversity forms the corner-stone of our national unity.

8.2 In view of above, the Anandapur Sahib Resolution in so far as it deals with Centre-State relations, stands referred to the Sarkaria Commission.

9. Sharing of River Waters

9.1 The farmers of Punjab, Haryana and Rajasthan will continue to get water not less than what they are using from the Ravi-Beas system as on 1st July 1985. Water used for consumptive purposes will also remain unaffected. Quantum of usage claimed shall be verified by the Tribunal referred to in para 9.2 below.

9.2 The claims of Punjab and Haryana regarding the shares in their remaining waters will be referred for adjudication to a tribunal to be presided over by a Supreme Court Judge. The decision of this Tribunal will be rendered within six months and would be binding on both parties. All legal and constitutional steps required in this respect be taken expeditiously.

9.3 The construction of the SYL canal shall continue. The canal shall be completed by 15th August, 1986.

10. Representation of Minorities

10.1 Existing instruction regarding protection of interests of minorities will be recirculated to the State Chief Ministers. (P.M. will write to all Chief Ministers)

11. Promotion of Punjabi Language

11.1 The Central Government may take some steps for the promotion of the Punjabi Language.

RAJIV GANDHI	SANT HARCHAND SINGH LONGOWAL
Prime Minister	President, Shirmoni Akali Dal

Appendix - VI

Peace Accords in Tripura

Memorandum of Settlement, 1988

Preamble

1. Government of India have been making efforts to bring about a satisfactory settlement of the problems of tribals in Tripura by restoring peace and harmony in areas where disturbed conditions prevail.

2. The Tripura National Volunteer (TNV), through their letter dated the 4th May, 1988, addressed to the Governor of Tripura and signed by Shri Bijoy Kumar Hranugkhawl, stated that keeping in view the Prime Minister Shri Rajiv Gandhi's policy of solution of problems through negotiations. TNV have decided to abjure violence, give up secessionist demand and to hold negotiations for a peaceful solution of all the problems of Tripura within the Constitution of India. The TNV also furnished its bye-laws which conform to the laws in force. On the basis, a series of discussions were held with representatives of TNV.

3. The following were the outcome of the discussions: **Deposit of Arms and Ammunition and ending of Underground Activities by TNV.**

3.1 The TNV undertakes to take all necessary steps to end underground activities and to bring out all undergrounds of the TNV with their arms, ammunition and equipment within one month of signing of this Memorandum. Details for giving effect to this part of Settlement will be worked out and implemented under the Supervision of the Central Government. The TNV further undertakes to ensure that it does not resort to violence and to help in restoration of amity between different sections of the population.

3.2 The TNV undertakes not to extend any support to any other extremist groups by way of training, supply of arms or providing protection or in any other manner.

Rehabilitation of Underground

3.3 Suitable steps will be taken for the resettlement and rehabilitation of TNV undergrounds coming over ground in the light of the schemes drawn up for the purpose.

Measures to Prevent Infiltration

3.4 Stringent measures will be taken to prevent infiltration from across the border by strengthening arrangement on the border and construction of roads along vulnerable sections for better patrolling and vigil. Vigorous action against such infiltrators would also be taken under the law.

Reservation of Seats in the Tripura Legislative Assembly for Tribals

3.5 With a view to satisfying the aspirations of tribals of Tripura for a greater share in the governance of the State, legislative measures will be taken including those for the enactment of the Bill for the amendment of the Constitution. The Constitutional amendments shall provide that notwithstanding anything contained in the Constitution, the number of seats in the

Legislative Assembly of Tripura reserved for Scheduled Tribes shall be such number of seats as bears to the total number of seats, a proportion not less than the number, as on the date of coming into force of the Constitutional amendment, of members belonging to the Scheduled Tribes in the esisting Assembly bears to the total number of seats in the existing Assembly. The Representation of the People Act, 1950 shall also be amended to provide for reservation of 20 seats for the Scheduled Tribes in the Assembly of Tripura. However, the amendments shall not effect any representation in the existing Assembly of Tripura until its dissolution.

Restoration of Alienated Lands to Tribals

3.6 It was agreed that following measures will be taken:

(i) Review of rejected applications for restoration of tribal land under the Tripura Land Revenue and Land Reforms Act, 1960;

(ii) Effective implementation of the law for restoration;

(iii) Stringent measures to prevent fresh alienation;

(iv) Provision of soil conservation measures and irrigation facilities in tribal areas; and

(v) Strengthening of the Agricultural Credit System so as to provide for an appropriate agency with adequate tribal representation to ensure easy facilities for both consumption and operational credit to tribals.

Redrawing of the Boundaries of Autonomous District Council Area

3.7 Tribal-majority villages which now fall outside the autonomous District Council area and are contiguous to such area will be included in in the Autonomous

District Council area and are contiguous to such area will be included in Autonomous District and similarly placed non-tribal majority villages presently in the Autonomous District on the periphery may be excluded.

Measures for Long Term Economic Development of Tripura

3.8 Maximum emphasis will be placed on extensive and intensive skill-formation of the tribal youths of Tripura so as to improve their prospects of employment including self-employment in various trades such as motor workshops, pharmacies, electronic goods, carpentry, tailoring, stationery, weaving, rice and oil mills, general stores, fishery, poultry, piggery, horticulture, handloom and handicrafts.

3.9 Special intensive recruitment drives will be organized for police and para military forces in Tripura with a view to enlisting as many tribal youths as possible.

3.10 All India Radio will increase the duration and content of their programmes in tribal languages or dialects of Tripura. Additional transmitting stations will be provided for coverage event of the remoter areas of the State.

3.11 The demands relating to self-employment of tribals, issue of permits for vehicles for commercial purposes, visits of tribal men and women to such places in the country as may be of value for the viewpoint of inspiration, training and experience in relevant fields will be considered sympathetically by the Government.

3.12 At least 2,500 Jhumia families will be rehabilitated in 5 centres or more in accordance with model schemes based on agriculture, horticulture including vegetable growing, animal husbandry, fisheries and plantations, with a view to weaning them away from Jhum cultivation. The scheme would also provide for housing assistance.

3.13 In the Autonomous District Council Area of Tripura, rice, salt and kerosene oil will be given at subsidized rates during lean months for a period of three years.

3.14 Conscious efforts will be made for effective implementation of the provision of the Sixth Schedule of the Constitution in so far as it relates to Tripura.

1. Sd/- Bijoy Kumar Hrangkhawl

Sd/-
(P.P. Shrivastav)
Additional Seceratary to the
Government of India
Ministry of Home Affairs

Sd/-
Ananta Deb Barma

Sd/-
Kartik Kalai

Sd/-
(I.P. Gupta)
Chief Secretary to the
Government of Tripura

Sd/-
Haripada Hrangkhwal

Sd/-
(Birenjoy Reang)

Sd/-
Binoy Deb Barma
On behalf of National Volunteer

Sd/-
Gen. K.V. Krishna Rao
Governor of Tripura
Dated: 12th August, 1988

In the presence of
(Sudhir Ranjan Majumdar)
Chief Minister of Tripura

MEMORANDUM OF SETTLEMENT, 1993

This indenture made on this the twenty third day of August one thousand nine hundred and ninety three BETWEEN the All Tripura Tribal Force (hereinafter referred to as the ATTF) of the ONE PART and the Governor of Tripura (which expression shall unless excluded by or repugnant to the subject or context include his successors in office and assigns of the Other Part.

Preamble

Whereas the Government of Tripura have been making concerted efforts to bring about an effective settlement of the problems of the tribals who are presently minority in Tripura and attempts have been made on a continuing basis to usher in peace and harmony in areas in which disturbed conditions have prevailed for long:

And

Whereas – All Tripura Tribal Force have given a clear indication that they would like to give up the path of armed struggle and would like to resume a normal life and they have decided to abandon the path of violence and seek solutions to their problems within the framework of the Constitution of India and, therefore, they have responded positively to the appeals made by the Govcernment of Tripura to join the mainstream and to help in the cause of building a prosperous Tripura:

And

Whereas on a series of discussions between the parties hereto and based on such discussions it has been mutually agreed by and between the parties hereto that the FIRST ATTF shall give up the path of violence and surrender to the Other Party the Government of Tripura along with all their arms and ammunition ending their underground activities and the Governor of Tripura will provide economic package and financial benefits and other facilities hereinafter provided.

Now it is Hereby Agreed and Decided between the parties hereto as follows:

1. Deposit of Arms and Ammunation and ending of Underground Activities by ATTF:

The ATTF hereby contends that –

(a) The ATTF undertakes to end all underground activities and to bring overground all their members with their arms and ammunition and equipment within 15 (fifteen) days of the signing of this Memorandum. Details for giving effect to this part of the Settlement will be worked out and implementd under the supervision of the State Government. The ATTF further undertakes to ensure that it will not resort to any manner of violence and will positively help in the restoration of amity and goodwill between different sections of the population of Tripura.

(b) The ATTF undertakes not to extend any support in any manner whatsoever to any other underground or extremist group by way of training, supply of arms, providing protection, providing shelter or in any other manner.

2. The Government of Tripura hereby convents that –

(a) Rehabilitation of ATTF Personnel:

Steps would be taken for the resettlement and rehabilitation of ATTF personnel coming overground on the basis of schemes already decided for the purpose.

(b) Action to be taken against Foreign Nationals:

Action would be taken in respect of sending back Bangladesh foreign nationals who have come to Tripura after 25th March, 1971 and are not in possession of valid documents authorizing their presence in Tripura.

(c) Restoration of Alienated Land:

Effective steps would be taken in terms of the Tripura Land revenue and Land Reforms Act, 1960 for restoring land alienated by tribals.

(d) Inclusion of Tribal Majority Villages in ADC Areas:

Tribal majority villages which now falls outside the ADC area and are contiguous to the ADC area, would be included in the TTAADC.

(e) Introduction of Inner-Line Permit:

The case for introduction of an inner-line permit system would be taken up with the Government of India. The State Government will insist on the Government of India to approve this demand.

(f) Village Police Force for the ADC:

The constitution of Village Police Force under the administrative control of the TTAADC is acceptable in principle to the State Government and the State Government will take up with the Government of India for Constitutional amendment, if required, to fulfil this demand.

(g) Increase in the Number of Seats for Scheduled Tribe Candidates in the TTAADC:

The demand for more representation for Scheduled Tribe members in the Autonomous District Council is acceptable to the State Government in principls and efforts will be made for amendment of the Rules which deals with reservation of seats for Scheduled Tribes in order to increase the number of reserve seats to 25 (twenty five).

(h) Setting up of a Cultural Development Centre:

Upajati Sanskritik Vikas Kendra (Tribal Cultural Development Centre) with arrangements for training would be set up in the TTAADC area.

(i) Improvement of Kok Borak and other Tribal Languages:

A Bhasa Commission would be set up for the improvement of Kok Borak and other Tribal languages. Steps would also be taken for the introduction, in phases, of Kok Barak at pregressively higher levels of education.

(j) Prevention of Ujjyanta Palace as a Historical Monument and Shifting of Tripura Legislative Assembly:

Respecting the sentiments of all section of the population, especially the tribals of Tripura, steps would be taken to construct a separate building for the Tripura Legislative Assembly and to retain the Ujjayanta Palace as a Historical Monument.

(k) Re-naming of Villages, Rivers etc.:

Steps would be initiated to ensure all villages and reivers which earlier had tribal names and which were subsequently renamed, are given their original tribal names.

(l) Jhumia Resettlement:

Area based resettlement of jhumias would continue to be implemented in order to provide for a strong economic base or the Jhumias of Tripura.

(m) Industrial Development of the TTAADC Area:

All necessary steps would be taken to ensure the promotion of industrial activities in TTAADC areas.

(n) Secured Accommodation and Escorts for Office Bearers:

The President, Vice-President, Convenor and 4 (four) other members of the Executive Committee of the ATTF will be given secured accommodation subsequent to their surrender and they will also be given personal security guard for such period as may be decided by the Government. They will be provided with police escort during their movement outside Agartala as and when required.

(o) Housing Facility:

After surrender, ATTF personnel shall be provided, with a house with GCI sheet roofing with a floor area of 220 square feet for their accommodation as early as possible ans the ATTF personnel shall take part in constructing such houses, provided that the cost of each house shall not exceed Rs. 20,000/- (Rupees twenty thousand).

(p) Drinking Water Facilities:

Steps should be taken by the State Government to provide drinking water in the resettlement colonies set up by the Government to resettle the ATTF personnel.

(q) Government Employment or Economic Package:

All ATTF personnel, on their surrender, will be provided with Government employment according to their qualification or economic facilities as provided herein and till such Government employment or economic facilities are given, each surrendered ATTF personnel shall be paid subsistence allowance at the rate of Rs. 500/- (Rupees five hundred) only per month, so, however, that the subsistence allowance shall not be paid beyond a period of 10 (ten) months.

In witness, whereof the ATTF being represented by (1) Shri Lalit Debbarma, President, ATTF, (2) Shri Ramendra Reang, Vice-President, ATTF, (3) Shri Rabindra Reang, General Secretary, ATTF, (4) Shri Dilip Deb Barma, Treasurer, ATTF and (5) Shri Santaram Reang, Accountant, ATTF, and the Governor of Tripura being represented by Shri M. Damodaran, Chief Secretary to the Government of Tripura, have hereunto set their hand on the date, month and year as afore-mentioned.

Signed on behalf of First Party ATTF by

Signed for and on behalf of the Governor of Tripura

1. Sd/-
(Shri Lalit Deb Barma)
President ATTF

2. Sd/-
(Shri Ramendra Reang)
Vice-President, ATTF

Sd/-
(Shri M. Damodaran)
Chief Secretary
Government of Tripura

3. Sd/-
(Shri Rabindra Reang)
General Secretary, ATTF

4. Sd/-
(Shri Dilip Deb Barma)
Treasurer, ATTF

5. Sd/-
(Shri Santaram Reang)
Accountant, ATTF

In the presence of

Sd/-
(Shri Dasharath Deb)
Chief Minister, Tripura

Sd/-
(Shri Baidyanath Majumdar)
Minister, PWD etc. Dept., Tripura

Index

❑❑❑